WHAT CHRISTIANS THINK ABOUT
HOMOSEXUALITY

WHAT CHRISTIANS THINK ABOUT
HOMOSEXUALITY

Six
Representative
Viewpoints

by L. R. Holben

BIBAL Press
North Richland Hills, Texas

BIBAL Press
An imprint of D. & F. Scott Publishing, Inc.
P.O. Box 821653
N. Richland Hills, TX 76182
(817) 788–2280
info@dfscott.com
www.dfscott.com

Printed in the U.S.A.

03 02 01 00 99   5 4 3 2 1

Library of Congress Cataloging-in-Publication Data
Holben, L. R. (Lawrence Robert), 1945-
 What Christians think about homosexuality : six representative viewpoints / by L.R. Holben.
  p. cm.
Includes bibliographical references and index.
ISBN 0-941037-83-5
1. Homosexuality—Religious aspects—Christianity. I. Title.
BR115.H6 H58 2000
261.8'35766—dc21
                                99-050584

Unless otherwise indicated, biblical quotations are from the New Revised Standard Version Bible, copyright © 1989 by the Division of Christian Education of the National Council of the Churches of Christ in the United States of America.

Quotations from "Focus on the Family Position Statement on Homosexual Rights" and "Focus on the Family Position Statement on Violence Against Homosexuals," both released October 1, 1998 (Copyright © 1998, Focus on the Family. All rights reserved. International copyright secured), used by permission.

Quotations from Andrew Comiskey, *Pursuing Sexual Wholeness: How Jesus Heals the Homosexual* (Lake Mary, FL: Creation House, 1989), used by permission.

Quotations from Greg L. Bahson, *Homosexuality: A Biblical View* (Grand Rapids: Baker Book House Company, 1978), used by permission.

Book design by April McKay
Back cover photograph by Loyd Sherwood

Dedicated to two dear friends
Rose Marie Springer,
who encouraged me to develop these materials
and
Dana Alexander,
who insisted that I turn them into a book

CONTENTS

ACKNOWLEDGMENTS

T his book would not exist were it not for the two people to whom it is dedicated.

Rose Marie Springer has encouraged the development of these materials since the early 1980s when she was instrumental in my being invited to lecture on the subject of Christian faith and homosexuality at the Westmont College Urban Program in San Francisco. She has been a faithful and caring friend for over two decades, a powerful model of thoughtful Christian integrity and a perceptive reader and critic of early drafts of the manuscript. Like so many others fortunate enough to know her, I have uniquely experienced the generous grace of God through her loving support and her at times inexplicable belief in me.

Dana Alexander, with whom I share a deep and cherished friendship stretching back to our college years, not only convinced me to turn my lecture notes into something more substantial, he provided consistent research support, tracking down bibliographical information, sending me articles and suggesting additional sources. He has generously read and commented upon a number of drafts of the manuscript and, going far beyond the extra mile, has given much time and effort assisting me to obtain permission for reproduction of the considerable amount of copyrighted material cited. His steadfast and robust conviction of the worth of this work has been the greatest of gifts.

The Reverend Dr. Kenneth Schmidt, Rector of All Saints' Episcopal Church, San Francisco, whom I am blessed to know both as my parish priest and spiritual director, gave a particularly insightful theological critique of one of the later drafts of the manuscript. I offer him both my heartfelt thanks and my apologies for any lingering defects in the work. I am grateful as well to my dear friend, the Reverend Sue Singer, Education Coordinator for the Episcopal Diocese of California, for her astute review of the manuscript.

I thank Steven Schultz, director of the Westmont College Urban Program, for his warm and courageous support of my presentations at the program over a number of semesters. Without the opportunity he provided me to hone these materials in interaction with students, I doubt I would ever have reached the point of writing this book. I also thank Jane Higa, vice president for student life and dean of students of Westmont College, Santa Barbara, along with the entire Student Life staff, for a gracious welcome and moving sensitivity and openness in a "trial run" of the manuscript as the basis for a daylong seminar at the college in the fall of 1997. That experience was a source of very important encouragement during the sometimes daunting process of finding an appropriate publisher.

In that process, I was very fortunate to be the recipient of "the kindness of strangers" in three singular instances. Although I have yet to meet any one of them face-to-face, I thank Frederica Mathewes-Green for her generous and early support for the work, Kathy Yanni of Alive Communications for a number of extremely helpful editorial suggestions and Father Robert Nugent, formerly of New Ways Ministry, for his cogent critique, in particular his suggestions for eliminating traces of bias.

Finally, I thank my boss at my "day job," attorney Cliff Palefsky, for his very practical support, as well as for his tolerance of my sometimes divided attention during both the writing and the submission process.

PREFACE

This book aims to provide a straightforward, objective presentation of the spectrum of opinion held by professing Christians on the "issue" of homosexuality and the church's response to the homosexual person. It is not my intention to arrive at a definitive determination as to what the correct Christian viewpoint on that issue is or should be. Numerous books and articles already exist arguing one or another viewpoint as the only legitimate Christian option. More often than not, these works to at least some extent misrepresent the views they reject, while at the same time sidestepping, or simply ignoring, the difficulties or inconsistencies of their own perspective.

My hope is that an in-depth exploration of the various viewpoints, each of them articulated—and critiqued—as fairly as possible, will be a useful tool in a process of personal or group reflection and discernment. To that end, six points along the spectrum of conviction are discussed, with twelve questions addressed to each. Representative denominations and/or parachurch groups are noted and a cross-perspective critique is made, followed by a short rebuttal section from the perspective of the viewpoint under consideration. After this presentation of the six viewpoints, a brief summary of the differing interpretations that are applied to commonly cited scriptural texts is provided, along with an annotated bibliography of some of the more widely read books on the subject.

As with any comparative construct addressing a continuum of belief, the six viewpoints identified are to some extent artificial. The reality of any given individual's or faith community's opinions may not be an exact fit with any one of them. That this is true does not, I believe, invalidate the general outlines of the discrete perspectives being compared, each of which has its own distinctive presuppositions, its own internal logic and its own most likely inevitable conclusions.

The Viewpoints

Across the spectrum of conviction from Condemnation (on the far "right") to Liberation (on the far "left"), the six viewpoints to be explored are:

+ Condemnation
+ A Promise of Healing
+ A Call to Costly Discipleship
+ Pastoral Accommodation
+ Affirmation
+ Liberation

The title I have given to each viewpoint is not intended to imply any sort of verdict on the merits of that particular viewpoint or its arguments, but simply to reflect how those holding such a perspective might describe themselves. Thus, for example, the use of "pastoral" in one of the titles is not meant to imply that other viewpoints are somehow less interested in effectively mediating the call of the gospel to individual lives. Similarly, the reference to "discipleship" in another title should not be understood as an indication that other viewpoints do not concern themselves with the formation of genuinely Christian character. Proponents of each of the views presented would presumably consider their approach to be appropriately pastoral and their goal to be the fullness of that new life in Christ which is the substance of discipleship.

The Questions

The following twelve questions form the comparative grid through which we will examine the six representative viewpoints discussed. Questions 1 through 8 have to do with presuppositions. Question 9 is the moral conclusion reached as a result of those presuppositions. Questions 10 through 12 deal with the practical consequences of that conclusion for individuals, churches and society at large.

Question 1
What is the ultimate authority upon which any moral judgment regarding homosexuals and/or homosexual acts is to be based?

Question 2
What is the God-given intent or design for human sexuality?

Question 3
What are the necessary criteria for morally legitimate sexual expression?

Question 4
Is there a "homosexual condition" (orientation) and, if so, what is its cause or origin?[1]

Question 5
Can a legitimate moral distinction be made between a homosexual condition (orientation) and homosexual acts?

Question 6
What is the psychological significance of homosexuality?

Question 7

What is the spiritual significance of homosexuality?

Question 8

Can a homosexual become heterosexual (the question of "cure")?

Question 9

What is the moral opinion arrived at, given the responses to Questions 1 through 8?

Question 10

What is the personal call of Christ for the gay man or lesbian?

Question 11

What is the pastoral call of Christ to the church on the issue?

Question 12

What is the political call of Christ to society on the issue?

It is my hope that this grid will provide not only a structure for examining the internal logic of each viewpoint, but will also facilitate comparison of various viewpoints' arguments on particular points of contention.

The Matter of Bias

I am not unaware of the fact that, by treating each of the six viewpoints considered as a perspective affirmed and lived out by authentic Christians within the larger community of faith, I am taking a position. That this is a position which will occasion strong criticism in certain quarters goes without saying. Many conservatives will no doubt see my approach as a sort of moral indifferentism at odds with the clear teaching of Scripture. Many liberals, on the other hand, may well insist with equal passion that any attempt at a sympathetic treatment of views which justify continued discrimination against God's gay and lesbian children does great violence to the primacy of justice and love proclaimed in Christ's teaching. Deeply committed men and women whose views fall at nearly every point on the spectrum (but in particular at the extremes) may be convinced not only that theirs is the only truly Christian viewpoint, but that those who disagree with them hardly deserve the name "Christian" at all.

On this point, it may be helpful to look at another issue on which Christians have long "agreed to disagree" without questioning each others' salvation or sincerity: pacifism.[2] From the perspective of those upholding what they see as the unequivocal gospel call to absolute nonviolence, Christians who support and participate in war are, quite literally, supporting or committing murder. On the other side of the question, many would argue that Christians who refuse to join in the defense of the common good are in a profound sense failing in that love of neighbor as oneself which is the second half of Christ's summary of the Law and the Prophets. Yet it is rare, however rancorous the disputation, for either side to insist that its opponents—because of their views on the issue or the actions which result from such views—are damned to eternal separation from God or are not "true Christians." Mennonites and Southern Baptists may disagree strongly on military service or the payment of war taxes, but they disagree as, in some sense, brothers and sisters in the Lord.

It is difficult to see how so weighty a moral question as the taking of human life (or participation in the preparations for doing so) should be any less significant or divisive for Christians than the question of morally appropriate uses of human sexuality. And, however their proponents may judge each other, it is a fact that all six of the viewpoints we will be discussing are held by self-professed, practicing Christians whose lives appear to evidence those "fruits" that have always been believed to be the marks of the work of the Spirit in the human heart. Nonetheless, it must be candidly acknowledged that the approach I take in this book (indeed, the fact that I wrote such a book at all) evinces a particular "bias" and that the legitimacy of that approach would be vigorously disputed by some participants in the current debate.

To further complicate matters, even the choice of terminology is problematical in discussing such a passionately contested subject.

In the first place, the words we use have connotative as well as denotative meaning. Consider the quite disparate images called up by "fag," "homosexual" and "gay" (or their antonyms "breeder," "heterosexual" and "straight"). While all three words in each grouping describe the same object, each one tells us something quite different about the speaker's attitude toward that object.

Depending on one's perspective, each may also carry significant emotional and rhetorical baggage. Many conservative Christians, for example, bridle at the word "gay," since for them this term calls up a whole web of associations centering around an assertion of the goodness and legitimacy of a "homosexual lifestyle" which they are convinced is a particularly brazen example of human rebellion in the face of God's clearly revealed will.[3] Some of these same conservatives would object to the term "homosexual person" as used in the first paragraph of this preface as well, arguing that there is no such thing as a "homosexual person," there are only ontologically heterosexual people who have deliberately chosen to act in ways that pervert and violate their essential nature.

Numerous gay men and lesbians, on the other hand, reject the word "homosexual" as reflecting a negative, pseudo-scientific judgment upon them, as well as limiting their whole personhood to their erotic and emotional "targeting." At the same time, many "women who love women" have come to spurn the label "gay" as coming out of the male homosexual community and therefore inappropriate for them. Gays are men, they insist. They are lesbians.

Even more recently, a growing number of gay men and women have defiantly embraced what was once understood by many heterosexuals to be the ultimate term of opprobrium for the homosexual—"queer"—as their appellation of choice.[4] They have done so to indicate, among other things, their determined rejection of the negative judgments attached to the word by many heterosexuals.[5] It should be noted that such usage is more than a matter of chants at a gay pride demonstration: "We're here, we're queer, get used to it!" In academia, there has arisen a subdiscipline of "Queer Theory." Some gay or lesbian advocates argue for a

"Queer Nation" that stands outside of and in resistance to what are perceived to be the self-serving pieties and patriarchal structures of "straight" society. For many who insist on self-definition as "queer," the conventionally acceptable terms are (sometimes vehemently) repudiated as voicing a subtle putdown similar to that which led African-Americans to reject the once polite term "Negro."

In short, the mercurial demands of political correctness, or even respectful sensitivity, can defeat the best intentions. Yet one must finally make a choice as to terminology—or give up discussing the subject altogether. In the materials that follow, then, the terms "gay," "gay and lesbian," "gay person" and "homosexual" will be used interchangeably.

But what, precisely, will they be used to describe? Beyond the emotionally loaded matters of connotation and political rectitude, it is important to be absolutely clear as to the phenomenon one intends to reference by whichever words one ends up employing.

In what follows, when referring to gay people, gays and lesbians or homosexuals, I will not be talking about an individual who might have had several sexual experiences with someone of the same sex. Neither will I mean to indicate a person who, at one point or another, has had strong, even passionate, feelings about a same-sex friend. Nor will I be referring to someone who doesn't happen to fit current cultural stereotypes as to appropriate male or female interests, activities, skills or appearance.

Most importantly, in referring to the gay, lesbian or homosexual person, I will not have in mind mere erotic itch, what "turns one on" physically and nothing more. Rather, I will be speaking of a person in whom not only the sexual drives but also the deepest emotional and psychological urges for self-revelation, intimacy, connectedness, bonding, closeness and commitment—all that we call romantic/erotic love—find their internal, spontaneous fulfillment not in the opposite sex but in the same sex.

To assert such a definition is, again, to admit a certain bias, since some on the conservative end of the spectrum reject as a matter of fundamental principle the idea that what homosexuals feel for each other can be in any way equated with heterosexual love. Indeed, the contrasting of heterosexual *love* with homosexual *lust* is something of a polemical staple for the viewpoint I have titled "Condemnation." As one conservative writer puts it, in describing how he explained homosexuality to his children: "A homosexual is a boy who *has sex* with other boys or a girl who *has sex* with other girls. A heterosexual is like Mommy and Daddy, a man and a woman who *make love* to each other."[6]

While admitting that my understanding of the gay or lesbian person's emotional and erotic same-sex attraction is itself a disputed point, I would argue that this does not, in and of itself, "decide" the question of the legitimacy of homosexual expression in favor of a more liberal answer. Many of those holding to viewpoint 3, for example, which I have titled "A Call to Costly Discipleship," acknowledge that romantic love and sexual desire are essentially the same phenomena whether experienced by gays or straights, but still understand the demands of gospel faithfulness to require absolute abstinence from homosexual acts.

Yet another issue relating to bias or the perception thereof needs to be addressed, as well. It was interesting to me that pre-publication evaluations of this book in manuscript form sometimes assumed bias on my part (generally a bias against the reader's own viewpoint) when I was, in fact, merely reporting the criticisms put forward by a particular viewpoint's opponents. Given this reaction, I think it is important to emphasize that, just as I do not necessarily agree with all the arguments put forth by any particular viewpoint in its own defense, neither do I necessarily agree with every critical comment I report. While I have not repeated criticism involving factual assertions I know to be false, I have attempted to represent fairly the arguments of those opposing each viewpoint, even when I myself find some or all of these arguments unconvincing.[7]

A final caution is probably in order. In such contentious questions as those we will be considering, even a seemingly innocuous matter of punctuation—specifically, quotation marks—can be taken to imply an editorial judgment or bias. This is due, in part, to the fact that in common usage a term is enclosed in quotes not only when it is a term with a particular, specialized meaning within the subject or viewpoint under discussion, but also, sometimes, when that meaning is being disputed, even ridiculed, by the writer. In order to avoid as much as possible the second implication, my practice has been to do my best to mirror the voice of those for whom I am speaking at any given point. Therefore, I put specialized or contested terms in quotes the first time (but only the first time) they appear in the affirmative statement of any viewpoint, but render them without quotes from then on. When stating the perspective of those critical of a particular viewpoint—for whom the legitimacy of such terms is itself a matter of sometimes great controversy—I set the contested term in quotation marks throughout. When presenting the arguments of the "ex-gay" movement (viewpoint 2) regarding "healing" or "change," for example, I make use of quotation marks only in the first instance these terms appear in that section of the chapter. In the cross-perspective critique, however, since these words and their purported misuse are major points of debate, I retain quotation marks each time they are used.

In the final analysis, of course, no amount of authorial apology or explanation can build the necessary bridge of trust between writer and reader. Only what is written can allow that delicate connection to take place. My hope is that readers of every viewpoint will have reason to feel that their own viewpoint has been respected and well served and will, therefore, trust my presentation of less familiar or comfortable perspectives as well.

L. R. Holben
Epiphany, 1999

INTRODUCTION

THE HISTORICAL CONTEXT

W hile it was once believed that few things could be more "objective" than history (after all, something either did or did not happen), contemporary historians are quite aware of the part interpretation and perspective play in our assessment of the past. Given that reality, it is not surprising that difficulties quickly arise in any attempt to provide a "neutral" statement of even the briefest history of gays and lesbians in Western society, whether from a religious or a secular perspective.

What some would articulate as the outrageously unjust oppression of gay people over the centuries will appear to others as the legitimate attempts of communities to fulfill their divinely ordained responsibility for enforcing moral order. What some would celebrate as the long-delayed ascendancy of enlightened justice for homosexuals, others would decry as unparalleled evidence of societal degeneration.

In this context, finding a suitably objective tone for any historical discussion is nearly as problematical as choosing the appropriate terminology for referring to the gay or lesbian person. Does one describe the first decorous demonstrations on behalf of homosexual rights in the mid-50s as "courageous," for example? Given the severity of the social and criminal penalties faced by gay people in America at the time, it certainly took what we would usually consider extraordinary courage to appear in public with placards protesting discrimination against homosexuals. Yet, from the

1

perspective of many conservatives, these very acts express a defiant shamelessness completely at odds with that courage traditionally esteemed as a high moral virtue. In the end, it would seem one is left with little choice but simply leaping in and beginning to tell the story, aware that nearly every word choice will inevitably be "loaded."

The Social Matrix

In his widely read study, *Christianity, Social Tolerance, and Homosexuality*,[1] the late Yale scholar John Boswell argues that, in pre-Christian Roman society:

> Gay people were in a strict sense a minority, but neither they nor their contemporaries regarded their inclinations as harmful, bizarre, immoral, or threatening, and they were fully integrated into Roman life and culture at every level.

While some of Boswell's critics question whether this extraordinarily sunny depiction is entirely accurate, the fact is that, until 533, two centuries after Christianity had become the de facto state religion, no legislation existed within the Roman Empire which explicitly outlawed homosexual acts. In that year, the emperor Justinian promulgated codes which for the first time placed sex between males in the same legal category as adultery—which was itself, at least in theory, a capital offense. Following the enactment of further laws on the subject in 538 and 544, the emperor issued a directive that men found guilty of engaging in homosexual practices were to be castrated. This decree resulted in large numbers of such men being arrested, convicted and emasculated—with the majority of them dying as a result. As Boswell notes, in the Christian West, "[f]rom that time on, those who experienced sexual desire for other males lived in terror."[2]

In the Middle Ages, acting as the agent of church law which could not pronounce a death penalty through its own ecclesiastical courts, European criminal statutes made homosexual conduct a capital offense, with the usual method of execution being—as it was for heretics—death by fire. Capital punishment for "sodomites" was not limited to the so-called "Dark Ages" in Europe, however. There are records of executions for "vile buggerie" in colonial America, as well.[3] While, with the Enlightenment, the death penalty ceased to be applied in most (but not all) cases where homosexuality was uncovered by the civil authorities, the lot of the homosexual male (except in certain extremely wealthy, artistic or criminal circles) was one of isolation, necessary secrecy and fear of exposure. And even in the most privileged of contexts, the homosexual could not count on toleration forever, as Oscar Wilde discovered to his regret in Victorian England.

The situation of lesbians over the centuries was somewhat different, given the fact that Western societies have always accepted a degree of emotional intensity and physical intimacy between women that has rarely been allowed men. It is true that the romantic cult of male friendship which thrived in England and America during the late eighteenth and nineteenth centuries encouraged a highly florid sentimentalization of masculine affection—and also permitted certain levels of familiarity that would be certain to raise questions today (Abraham Lincoln, for example, as a young man shared a bed for four years with his good friend Joshua Speed, and suffered significant emotional distress when circumstances required that they part). Nonetheless, women drawn affectionally and erotically to their own sex enjoyed a range of freedom far greater than that available to men of similar inclination. It was permissible for women to live together in lifelong companionship (sometimes referred to as a "Boston marriage"), to write with passionate abandon of their love for each other, and to touch and embrace in public in ways that would have been scandalous among males.

Certainly some of these relationships involved women who were in love with each other, whether they ever physically consummated that love or not. One such couple in turn-of-the-century England—the devoutly Evangelical widow of one Archbishop of Canterbury and the equally pious spinster daughter of another—slept in the same bed for decades, and the widow's diary reveals that for at least a period in their relationship they struggled (apparently successfully) against "carnality."

We can, of course, never know the true incidence of sexualization in same-gender friendships of previous generations. The uproar several years ago over whether Eleanor Roosevelt and her "special friend" Lorena Hickock were, in fact, lovers reveals something of our present inability both to understand the mores and sensibility of another, quite different era and to believe that there might be people who would choose, for whatever reason, not to act on those sexual feelings they might have. Be that as it may, whether many or few of the socially acceptable female partnerships of former generations included physical intimacy, the fact remains that male couples were afforded far less toleration. While two "confirmed bachelors" might in certain circumstances live together for years without provoking the sort of suspicions such an arrangement would automatically raise today, in general men sexually and emotionally drawn to other men either suppressed their "impulses" and lived as heterosexuals, or led secret lives on the underbelly of society while maintaining the appearance of normality, or became sexual outlaws.

It should be noted that some academics currently working in the area of "Queer Theory" now argue that, until the creation of the psychological classification "homosexual" in the late nineteenth century, no gays or lesbians, as we presently understand these terms, existed. These theorists contend that homosexuality—understood as an intrinsic psychological condition distinct from and parallel to heterosexuality, with similar dynamics but a different target—is an abstract construct superimposed upon the widely diverse reality of human experience. Definition, as it were, preceded and produced that which it now defines.

As evidence for such a hypothesis, these scholars and polemicists point to the wide variance in homosexual practice over the centuries. In ancient Greece, for example, an adult male's sexual relationship with a pubescent youth (which we would now consider both criminal and pathological), was celebrated by Plato and others as the highest form of human love, while sexual love between two adult males of equal age and status was condemned as aberrant and shameful. In contemporary Latin cultures, only the passive partner in male same-sex activity is perceived as homosexual, while the penetrator remains robustly "macho" so long as he does not adopt the contemptible "female" role. In Victorian and Edwardian England, age and class differences were significant in the typical homosexual encounter: lower class males (often soldiers) and boys accepted money for sex with older men of a "better class" (most often in houses of assignation or male brothels) without the lower class partner ever considering himself other than a "normal" man, even if he played the passive role. In the immigrant working class neighborhoods of eighteenth- and nineteenth-century New York, "molly houses" provided opportunities for men who would have considered themselves thoroughly "straight" (had such a distinction existed at the time) to have sex with male transvestites who dressed and acted as "females," and it is noted that the mollies did not have sex with each other, only with "real men."

Such "social constructionist" theories parallel current arguments that contemporary heterosexual notions of romantic love, marriage and the nuclear family, far from being eternal verities built into the human psyche, are on the contrary arbitrary arrangements of relatively recent vintage. While constructionist views—in particular the theories of French philosopher and social critic Michel Foucault[4]—are at this point ascendent in academic circles, a number of gay writers (usually termed "essentialists"), though admitting that there has been and continues to be wide variation in the social, economic and philosophical context in which homosexuality is understood, nevertheless insist that the phenomenon we now call the gay or lesbian person, one who is emotionally and erotically drawn to his or her own sex, has always been part of human experience. Furthermore, they argue, this "common experience of men loving men and women loving women in all times and in all places is more important than variances between cultures, classes, gender and economic systems."[5]

The late gay author Paul Monette, speaking for the essentialist viewpoint, wrote often and passionately of this generally ignored history of his "tribe," noting the resonating familiarity to the contemporary gay ear of lyrics by the Greek poet Sappho—such as these lines directed to another woman of her circle on the Isle of Lesbos in the sixth century BCE:

Without warning,
As a whirlwind
Swoops on an oak,
Love shakes my heart.

Robert Goss,[6] on the other hand, argues that, while contemporary gay men and lesbians "may share same-sex sexual practices with particular Greek men in Athens and women on Lesbos during the fourth [sic] century BCE . . . those similar sexual practices have different social constructions of meaning."

Wherever the truth may lie in the constructionist/essentialist debate, the term "homosexual" did not appear in any European language until 1869, when its German form[7] was coined by a Hungarian writer, K. M. Kentbeny (who had previously gone by the last name "Benkert"), for use in two pamphlets he wrote arguing against extension of Prussia's severe anti-sodomy statutes to other areas of the newly forming German confederation. During the same period, Karl Heinrich Ulrichs, a lawyer/journalist from a more liberal section of the confederation, began publishing his own series of pamphlets arguing a personally developed theory that same-sex erotic and romantic attraction (Ulrichs himself was particularly drawn to handsome young soldiers) evidences the fact that there exists alongside conventional males and females—the gender of whose souls conforms to that of their bodies—another category of human being: men who are outwardly male but female in their souls and women who are male in soul. These unique men and women Ulrichs termed *Urnings* (often translated into English as "Uranians").

Although the initial campaign against extension of Prussian law regarding male homosexual acts failed, activism against the statutes was revived in the 1890s under the leadership of Dr. Magnus Hirschfeld, who began a petition drive for repeal which, by the time he presented it to sympathetic Socialists in the German parliament, had garnered over 5,000 signatures. More importantly, in support of his efforts on behalf of what—echoing Ulrichs's *Urning* theories—he termed the "intermediate sex," Hirschfeld founded the renowned Institute for Sexual Science, which collected and published research on sexuality, and in particular homosexuality, from throughout the world.[8]

Pioneer though he was, Hirschfeld was not pursuing his scholarly activism in a cultural vacuum. In the early decades of this century, there were strong homoerotic elements in much of the emerging German "body culture" and nudist/nature worship movements, which elements reached an apotheosis of a sort in the theories, photographic art and publications of the "Community of the Special" movement, which grounded its affirmation of male erotic friendship in traditional German notions of sentimental attachments between comrades in arms. In the 1920s, between the world wars, there developed in Berlin an increasingly open and politically active homosexual subculture which many historians today consider to be the first "gay community" in the contemporary sense of the term. However accurate that assessment may be, this community disappeared in the Nazi death camps, where "pink triangles" (the identifying insignia for gay men) and "black triangles" ("anti-socials," that is, lesbians who refused to do their patriotic duty and bear children for the Reich) were exterminated along with Jews, Gypsies, Communists, anarchists, Christians and other "undesirables."

As for America, where today gay men and lesbians are a significant element in the urban social, cultural and political landscape, and where positive gay characters appear almost nightly on the most popular television sitcoms, it is perhaps easy to forget that over the last hundred years gay men in this country have been castrated, imprisoned, confined in mental hospitals, subjected to electroshock "treatment," blackmailed, driven to suicide and cynically harassed by law enforcement for political purposes. As recently as the 1970s, it was a regular practice in many American cities for the names of men arrested for violation of the public decency statutes—or even for being present in an establishment known to cater to homosexuals—to be published in the newspapers the following day. It was not uncommon for calls to be made directly to employers, landlords or families, as well. Those who were so identified lost spouses, children, friends, jobs and housing. Indeed, the price one could pay for being publicly identified as a homosexual was so great that the first American organization for gay men, The Mattachine Society, organized in 1951,[9] for many years kept its membership lists secret and used only first names in society meetings.

Lesbians, as already noted, experienced far fewer and less obvious strictures—a fact which reflects a disinterest in female sexuality going all the way back to the Old Testament, which dictated the death penalty for at least certain male homosexual activity[10] but had not a word to say about lesbian acts. Nonetheless, the lives of gay women, too, required circumspection and were always shadowed by the possible consequences of discovery, even if these consequences might be somewhat less draconian that those faced by gay men.[11]

This overriding need for secrecy, for both gay men and lesbians, had much to do with the evolving nature of "The Life," as it came to be called in some gay circles in this country. The Life was urban, since cities provided essential anonymity. For all but a privileged few whose wealth, social connections or beauty made them part of the international gay elite, The Life was lived beyond the fringes of respectable bourgeois culture, in ghettos and slums, in basement bars and Mob-run clubs. The Life developed its own dress, jargon, and coded signals, so that its members could find and communicate with each other freely under the oblivious eyes of the wider society.

Despite the founding of The Mattachine in 1951 (and of its lesbian counterpart, The Daughters of Bilitis, a few years later), and even though a few public protests of anti-gay discrimination were organized by these groups in the mid-1950s on behalf of what was then usually termed the "homophile movement," it was only during the civil rights struggles of the '60s that larger numbers of gay men and women began to draw parallels between what they experienced at the hands of mainstream American culture and the oppression being challenged by racial minorities at that time. What turned these isolated reflections into the basis for a movement, what gave birth to "gay liberation" and the assertion of "gay pride," was a group of drag queens (transvestites)—most of them "men of color" (Puerto Ricans and African-Americans)—who frequented a run-down bar called The Stonewall Inn on Christopher Street in New York's Greenwich Village.

As was common in many American cities at the time, it was illegal in New York State for "deviants" to congregate in public places and it was also illegal to serve them liquor. As a result, establishments catering to gays were usually operated by organized crime—which paid corrupt law enforcement officials handsomely for the privilege of making money "off of the queers." Even with such payoffs, gay bars like the Stonewall were subject to periodic vice raids. On one hot June night in 1969, police moved in on the Stonewall to make what they no doubt assumed would be just another routine raid. On this particular evening, however, the Stonewall patrons resisted, setting off several nights of confrontation between police and gays which came to be known as the

"Stonewall Riots" and were the effective birth of the political movement for gay rights.

On the individual level, "coming out" soon came to be understood within the movement as the fundamental political act. The term "coming out of the closet" is conventionally understood to have originated in drag culture, referring to that moment when the cross-dresser ceases wearing his woman's finery only in the privacy of his own closet and steps out onto the street in his new drag identity. Samuel R. Delany is one of a number of authors arguing an alternative derivation, however. In his contribution to *Boys Like Us: Gay Writers Tell Their Coming Out Stories*,[12] Delany recalls that, prior to Stonewall, "coming out" was associated with the debutante balls of high society, in which a young lady had her "coming out" when she was "presented" socially. By ironic parallel, one "came out" into gay society through having one's "first major homosexual experience" and beginning to move within gay circles as a self-defined member of the subculture. Sometimes one's gay friends even threw a party to celebrate the event.

Whatever its etymology, as co-opted by the gay liberation movement, "coming out" meant accepting one's homosexuality as an immutable given (and therefore no longer fighting or attempting to change it), celebrating it as a gift to be embraced and rejecting the shame society would attempt to impose on account of it by living openly and unapologetically as a gay man or lesbian. There could, of course, be degrees of "outness." One might be out to family and friends, but closeted at work. Or—a common situation— one might be out in one's work and social life (often in a city far distant from one's home of origin), but still in the closet to one's family. For the movement as a whole, however, it was deemed vitally important, both for personal mental health and for progressive change in social attitudes, that gays and lesbians come out fully in every area of their lives.[13] In that spirit, the movement boldly claimed even such a stigmatizing symbol as the Nazi pink triangle as an insignia of personal and group pride.

Since 1969, the movement for "gay rights"—which soon became the movement for "gay and lesbian rights" and has, in more recent terminology, been expanded to include the rights of the "lesbian/gay/bisexual/transgender[14]/questioning community," often abbreviated "L/G/B/T/Q"—has moved with what has seemed to its opponents ruinous speed and to its supporters unconscionable delay toward the goals of full equality under the law for all sexual minorities and unqualified social acceptance of alternative sexual "lifestyles." Within the elite liberal culture of academe and the media, the movement's gains would seem to have been significant—even extraordinary considering that they have been achieved within no more than a quarter century. But in the mainstream culture, as reflected in particular in governmental policy, much—from the perspective of the movement itself—remains to be done. The movement's opponents would, of course, argue that far too much has been "done" in contravention of traditional moral values already.

At the turn of the millennium, activists within the American lesbian and gay (or L/G/B/T/Q) community continue to work for increased governmental funding for AIDS research and treatment, legal recognition of same-sex partnerships, repeal of those state and local anti-sodomy statutes which remain on the books, statutory protection of gay people from discrimination in employment, housing, insurance and public services, and the right of gays and lesbians to serve in the military on an equal basis with heterosexual soldiers (including the prerogative of being sexually active in their private lives off duty). From the right, conservative religious and political forces are becoming increasingly organized in their efforts to oppose these and other similar initiatives and to reaffirm society's traditional "preferential option" for heterosexuality. It is in the very center of the contending convictions and impassioned debate of this struggle for the moral and cultural high ground that the Christian churches find themselves today, with their own divisions over the subject mirroring those of the society around them, and with many on right and left alike looking to these churches and their people both for theological justification and practical support.

The Community of Faith

As recently as fifty years ago, it would have been inconceivable to most Christians that their faith might have anything whatever to say about homosexuality other than to condemn it unequivocally.

After all, Leviticus was surely clear on the subject, imposing the death penalty on any man who lay with another man "as with a woman."[15] And the notorious sin of Sodom,[16] as interpreted by generations of exegetes, had even given a generic name to practices so despicable that many decent people were probably not entirely clear as to what they actually involved.

When they allowed themselves to think about so distasteful a subject at all, most Christians no doubt contented themselves with the conviction that it was in pagan antiquity that homoerotic activity had flourished and that it was the ascendancy of the Christian church which had put an end, if not to the practice, certainly to any general acceptance of the "sin against nature." Whatever homosexual behavior might continue to exist was surely confined to the demimonde of criminals, artistic bohemians and self-declared infidels.[17]

Indeed, St. Paul was believed to have made specific in his Epistle to the Romans[18] a clear connection between homosexual "perversion" and idolatrous spiritual rebellion. This implicit linkage between deviant sexuality and apostasy was so clear to the medieval mind, in fact, that it was common practice to ascribe the sin of buggery to any and all heretical groups simply as a matter of course, irrespective of what their actual sexual practices might be.

That there have been gay men and lesbian women in the church throughout its nearly two thousand year history is well documented by John Boswell in his *Christianity, Social Tolerance and Homosexuality*.[19] There have been homosexuals among the clergy and in religious orders. At least one canonized saint (Aelred of Rievaulx, who died in 1167 and is best remembered for his luminous writings on spiritual friendship) is known to have been romantically attached to other men, although he lived faithfully to his vows as a celibate monk. Nonetheless, it was the official teaching of the medieval church that homosexual acts violated not only the moral law revealed by God in sacred Scripture, but also natural law—that law imprinted on our very being by the Creator.

St. Thomas Aquinas, arguably the most influential Roman Catholic theologian in the church's history, saw homosexual activity as a sin more heinous even than adultery or rape. This was because, St. Thomas reasoned, although in those cases there is a sin against a human victim (either the betrayed spouse or the woman being violated), as there is not in consensual homosexual activity, in homosexual acts there is another victim: God himself, whose design for human coupling is blasphemously rejected by the homosexual partners. With the Reformation, Aquinas's teaching on this subject was adopted without significant alteration by Protestant divines, becoming part of the common theological heritage shared by Catholics and Protestants alike.

And so things to all intents and purposes remained for the church until the latter half of the twentieth century. By the late 1950s, it is true, a few liberal theologians and biblical scholars had been quietly proposing theological and pastoral alternatives to traditional moral judgments and scriptural interpretations regarding homosexuality, the first of which to gain any significant audience beyond academic circles was Derrick Sherwin Bailey's *Homosexuality and the Western Christian Tradition*.[20] Such scholarship had little or no practical impact on the attitudes of the laity or the pastoral practice of the churches, however. Even such radical departures as a 1963 statement by the British Society of Friends suggesting that homosexual and heterosexual acts are subject to exactly the same moral criteria made little impression in the wider Christian community.

True, certain more liberal denominations (at least in sophisticated urban centers) were understood to look the other way when socially acceptable, "discreet" homosexuals joined their congregations, and from time to time there were local attempts on the part of mainline churches to reach out to the homosexual community— as when, in 1964, a group of liberal clergy in San Francisco founded the Council on Religion and the Homosexual to defend gay men against police entrapment and harassment.

But the fact is that the current widespread discussion and extensive publication in the area of the relationship between Christian faith and homosexuality are, in their entirety— whether the views argued be conservative or liberal—a phenomenon of the last quarter century and they exist either as a result of or in reaction to the secular "gay movement" and, more particularly, to the rise of a "gay theology" which was initially popularized in the ministry and writing of the Reverend Troy Perry, founder of what came to be the Universal Fellowship of Metropolitan Community Churches.

Alternatives to the church's traditional teaching on the homosexual question have now been proposed in books and articles from an extensive range of Christian theological contexts. Among the more widely read authors of the "first generation" of this new thinking were Father John McNeill, S.J., a Roman Catholic, Norman Pittenger, an Anglican, and evangelicals Ralph Blair, Virginia Mollenkott and Letha Scanzoni. The post-Stonewall decade also saw the founding of gay organizations within nearly all the mainstream churches, among them Dignity (Roman Catholic), Integrity (Episcopalian), the non-denominational Evangelicals Concerned, and Presbyterians for Gay and Lesbian Concerns.

In the 1980s and '90s, a new generation of revisionists, strongly influenced by the work of North American feminist and Latin American liberation theologians, pushed the boundaries of the debate considerably further. For lesbian theologian Carter Heyward, as for Marvin Ellison (Professor of Christian Ethics at Bangor Seminary), Richard Cleaver (whose theological roots are in the radical Catholic Worker movement) and others of similar perspective, the call of Scripture is an unambiguous summons to liberation on every front—political, economic, spiritual and sexual. As Cleaver writes:

> . . . the God of history is revealed most clearly in liberating activity. Thus, whenever we see people being liberated from oppression we see, with the eyes of faith, God at work.[21]

Therefore, according to these theologians, it is not for the "bourgeois church" (as Cleaver characterizes it, drawing his term from "political theologian" J. B. Metz[22]) to make moral judgments on the lives of gay and lesbian people, but rather it is the right of "oppressed" gays and lesbians "to demand that any pronouncement of scripture or ecclesiastical authority be judged [*by us on the basis of*] whether it helps or hinders our liberation, our becoming subjects of history, not victims only."[23]

On the conservative side of the issue, a number of ministries focusing on promises of "healing" or "change"[24] for gays and lesbians have arisen within or with the support of various evangelical and charismatic churches. Exodus International, founded in 1976, now claims eighty-three chapters in thirty-five states[25] and serves as networking umbrella organization for these "ex-gay" support groups and ministries. Exodus has been in the forefront of the debate over the question of a spiritually-based "cure" for the homosexual.

Although the ex-gay movement has had a fairly high profile for a number of years within conservative Christian circles, the movement's claims were until recently most often ignored by the wider culture, in particular the mass media. That state of affairs changed dramatically in July of 1998, however, when ex-gay proponents seized the offensive with a series of full-page advertisements in major American newspapers (including the *New York Times*, the *Washington Post*, the *Chicago Tribune* and the *Los Angeles Times*),[26] one of which featured the testimony of "wife, mother, former lesbian" Anne Paulk. A month later, Paulk and her ex-gay husband John, the Exodus national board chairman and a former transvestite, appeared on the cover of the August 17, 1998 *Newsweek* under the headline "Gay for Life? Going Straight: The Uproar Over Sexual 'Conversion.'" In the accompanying cover story,[27] Anthony Falzarano (who, according to *Newsweek*, describes himself as "one of the top five ex-gays"), reported that movement spokespersons had "done thirty-seven interviews in the last ten days"—one of which was an appearance by the Paulks on *Good Morning America*.

Publication from this side of the controversy has been extensive, ranging from personal testimonials, including John Paulk's *Not Afraid to Change: The Remarkable Story of How One Man Overcame Homosexuality*,[28] to the practical and theoretical works of therapist Elizabeth Moberly, inner healing practitioner Leanne Payne and ex-gay leader Andy Comiskey,[29] to sympathetic treatments by evangelicals outside the ex-gay movement such as Richard Lovelace and Thomas Schmidt.

Psychological Interpretations

Until the late nineteenth century, secular European and American opinion generally followed Christian conviction in holding that there is no homosexual condition, per se. Everybody, it was believed, is heterosexual in the ontological reality of his or her intrinsic being.

The fact that some individuals feel sexual desire for people of their own gender was seen, first of all, as a result of their having deliberately turned away from God (following the common understanding of St. Paul's words in the Epistle to the Romans[30]), and secondly, as a willful perverting of the authentic structure of what we would now call their personalities. This choice to act against one's created heterosexual "nature" by experimenting with "unnatural vice" was believed to occasion a very specific consequence: perverse lust was given unbridled reign in the heart.

According to this traditional view, therefore, homosexual activity is a sinful choice which, once made, is punished by becoming an enslaving habit. Further, if everyone is fundamentally heterosexual, it follows that the "spread" of homosexuality is effected primarily through seduction. Those already given over to depraved lusts tempt others to sin, with the result that these new recruits discover their own desires have been turned habitually to perversion.

Late in the nineteenth century, there began in Europe what might be termed a "campaign" on the part of some medical professionals to change the perception of homosexuality from that of being a "sin" to being an "illness" (there is a certain irony to the fact that this interpretive shift was then considered to be extremely liberal). At approximately the same time that Kentbeny (Benkert) in Germany was introducing his coinage "homosexual," a number of other terms, including "counter sexual feeling," "inversion," and "the third sex," were also being proposed by medical professionals to describe a phenomenon which, until then, had never been recognized by either clinicians or the wider culture: a lifelong "condition" of erotic and emotional attraction to the same rather than the opposite sex out of which specific homosexual acts might arise.

The pioneer "sexologists" of the turn of the century, preeminently Krafft-Ebing and Havelock Ellis, generally sought organic or biological explanations for this newly acknowledged reality. The general consensus was that homosexuality represented "faulty heredity" or, as Krafft-Ebing more elegantly put it, "hereditary neuropathic degeneration.[31]

Sigmund Freud—whose views revolutionized the West's concept of the human personality and human sexuality—rejected the idea of an inborn or physical cause for either homosexuality or heterosexuality.[32] Rather than assuming that we are all born heterosexual, Freud argued that we come into the world what he termed "polymorphous perverse," that is to say, with sexual drives that are without any specific target. These drives simply *are*, like a hunger that can be satisfied by anything edible. Freud went on to posit a "normative" pattern of growth *into* heterosexuality, which was understood to be the mature sexual state, through a period of pre- and early pubescent homosexuality. This homosexual "phase" in the growth process—when girls and boys hate each other and bond closely with their own sex, when young women develop intense crushes on older female role models and young boys explore their burgeoning sexual drives in the privacy of a community of male peers—was understood as natural, healthy and necessary, so long as it was temporary.

Adult male homosexuality, as Freud saw it, is the result of a failure to move past the "Oedipal phase" in which the prepubescent boy experiences an unconscious libidinal attraction to his mother and an equally unconscious competition with his father for the mother's affections. Normally these feelings are overcome during puberty and the young man moves on to adult heterosexuality. The process by which this transition from the Oedipal stage occurs involves the "castration complex"—the boy's unconscious fear that his father will genitally mutilate him in retaliation for his incestuous desires for the mother. This complex drives the boy to withdraw from the mother libidinally and bond with his father defensively, thereby identifying with him in secure heterosexual masculinity.

Despite such theorizing, Freud seems to have taken a rather phlegmatic attitude toward homosexuality: "assuredly no advantage, but . . . nothing to be ashamed of, no vice, no degradation," as he wrote in a now-famous letter to an American mother concerned about her gay son, adding that it "cannot be classified as an illness."[33] In his classic *Three Essays on the Theory of Sexuality*,[34] the founder of psychoanalysis wrote:

> Inversion [*homosexuality*] is found in people who exhibit no other serious deviations from the normal. It is similarly found in people whose efficiency is unimpaired and who are indeed distinguished by specially high intellectual development and ethical culture.

Freud's followers in the psychoanalytical tradition, however, especially those in America, were quick to depart from his convictions on this point and apply medical models of "sickness" or "pathology" to adult homosexuality. As *Homosexuality: A Report by the Committee on Public Health of the New York Academy of Medicine*[35] asserted in the early 1960s:

> Homosexuality is indeed an illness . . . [*it*] fulfills all the requirements to place it in the category of illness. In a strict sense it is a symptom of illness.

The problem with the homosexual, Freud's American disciples argued, was that he or she had become fixated at an immature, incomplete level of psychosexual development, never completing the psychic journey to mature heterosexuality. This failure to mature was a form of neurosis, of emotional or psychic sickness. The homosexual's erotic and emotional drives toward his or her own sex were a matter of "arrested development." The source of this arrested development was to be found in unresolved conflicts with psychologically unhealthy parents in dysfunctional family units.

It comes as no surprise to feminists that the primary (indeed, nearly exclusive) focus of this work was the male homosexual. For some Freudians, the chief causative factor for the homosexual adult was a smothering, overly protective, seductive mother who so cut the young boy off from his primary male role model—his father—that he was never able to see himself as a real man, responsive to women, and thus sought out male partners instead, limping through life as a kind of pseudo-female. Alternatively, this same seductive mother was claimed by other analysts to create such conflict between the boy's incestuous cravings for sexual union with her and his internalized incest taboos that—perceiving all women through the grid of this neurotic relationship—he avoided reliving these conflicts with other women and turned to men for sexual and psychological relief. Other psychoanalytical theorists argued that the very oppressiveness of the dominant, seductive mother's power in the boy's life led to a generalized hatred of all women as castrators and manipulators, so that homosexuality was not so much a matter of attraction to men as it was of recoil from women.

Still others turned away from the mother altogether, suggesting that a cold, distant or absent father, unable to give affection and intimacy to his son, was the ultimate causative factor in the formation of homosexual orientation, leaving the homosexual on a life-long quest for the masculine approval and, more importantly, the masculine identity, denied to him by his father and therefore sought in male sexual and emotional partners.

Whichever of these paradigms, or combinations thereof, was argued as determinative (always with the support of apparently compelling case histories), the American Psychiatric Association classified homosexuality as a category of mental illnesses. Certain common themes consistently emerged in the psychiatric literature and rapidly moved from there into the popular culture by way of novels, plays, films and non-academic magazine articles: homosexuals were immature, emotionally arrested and neurotic; unstable, unhappy and potentially dangerous to society. They were doomed to live tragic lives because their affliction was *global*—that is, it affected every part of their personality. As psychiatrist Edmund Bergler wrote:

> In objective reality, [*the homosexual*] is a diseased person. He just won't admit to that . . . He is diseased in his personality.
>
> Homosexuality is a neurotic distortion of the whole personality. . . there are no healthy homosexuals . . . the homosexual is an emotionally sick person.[36]
>
> Every homosexual is . . . a psychic masochist.[37]

Later critics have pointed out that every study of homosexual men published during this period from the conventionally orthodox perspective (including what was purportedly the most comprehensive of them all, that of Irving Bieber, released in 1962[38]) used as subjects only individuals who had either sought out treatment because they were unhappy about being homosexual or who had been referred from the courts following convictions for sex crimes. While the majority of therapists and theorists of the time accepted the validity of such a research model without question, a few began to challenge the methodological integrity of studies purporting to describe all members of a class only by those whose inner conflicts drove them to seek psychological intervention or to commit antisocial acts that landed them in court. What sort of picture would one get of *heterosexuals*, these therapeutic mavericks asked, if the descriptive sampling were limited to those whose sexual problems required professional counseling and criminal sex offenders?

Evelyn Hooker, whose first landmark research was released in 1957, also questioned the legitimacy of arguing global damage from one particular element in the whole personality. In a now-famous study,[39] she gave a battery of psychological tests to two groups, one a cross-section of homosexual males and the other a cross-section of heterosexual males. When the results of this testing were presented "blind" to a group of therapists, these professionals were unable to determine which subjects were gay and which straight. This, of course, should not have been the case if homosexuality were truly, as Bergler puts it, "a neurotic distortion of the whole personality."

In the late 1960s, following the rise of the gay rights movement, increasing numbers of gays and lesbians began coming to the conclusion that their disenfranchisement and oppression at the hands of straight, mainstream society were grounded, at least to some extent, in the mental health community's labeling of them as unhealthy, emotionally sick and incapable of positive integration into or contribution to the larger society simply because of their sexual orientation. Further, the conviction grew that much of the observable neurosis among gay people had nothing to do with the fact of their being homosexual, but was rather a result of their being forced to cope with the hostility of the surrounding culture— a hostility which effectively ignored the reality and legitimacy of their needs and experience and, furthermore, a hostility which they themselves all too often internalized in self-loathing and self-destructive life patterns.[40] In this view, it was not the homosexual who was inherently sick, it was the homophobia (anxiety and fear manifested as irrational loathing of homosexuals) of heterosexual society that was sick, and it was this homophobia that was causing whatever sickness there was among gay men and women.[41]

Prayers for Bobby

As a result, along with pressing demands for an end to discrimination and legal harassment, gay activists mounted a campaign to have homosexuality declassified as a mental illness by the professional psychiatric and psychological organizations representing the American therapeutic community. This campaign included not only enlisting the support of the growing number of younger therapists whose experience was leading them to doubt conventional psychiatric wisdom as to the health of homosexual people, it also involved more direct forms of confrontation borrowed from the student and minority movements of the times: disruption of professional meetings and conferences, picketing, and other forms of political pressure.

This pressure—combined with a growing conviction on the part of many therapists that the older studies were methodologically flawed and that professional treatment was failing in its attempts to cure homosexuals (a failure, it was noted, which Freud himself had predicted)—led, in December 1973, to the Board of Trustees of the American Psychiatric Association removing homosexuality from the association's *Diagnostic and Statistical Manual*. No longer was homosexual orientation, in and of itself, to be considered a mental illness. Rather, under new language, if someone who was homosexual could not accept or adjust to his or her condition, with resulting stress, anxiety or maladaptation, then that person was said to be suffering "Sexual Orientation Disturbance." This condition was presumably treatable—not by attempting to change that person's orientation to heterosexuality but rather by enabling him or her to accept the given homosexual orientation and function productively within it. The new *Manual* was unequivocal: "Homosexuality by itself does not constitute a psychiatric disorder." The following year the board's decision was ratified by a general vote of the membership of the association, and in January 1975 the American Psychological Association followed suit.[42]

This apparent triumph and vindication for the gay movement was qualified somewhat by the fact that the general membership vote was bitterly contested and carried by only a slim majority. Further, opponents of the change claimed that many younger therapists had made a political rather than therapeutically-based decision, believing that retention of the traditional classification would encourage continued violations of the civil rights of gay people. On the other hand, those professionals who came down on the side of reclassification pointed to the fact that the anti-revisionists had years of professional commitment to traditional understandings at stake and were unable to admit they had built therapeutic careers on a diagnostic error. While some still contend the association's decision was nothing more than capitulation to intimidating political pressure, defenders of that decision argue that the removal of homosexuality from the *Manual* was, in fact, based upon scientific standards which were consistently applied to the entire document.

Despite the diagnostic reclassifications of the associations, an active and vocal minority of therapeutic professionals continues to hold that homosexuality is a mental illness which can and should be treated. United under the banner of their own professional organization, The National Association for Research and Therapy of Homosexuality (NARTH), these clinicians generally espouse some form of what has come to be termed "reparative therapy."[43]

Reparative therapists view homosexuality as essentially a "gender-identity disorder" brought about, in male homosexuals,[44] by a failure to appropriately bond with the father (and, to a lesser extent with male peers) in early childhood. Martin Silverman, in a paper presented at the 1996 NARTH annual conference,[45] describes in broad but compelling strokes the archetypal family dynamic held to lead to such gender identity confusion in a boy:

> [He is] born to a basically depressed mother whose depression may not always be overly apparent . . . She reacts to the birth of a son by investing in him as a means of completing herself, fulfilling her yearnings, and endowing herself with the capacity to feel whole, self-reliant, and protected against the pain of loss, abandonment and unfulfilled need . . . She communicates . . . from the very beginning that he can remain in her good graces as her loved and cherished child only if he gives up his aspirations to be separate, independent . . . The father tends to be passive . . . to feel powerless to oppose his wife's insistent dominance of his son's increasing effeminacy . . . to be under assertive and under aggressive, or given to intense though short-lived, impotent rages . . .

The child in such a family is torn between, on the one hand, his innate drive to bond and identify with his father, thereby asserting his independence from his mother and claiming his identity as a male, and, on the other hand, an overpowering need to remain connected to his "all-powerful, all-providing mother."[46] Not surprisingly—given the lack of a psychological power center in the distant father—such a boy often opts to sacrifice the drive to independence and male identity so as to retain the security of the overwhelming and protective attachment to the mother. This failure in gender identity formation, which results in an inability to experience himself as fully or adequately male, leads to a defensive withdrawal from and resistance to appropriate nonsexual intimacy and mutuality with other males and a rejection of their pursuits, interests and emotional style.

Despite this "defensive detachment" from the masculine principle, there remains a "reparative drive" for gender wholeness. At puberty, this reparative drive becomes eroticized as sexual desire for other men, but what the psyche is truly seeking is the forfeited masculine self, not psychosexual union with another man. Appropriate treatment, therefore, aims at bringing the homosexual to a recognition of the origins of his condition and an understanding that the psychic goal of what he experiences as homoerotic attraction is actually his own lost masculine identity. Having attained this awareness, he must then do the hard psychological work required to reclaim that identity. Various methodologies are put forward for accomplishing this task, but all of them aim at creating a solid sense of masculine selfhood. Finally, having completed the aborted gender identity work of his childhood, the former homosexual is ready to relate to other men and to women as a whole male.

The majority of mainstream therapeutic professionals would probably agree with University of California at Davis research psychologist Gregory Herek that NARTH inhabits "the fringe of the mental-health establishment."[47] This professional marginalization of reparative therapists and their work was formalized in December 1998 when the Board of Trustees of the American Psychiatric Association voted unanimously to accept a Position Statement proposed by the APA's Committee on Gay, Lesbian, and Bisexual Issues three months earlier. Citing a 1997 APA "Fact Sheet" to the effect that "there is no published scientific evidence supporting the efficacy of 'reparative therapy' as a treatment to change one's sexual orientation," the Position Statement approved by the APA argues that "the potential risks of 'reparative therapy' are great, including depression, anxiety and self-destructive behavior, since therapist alignment with societal prejudices against homosexuality may reinforce self-hatred." While acknowledging that, "in the course of ongoing psychiatric treatment," there could be circumstances in which it would be appropriate to attempt to change certain sexual *behaviors*, the statement concludes with the unequivocal declaration that "the American Psychiatric Association opposes any psychiatric treatment, such as 'reparative' or 'conversion' therapy, which is based upon the assumption that homosexuality per se is a mental disorder or based upon the a priori assumption that the patient should change his/her homosexual orientation."[48] In the press release announcing this decision,[49] APA President Dr. Rodrigo Muñoz asserts that there is no "scientific evidence that reparative or conversion therapy is effective in changing a person's sexual orientation" and, furthermore, that there is "evidence that this type of therapy can be destructive." Dr. Nada Stotland of Rush Medical College in Chicago, head of the APA's Joint Committee on Public Affairs, went even further. In an interview given in conjunction with the APA announcement, Stotland contended that not only are such therapies dangerous for those who undergo them, but that the "very existence of therapy that is supposed to change people's sexuality, even for people who don't take it, is harmful because it implies that they have a disease."[50] Reparative therapy advocates counter that the larger professional community has simply caved in to the aggressive political and social pressure of gay activists and their liberal supporters, abandoning professional responsibility and scientific objectivity in favor of cultural acceptability.

Not surprisingly, reparative therapy is anathema to most gay apologists, who denounce its practitioners as homophobes, its theories of etiology as nothing but a stale rehash of discredited neo-Freudian doctrine, and its claims of effecting change in sexual orientation as wishful thinking unsupported by the evidence. Nonetheless, noted neoconservative and openly gay Roman Catholic cultural critic Andrew Sullivan argues in a recent work[51] that gay men need to admit that the etiological model proposed by reparative therapists cannot simply be dismissed as "an improvised rationalization of bigotry."

> Its . . . observations are too acute . . . The range of homosexual experience is truly vast, but it is still undeniable that certain patterns seem common, in particular an often deep and powerful bond with a mother, an estranged relationship with a father, and often dysfunctional sexual and emotional relationships . . . To say this is not, I think, a function of self-hatred. It is a function of honesty.[52]

Apart from the similar, though not entirely identical, etiological models of American neo-Freudians and the reparative therapists, research and speculation have been ongoing as to why a certain, apparently fairly consistent, percentage of the population[53] grows up to find its primary erotic and emotional fulfillment in same-sex partners.

Some have looked to the analytic psychology of Carl Jung for an explanation. Believing that humankind's myths are symbolic representations of psychological realities contained in a "collective unconscious" shared by all human beings, Jung found it significant that a number of ancient cultures preserved myths of an originally unified, hermaphroditic human creature containing within it both the masculine and the feminine principles.[54] According to these myths, some primal catastrophe split this unified being into two parts, male and female, and as a result man and woman forever after seek reunion through sexual congress and emotional bonding.

According to Jung, the psychological reality expressed through these myths is the fact that every male personality contains within it a subordinated female principle (which he termed the *anima*) and every female personality a secondary male principle (the *animus*). What attracts men to women and women to men, Jung believed, is a search for psychic completion every bit as powerful as the quest for physical wholeness expressed in the ancient myths: the male seeks fulfillment of his *anima* in a female partner, the female the completion of her *animus* in a male partner. Either is in some mysterious but profound sense incomplete without the other.

Drawing on Jung's model, some theorists have suggested that, in homosexuals, the internal balance between *animus* and *anima* is reversed, with the result that the quest for psychological "wholeness" is directed toward one's own sex. The gay man seeks fulfillment of his secondary *animus* in male partners and the lesbian looks to other women to complete her subordinated *anima*. Whether such *animus/anima* reversal is an inborn trait or a result of early childhood experience (or a combination of the two) is a matter of debate among those advancing this theory.

Other therapists and researchers suggest what might fairly be described as a "demythologized" Jungian viewpoint, holding that homosexual attraction has its source in a weak or damaged self-image that attempts to "cannibalize" certain same-sex characteristics the homosexual feels he or she lacks through incorporation of the same-sex partner's gender "power" or specific admired attributes.[55] Reflecting a similar perspective, but enlarging it significantly, C. Tripp in the mid-1970s argued in his *The Homosexual*

Matrix[56] that *all* erotic attraction, gay or straight, is finally a matter of "import/export"—that is, of individuals seeking completion of their subconsciously perceived deficits in the qualities of the desired sexual partner. Heterosexuals find this completion in the opposite sex, homosexuals—for reasons which Tripp never makes entirely clear—come to value same-sex qualities more highly and therefore their erotic targeting is toward their own sex.

It has also been claimed by some that male homosexuality seems to be more prevalent in societies with highly competitive, aggressive and eroticized male gender expectations (societies such as our own or that of ancient Greece), whereas it is relatively uncommon in cultures in which the male role model is one of cooperation, accommodation and relative passivity (contemporary China, for example). Whether or not—given the difficulty of making accurate demographic comparisons across cultures and centuries—there is any way to demonstrate a factual basis for such a theory, it does nothing to account for lesbianism.

While some theorists continue to explore psychological explanations, others look to physical causes for homosexuality. At one point, for example, some research seemed to suggest that male homosexuals showed lower levels of testosterone than did a comparable sampling of straight men. After a flurry of excitement, however, it was discovered that administering large doses of the hormone to gay men did nothing to change their orientation. It merely made them much randier homosexuals—and gave them a recurrence of adolescent acne.

Recently, there has been renewed interest in possible genetic causes for variant sexual orientation, with a good deal of research focusing on a search for what *Time* magazine rather misleadingly referred to as the "gay gene."[57] Despite a brief stir of media attention, however, science at this point is far from any definitive proof that individuals are, or are not, born with a predisposition to a particular sexual orientation. Nonetheless, it has been argued by many for years that certain people are simply "born gay"—just as some people are born left-handed.[58] Whatever the merits of that claim, a large body of anecdotal testimony from gays and lesbians themselves would certainly seem to indicate that, for most homosexuals, there was never any conscious "decision" or "choice" to become gay[59] and that recognition came very early on, well before puberty, that they were somehow "different."[60] In the matter of self-recognition, however, there does seem to be a significant divergence between the experience of gay men and lesbians. Most gay men report a fairly early awareness of their orientation. While some lesbians state that they recognized they were erotically and romantically attracted to other women from an early age, there appears to be a much higher percentage of gay women than men who come to the conclusion that they are lesbian only after— sometimes well after—puberty.

Despite absolutist statements regarding etiology from experts on both left and right, it would seem fair to say that, at present, we have no certain scientific knowledge of what makes some people homosexual and others heterosexual.[61] The view most commonly accepted professionally would tend to see all sexual orientation— gay, straight or bisexual—as a result of the delicate interplay of a complex web of factors, both predispositional and environmental, an interplay which can vary from individual to individual. Accordingly, in some people, a particular, unique combination of inborn psychological (possibly genetic) factors, interacting with particular familial and social dynamics, results in the budding psyche forming patterns of response, self-identity and reality construction that produce an emotional and erotic nature which at puberty, spontaneously and without calculation or conscious decision, finds its target in the same, rather than the opposite, sex. It is the opinion of the majority of therapists and researchers that, for most people, sexual identity is "set" by the age of six or before.

As already noted, for a good number of today's gays and lesbians, even to raise questions of causality is taken as evidence of an at least subliminal homophobia. After all, they argue, nobody spends much time trying to figure out why most people are straight. Applying an etiological model to homosexuality, they insist, assumes that the psychosexual and emotional makeup of gay men and women is some sort of deformity, illness or impairment.

While there is clearly at least an element of truth in such concerns, questions of etiology would seem inevitable from a scientific perspective. Moreover, as we shall see, the whole issue of how people "become" homosexual has profound theological implications for various Christian views regarding the homosexual person and his or her calling and ethical options. As a result, particular theories of etiology have become issues of sharp debate, even—in some circles—matters of faith. That etiology is finally a scientific question, not a matter of revelation, does not seem to trouble either those who, out of a deeply conservative position, insist that the homosexual person has willfully chosen to be a homosexual or those who, from a liberal position, are convinced that God created them gay.

CONDEMNATION

W e begin with this most conservative viewpoint on the spectrum because it is, at least arguably and in its broader outlines, the view of longest standing within the Christian community.

Indeed, those who affirm it see themselves as defenders of a historic orthodoxy now under attack from both inside and outside the churches. Those mounting this assault, they believe, act not out of submission to the Spirit of God, commitment to scriptural truth or allegiance to the "faith once delivered." Rather, these moral iconoclasts proceed from a secular humanist worldview which—whatever the theological language in which it may drape itself—aims at nothing less than a wholesale abandonment of Judeo-Christian morality. The fact that anything other than the traditional unequivocally negative judgment upon homosexuality would even be suggested among people calling themselves Christians is evidence of just how far these liberalizing forces have moved toward achieving their goal. At work behind and through such efforts, however well-intentioned they might be on the part of some, is a spirit which can only be termed demonic.

From this perspective, there is only *one* viewpoint on the matter of homosexuality worthy of the name "Christian"—an absolute condemnation which is held to be the "clear teaching" of Scripture.[1] The alternative views now being proposed within the church are simply one of the more egregious expressions of a widespread apostasy which began with the acceptance of "higher" biblical criticism[2] in the mainstream denominations decades ago and has continued in rejection of scriptural authority, repudiation of traditional orthodox doctrine, and revolt against revealed moral standards. Having abandoned God's truth in favor of subjective human opinion, liberals now seek to conform the church and its divinely-mandated message to the convictions of the world, rather than judging the world by Christian truth.

In short, the current debate within the churches over homosexuality is in fact a manifestation of that perpetual spiritual warfare which exists between the rebellious spirit of sinful humanity and the revealed will of God. Today, however, rather than simply rejecting God's law outright and admitting themselves to be pagan, those opposing the traditional view are attempting to stake a claim for themselves within the household of faith.

Question 1:

What is the ultimate authority upon which any moral judgment regarding homosexuals and/or homosexual acts is to be based?

As is the case with any moral question, so with homosexuality: the Christian is bound by the unimpeachable authority of God's eternal law as set forth in the inspired Word of God, the Bible. Reformed theologian Greg Bahnsen puts it well: "For the true disciple of Christ, moral boundaries are never drawn by man but only and always by God . . . The supreme judge by which all religious controversies are to be determined and all human opinions are to be examined can be no other than the Holy Spirit speaking in the Scripture . . . Christian ethics does not have its source in human . . . authority, but in the revealed Word of God." For the believer, the authority of Scripture is not subject to debate, accommodation, obfuscating qualifications or revised understanding on the basis of opinions arising outside of revelation, however purportedly "scientific" the origin of such judgments might be or however prevalent their acceptance in secular society. As Bahnsen continues:

> Because God is omniscient, because He has created man with his specific nature . . . God does not depend upon man's modern research to make His law applicable or relevant to man's every historical situation. Being the eternal creator and sustainer of the world

30

[handwritten: but not static!]

and (unchanging) in His nature, God is not threatened with obsolescence; He and His law are relevant to every moment of finite man's existence.

That being the case, far from allowing the purported truths of scientific inquiry or biblical "scholarship" to call into question the objective truth of the divine law as declared in the Scriptures, the Christian will use the Scriptures and the law they proclaim to judge "the results and explanations of disciplines dealing with general revelation." The moral authority of the Scriptures, insists Bahnsen, "is not historically and culturally limited . . . Because [*scriptural*] law reflects the character of the immutable God, it too is unchangeable." While certain elements of Old Testament cultic law (e.g., circumcision, blood sacrifice) were "types" (prefiguring symbols) of the final work of redemption in Christ, and are therefore no longer binding on the Christian, the non-cultic commandments of God, as revealed in both Old and New Testaments, "are necessary to Christian morality, unquestionable in their requirement, relevant to every age, allowing no extrascriptural exceptions, and perpetually binding."

[handwritten margin notes: leads to moral casuistry & a God who is not dynamic (= dead)]

No one element of scriptural truth may be used "against" another portion of its message—as in liberal calls for a purportedly gospel-based "compassion" or "justice" for gays and lesbians that would take precedence over clear biblical proscriptions of same-sex activity. The Scriptures, having one divine author, speak one consistent truth, without internal contradiction of any kind. As for the matter of homosexuality, this consistency is evidenced by the fact that both the Old and New Testaments unequivocally condemn homosexual acts.

The Old Testament, both by precept (Lev 18:22; 20:13) and example (the story of Sodom, Genesis 18 & 19), pronounces such acts—by males—as an "abomination" worthy of the death penalty, whether that penalty is imposed by the civil authorities (as required by Leviticus) or directly by God (as with Sodom). In the New Testament, these acts—again by males—are judged a basis for exclusion from the Kingdom of God (1 Cor 6:9–11), that is, eternal damnation. They are also evidence—when committed by either males or females—of conscious rebellion against God (Rom 1:18, 24–28) Moreover, not once in the whole of the Bible is there *[handwritten: ✳]* *any* positive reference to homosexuality.

Traditional Roman Catholic moral theology has held that one may also look to human reason and the design of God's creation (together understood as "nature"), even in their fallen state, as a source for some forms of moral guidance. While St. Thomas Aquinas and numerous theologians following him developed highly refined conceptions of what precisely is to be understood by "nature" and "natural law,"[4] their sometimes abstruse reasoning trickled down into the common teaching of the church as an argument that simple observation of male-female sex differentiation and the function of that differentiation within the reproductive process makes clear to human reason, unaided by any special revelation in Scripture, the intended scope and purpose of sexuality.[5] Equally clear, in light of that purpose, is the fact that certain forms of sexual activity are "unnatural," contrary to nature.

Many conservative Protestants make a similar appeal to "nature" as an indicator of at least the broader outlines of the divine intent for sexuality. Some Reformed theologians, on the other hand, reflecting that school's suspicion of corrupted human reason as a source of any truth apart from the grace of special revelation, insist that we cannot look to the empirical data of nature or to human reasoning to determine what is "natural." Rather, the Bible instructs us in what is truly natural—that is, in conformity with God's created intent—and therefore normative. It is only in light of this revelation that we can then reflect on the evidence of God's sublime wisdom expressed in the specifics of the natural order.[6]

Question 2:

What is the God-given intent or design for human sexuality?

As is made clear in Genesis 1 and 2, confirmed in the explicit teaching of Jesus (Matt 19:4–6; Mark 10:1–10) and given sublime theological dimension in the writings of St. Paul (Eph 5:23–32), God's intention for human sexuality is the propagation of the species and the joining of husband and wife "as one flesh" in a monogamous, lifelong union which is, on the spiritual level, a symbolic expression of the relationship that exists between Christ and the church. Evangelical theologian Carl Henry puts the matter succinctly:

> From the Genesis creation narrative, which Jesus made part of his own teaching, we know that God ordained a heterosexual life for

mankind, and that the monogamous union of Adam and Eve as "one flesh" is the pattern of God's intention for the whole human family. In this framework of relationships both the procreation of the race and the sexual fulfillment of the individual were ideally and naturally to be found.[7]

Bahnsen writes similarly:

> The distinction enunciated in Genesis is more than incidental historical detail. It is a declaration of the proper creation order, cited with authoritative approval . . . by Christ . . . This creation of sexual differentiation by God from the beginning established heterosexuality as the normative direction for the sexual impulse and act. God the Creator gives created things their essential identity and function and defines man's proper relationships. Man's sexual function has been defined by God as male-female behavior.[8]

Question 3:

What are the necessary criteria for morally legitimate sexual expression?

The only context in which sexual expression is ever morally acceptable is the "creation ordinance" of heterosexual marriage. Sexual activity under any other circumstances (with or without actual intercourse) is sin. Further, following St. Paul's teaching that all other sins are "outside the body" while fornication is a sin against one's own body (1 Cor 6:18), it is sin of the most serious sort, a "mortal sin" in traditional Catholic moral theology—that is, sin which, unrepented, ensures damnation.

According to this same traditional Roman Catholic perspective, sexual expression retains a certain taint of sin even within marriage. Since sexual intercourse is necessary for the perpetuation of the race, however, it is licit—even a good thing—so long as it is potentially generative. On the other hand, if a particular sexual act (even between married partners) is not generative, it is sinful. Birth control, intercourse with a sterile partner and intercourse during menstruation are therefore forbidden even to husband and wife, as are various forms of sex play which result in orgasm without deposit of the seed in the womb. In recent decades, Catholic magisterial teaching has downplayed the church's historic negativity regarding marital sexuality and significantly expanded the legitimate significance of conjugal relations to include intimacy, psychological union and even a certain measure of mutual gratification. Nonetheless, the defining significance of generativity remains, most clearly evidenced by the church's continuing rejection of "artificial" birth control.

The primacy of generativity within the classic moral formulation makes it possible, while affirming that every sexual act occurring outside marriage is sin, to distinguish between two classes of sexual trespass. Some sexual sins—premarital sex, adultery, even incest—do not involve a negation of the fundamental biological purpose of the sex act. That is to say, although such sins violate the divine order of monogamous marriage for life set forth in God's specially revealed moral law, they do not transgress natural law: male mates with female and there is the possibility of conception. Other sexual sins—specifically, masturbation, homosexuality and bestiality—violate not only the revealed moral law but natural law as well. They are inherently unfruitful; they involve an unnatural use of the sexual organs. By their embodied denial of the essential meaning of sexual intercourse, they do profound violence to the harmony and balance of the Creator's design. On the level of value and meaning, such acts are contradictory, disordered and always a great moral evil.[10]

Conservative Protestants also strictly limit licit sexual expression to heterosexual marriage[11] and most would hold that homosexual acts are not only immoral but unnatural, echoing the traditional Catholic paradigm (although, as noted, some Reformed theologians have insisted that what is truly natural is determined by scriptural revelation, not by observation of the natural order). Since Protestantism from its inception has had a far less negative view of sex between spouses, however, Protestants have generally been less insistent that any morally acceptable sexual act must be open to conception.[12] Rather than upholding generativity as the sine qua non of permissible sexual expression, conservative Protestants generally contend that conformity to the God-given created order of monogamous heterosexual marriage—as set out in Genesis and confirmed by Jesus himself—is the essential element determining the morality of a given sexual act. While such a model obviously allows for a wider range of permissible sexual activity between spouses, it still excludes any homosexual act from moral legitimacy.

Question 4:

Is there a "homosexual condition" (orientation) and, if so, what is its cause or origin? *No*

Scripture knows nothing of a "homosexual condition" and, therefore, no such condition exists. Everyone is, ontologically, heterosexual. The notion that some people are homosexual by "orientation" is a self-serving rationalization invented to justify deliberately chosen perversity. What Scripture *does* recognize, however, is an "inner, spiritual depravity in men—a disinclination to good and a propensity for evil,"[13] i.e., original sin. It is out of this depravity that all sinful desires and acts (including homosexual desires and acts) come. The specific outworking of this general, universal depravity in any individual's life is the result of that person's whole history of reactions to circumstances, moral choices and acceptance or rejection of divine grace. Yet Scripture makes it clear that "original sin . . . is itself sinful in character and something for which its inheritors are held personally culpable."[14]

Those holding this view tend to discount much of contemporary psychology on the general principle that it is premised upon and promotes an un-Christian worldview.[15] On the popular level, however, many are willing to utilize certain elements of the older analytic tradition as regards homosexuality, at least to the extent of asserting that unhealthy families—in which the divinely ordained pattern of paternal headship is sacrificed to divorce, a domineering wife or a mother who works outside the home—may well have something to do with creating the sorts of gender confusions by which effeminate boys or overly-masculinized girls are created. At puberty, these damaged young people are most likely more susceptible than healthy teens to homosexual temptation, but they still have the power to resist that temptation and overcome it.[16]

It is true, however, that some people eventually find themselves consistently and exclusively drawn to homosexual lust. That this is the case was traditionally (and is sometimes still) attributed to a three-step process beginning with a conscious choice to sin) homosexual *experience* (either through injudicious experimentation or seduction) leads to *addiction*, which is itself God's punishment for the initial yielding to homosexual temptation. That addiction is then justified by the adoption of a false homosexual *identity* which becomes a sort of self-fulfilling prophecy.

exp / addictn / id.

Given this paradigm, the spread of homosexuality within a society is understood to be due to seduction of the young by self-identified homosexuals (who are by definition predatory). As the much-maligned Anita Bryant once put it: "They can't reproduce, so they have to recruit." Social tolerance of homosexuality also contributes to its spread, in that it encourages the impressionable young to experiment with homosexual activity and therefore find themselves caught in the inevitable sequence of experience/addiction/identity.

Bahnsen does not explicitly advance the experience/addiction/identity argument. Rather, he first notes that, even if the existence of a "homosexual disposition" distinct from homosexual desires and homosexual acts could be persuasively demonstrated (which he asserts has not been done), it would be morally irrelevant and could not "cancel culpability," since "the teaching of God's infallible Word" explicitly condemns both homosexual desires and homosexual acts as sin. Even without invoking the traditional etiological model, however, Bahnsen insists that homoerotic inclinations represent a "choice" on the part of the homosexual:

Of course homosexuality may not be a conscious and remembered choice . . . There may not have been a process of explicit deliberation, weighing the options, and coming to a decision . . . But that does not make homosexuality . . . any less chosen, in the sense of a voluntary, willful and personal preference.[17]

Question 5:

Can a legitimate moral distinction be made between a homosexual condition (orientation) and homosexual acts?

No. Under the classic etiological model (experience/addiction/identity), the so-called "homosexual condition" is nothing but the culmination of a series of choices to commit homosexual acts. Both the acts themselves and the false identity that is adopted to justify them (and is then the source of temptation to still further homosexual activity) are evidences of an unregenerate spirit that has not submitted to the saving work of Christ.

Bahnsen approaches the matter differently. Arguing that no homosexual orientation has been proven to exist, he contends that there are consequently only two relevant factors to be considered in a moral assessment of homosexuality: homoerotic desires and same-sex acts. Basing his argument upon the general scriptural principle that it is "not only evil to do immoral acts, it is also evil to desire to do immoral acts"[18] and, additionally, upon St. Paul's reference in Romans to the "impure lusts" (Rom 1:24) and "shameful passions" (Rom 1:26)[19] which lead men and women into homosexual behavior (which "lusts" and "passions" Bahnsen takes to describe all homoerotic desires), Bahnsen insists that "[i]f it were crucial to our moral judgments that we distinguish between innocent inversion and culpable homosexual acts, then certainly God would be aware of that distinction and bring it to light in His inspired Word for us." Since Scripture does not make any such distinction and, in fact, equally condemns both homosexual lust and homosexual acts, it is therefore:

> . . . plainly incorrect to hold that Scripture speaks only of homosexual acts and not of the homosexual desire and inclination. In forthright language Paul holds men and women morally responsible and under God's wrath for burning with homosexual desires . . . Scripture holds the homosexual fully responsible for his desires . . . as well as his overt activities.[20]

Question 6:

What is the psychological significance of homosexuality?

As already noted, those arguing for this viewpoint tend to be suspicious of psychology and its categories. Nonetheless, they generally expound a very clear psychological profile of the gay or lesbian person.

Homosexuals are incapable of love—their desires are always a species of lust,[21] never a matter of romantic or affectional attraction.[22] They are predatory and they pose a genuine threat to the young, since homosexuality and pedophilia are essentially the same thing.[23] Having crossed the line into perversity, any homosexual will—in accordance with an inflexible moral law built into the universe—sink into deeper and deeper levels of vileness and depravity.[24] Wilfully rejecting God's sovereign prerogatives over his creation, homosexuals seek the destruction or corruption of all that is good and wholesome on both the personal and the civic level.[25]

Question 7:

What is the spiritual significance of homosexuality?

As Saint Paul teaches in the first chapter of his Epistle to the Romans, homosexual desire is an indication of grievous spiritual rebellion.[26] It is by definition idolatrous, in that it sets up its own alternative "good"—homosexual gratification—in opposition to the manifest design of the Creator, thereby rejecting God's legitimate supremacy and authority over his own creation. Both homosexual inclination and homosexual acts are inconsistent with Christian discipleship.

Question 8:

Can a homosexual become heterosexual (the question of "cure")?

In much of their polemical literature, those holding to this view tend to focus more on the homosexual as an "enemy" to be resisted than they do on questions of cure.[27] Once the danger gay people allegedly pose to society is set aside, however, the assumption of many has traditionally been that one of the immediate results of conversion to Christ will be a "release" from homosexual addiction. This view is well put in a tract widely distributed in New York City's "gay ghetto" in the early 1970s by the evangelical ministry Teen Challenge:

> If you are desperate, if you are willing to turn your back on your sin of homosexuality, if you will receive Christ as your Savior today, you will be set free.[28]

Some Pentecostalists and charismatics likewise see the gospel as offering a promise of relatively instantaneous deliverance from homosexual desires and addictions. For them, however, homosexuality is more than merely one of the myriad forms original sin can take in the human personality—it is a species of demonic possession. Accordingly, they use exorcism to "cast out" the "demon" of homosexuality.

Bahnsen is willing to allow that "[t]he sin of homosexuality will not completely stop tempting the new convert any more than any other habitual sin immediately loses influence over a young believer. The problem will not necessarily disappear easily; it may take time, and it certainly will require pastoral counseling."[29] Nonetheless, Bahnsen writes at length and vigorously to the point that "[i]nverts must be assured that they *can* redirect their sexual desires, not by lengthy psychotherapeutic treatment but by ethical confrontation and the means of grace. They must be encouraged that, by God's Spirit they can indeed put their homosexuality behind them."

Such certainty follows logically from Bahnsen's understanding of homosexuality as a learned response: if it can be learned, it can be unlearned. Furthermore, according to Bahnsen's reading of 1 Cor 6:9–11—which includes two terms traditionally understood to refer to male homosexuals[30] in a listing of sins which will exclude one from the Kingdom but then goes on to affirm that "and such were some of you, but you have been washed . . . sanctified . . . justified" (verse 11)—St. Paul's words make it clear that:

> There *is* a way of escape for homosexuals. There is a better hope than that offered by secular psychology, a confidence that one can be delivered from the guilt and power of homosexuality. Paul knew people whom God had saved from this abomination; their homosexuality was now in the past tense, a matter of their preconversion lifestyle.

Given what Bahnsen takes to be the incontrovertible meaning of God's Word through the apostle, it follows that the converted homosexual must simply "channel his sexual drives in the right direction and exercise them, mentally and physically, under the limits set by God's will . . . assum[ing] the biblical attitude of repentance, resistance and redirection" toward his "sinful and perverse condition." The bottom line for Bahnsen is straightforward: "Because a person is a homosexual by will, and not by constitutional necessity, he can be changed and can reform his life."[31]

Some conservative Christians who, like Bahnsen, allow for the possibility of a less than instantaneous reordering of the sexual identity, do not likewise share his blanket rejection of all psychotherapeutic intervention. They suggest that at least certain forms of "Christian counseling" can be a legitimate tool in assisting the former homosexual in his or her turning away from sinful habits and inclinations. As the dean of evangelical Christian counseling, Clyde Narramore, writes:

Many men and women who have been engaged in overt homosexuality have become convicted by the Holy Spirit as they have surrendered their lives to Christ . . . After the question of salvation has been settled, then the counselor can help the counselee develop an effective program for spiritual development which, in turn, will have an important effect on his problem.[32]

Question 9:

What is the moral opinion arrived at, given the responses to Questions 1 through 8?

Homosexual acts or desires are always, without exception, sin. Homosexuals, without repentance and amendment of life, are destined for eternal damnation. No person can be a Christian and also be, in identity or in action, a homosexual.

Question 10:

What is the personal call of Christ for the gay man or lesbian?

The homosexual must repent of the sin of homosexuality, admit that his or her homosexuality is the result of conscious, sinful choice, and renounce that choice, claiming the saving work of Christ for forgiveness of both homosexual inclination and all homosexual acts committed. He or she should resist by the power of God's Spirit whatever further temptation may occur as a result of the habitual nature of sin, utilizing the ordinary means of grace (fellowship, Word, sacraments and pastoral counseling) in the ongoing work of sanctification which God's Word promises will eradicate both homosexual habit and desire. This sanctification, Bahnsen insists, cannot simply be a matter of the homosexual

> sublimating and being frustrated by his desires; such a halfway house is not where God intended to leave the homosexual when he delivered him from his sin. Since the homosexual has obviously not been given the gift of sexual abstinence, his restoration by God should eventually bring conformity to the creational order and a regaining of heterosexual desires. His final goal is God's ordained context and direction for sexual gratification—heterosexual marriage.[33]

Question 11:

What is the pastoral call of Christ to the church on the issue?

The church must stand firm and proclaim God's intended moral order, as well as its own adherence to biblical authority. It must speak God's judgment on a permissive culture that would promote toleration of so grave a moral evil as homosexuality. For the sake of those children who will be seduced, recruited or confused into homosexuality absent strong legal penalties against it, Christians must work tirelessly to oppose any social or legal legitimization of homosexuality, no matter how unpopular such a stand may be.

False notions of "sympathy" for homosexuals who "suffer" from an "involuntary orientation" have no place among true Christians. In the first place, there is no involuntary homosexual orientation.[34] In the second, "[p]ity or sympathy is inappropriate if we are to think God's thoughts after Him and have our emotions transformed by the Word of truth. We cannot sympathize with those who commit what God deems abomination and perversion . . . the child of God must be repulsed and outraged at this vile behavior."[35] The Christian who "delights in God's law"—as any Christian should—"burns with indignation toward the wicked who forsake it."[36]

Instead of offering misguided sympathy, the church must speak, with unapologetic clarity, God's condemnation of homosexual sin to individual gays and lesbians. As the editors of *Christianity Today* wrote in 1969, "The church had better make it plain that Christianity and homosexuality are incompatible even as it proclaims deliverance for the homosexual from his sinful habit through faith in Jesus Christ."[37] If homosexuals are found within the church, they should be confronted with their sin and, if recalcitrant, expelled and shunned, following the teaching of Jesus regarding such situations (Matt 18:15–17). While such adherence to biblical principle may be denounced by the wider culture or by liberals within the churches as "unloving" or "discriminatory," anything less is nothing but "cheap grace" willing to abandon homosexual sinners to eternal separation from God in order to spare their temporal feelings. Harold Lindsell articulates this viewpoint forcefully in a 1973 *Christianity Today* article:

A church that decides to show compassion toward the homosexual by admitting him to full rights and privileges shows a false compassion that confirms the sinner in his wicked ways . . . It is discrimination on the part of the church to exclude homosexuals, but it is not oppression. Discrimination lies at the heart of Christianity. The ax of God's holiness and righteousness divides the saved from the lost.[38]

On the other hand, the church's obligation goes beyond an unflinching pronouncement of God's just judgment upon homosexuality. The church must also, with equal clarity and force, announce the Good News "as the power of God unto salvation, so that as repentant believers homosexuals may become fellow-members in the body of Christ."[39] And there is yet another responsibility incumbent upon the Christian community as well: it must "support and encourage" redeemed former homosexuals in their growth into a "transformed lifestyle." It must "not only require a change of direction, but extend aid to the former homosexual in his Christian growth and in resisting temptation." That being the case, "a lack of concern, an unhelpful and cold attitude toward the converted homosexual in the church is especially inexcusable. Christian fellowship . . . can help reshape a person's lifestyle, schedule, interests and acquaintances. It can prevent loneliness and despair. It provides a shelter in temptation . . ."

Despite the unfeigned welcome and ongoing support the church is called to give repentant homosexuals, however, consistent homosexual temptation is evidence of refusal to submit to the sanctifying work of God in one's life, and therefore even a celibate homosexual is unfit for any leadership role in the church.

Question 12:

What is the political call of Christ to society on the issue?

Civil government is established by God with a mandate to foster righteousness and punish wickedness. If it fails in this responsibility, it rightly falls under the judgment of God. Human law, if it is to be legitimate, must mirror and give civil force to God's eternal law. Societies that promote or even tolerate grievous sin lay themselves open to divine retribution. It is the duty of the state, as well, to protect the weak and the innocent from the depredations of the depraved.

Homosexuality represents the "cultural culmination of rebellion against God . . . the 'burning out' of man and his culture." Its public toleration or acceptance is symptomatic of "a society under judgment, inwardly corrupted to the point of impending collapse."[40] Homosexuality, therefore—countenanced at any level—is a profound threat to the common good. Criminal law should restrict and penalize it severely and Christians should work actively to that end. Conversely, antidiscrimination statutes should be vigorously opposed, since legal "neutrality" toward homosexuals implies a moral parity between homosexuality and heterosexuality and deprives Christians of their right to hold themselves and their families apart from ungodliness and to "shun moral perversion." Society *should* discriminate against homosexuals, just as it "discriminates" against thieves, murderers and other antisocial elements.

Bahnsen sets out a detailed argument in support of the contention that homosexual acts are not only sin but a crime to be punished by civil authority. He begins by acknowledging that not all sins are, in fact, crimes—"there is a realm of private morality and immorality which is *apart from* the public claims and corresponding duties that the state enforces with civil sanctions." But how, then, are we to know which sins inhabit this private realm and which are legitimately the concern of the state? For Bahnsen the answer is simple: "the believer has no choice but to settle the issue of society's proper response to the homosexual on *scriptural* grounds . . . we should decide whether homosexuality is a crime on the basis of God's infallible Word." This being the case, the fact that a criminal penalty for homosexual acts is set forth in Lev 20:13 ("If a man lies with a male . . . they shall [*both*] be put to death; their blood is upon them.") makes it clear that such acts are intended by God to fall under the jurisdiction of the state, that they are not merely private sin but public crime. If Christians are to be true to the Word of God, they have an obligation to urge the state to forbid these acts by statute, both through legal discrimination against and punishment of those who commit them.[41] Furthermore, in terms of the nature of such punishment, "[t]o treat the criminal homosexual as a subject for rehabilitation rather than retribution is to dismiss the restraining function of God's revealed law . . ."[42]

Addressing directly the libertarian argument that criminal law exists only to protect innocent victims, not to control the private behavior of consenting adults, Bahnsen counters that such an argument is erroneous on its face, since even those who argue most strenuously for the "liberty ideal" admit that there are exceptions to it (e.g., restrictions on the sale and use of drugs, disallowance of the consent of the victim as exculpatory in assisted suicide). Civilization requires that we "recognize that there are certain standards of behavior that society ought to require to be observed, completely apart from considerations of personal freedom and consent." The real question, then, is what authority will be relied upon to determine what those standards should be. For Bahnsen, there can be only one answer to this question: the authority of God's revealed moral law. Furthermore, Bahnsen insists, the libertarian argument is fallacious in claiming that socially sanctioned homosexuality has no victims, since tolerated, openly flaunted homosexuality *does* victimize others: "[i]f homosexual relations are tolerated by civil law, thereby failing to witness against their abnormality and perversion and refusing to restrain their occurrence, the state allows a progressive degradation and permissiveness toward sexual matters. This is detrimental to the society's moral stability, the dignity of human beings, the attempts of people to live—and to raise their children to live—chaste lives, and the monogamous foundation that has been found crucial to all civilized societies."

As for the often repeated charge that the imposition of biblical law upon a pluralistic society (in which many do not accept the authority of the Judeo-Christian Scriptures, or interpret that authority differently than do conservative Christians) would constitute a violation of the separation of church and state, Bahnsen contends that Christians must "repudiate a dichotomy between a sacred realm of grace (or religion) where God's revelation is followed and a secular realm . . . where autonomous standards of thought and behavior govern . . . [E]very aspect of life [*must*] be brought under the dominion of God and consecrated to His ends." Furthermore, the fact that Christian believers "distinctively acknowledge the [*biblical*] ethic as objectively valid due to God's work of redemption in their lives does not reduce their moral standards to mere private opinion . . . God is the Creator of all men, as well as the Redeemer of His elect; consequently, His moral standards are . . . universally valid and applicable . . . as absolute as the character of God, to whom all men are responsible." Therefore, "God's law is to be promoted publically" and not just in the private lives of Christians. "Christians are obliged to reprove the unfruitful works of darkness." If they fail in this obligation, "they share in the guilt of sins committed through consent." Thus, Bahnsen concludes, while "[n]ot all sins are crimes . . . those which God's Word defines as crimes (punishable by the civil magistrate) are to be treated as such in society."

Few proponents of this viewpoint have argued the political consequences of the viewpoint as exhaustively as Bahnsen. But all are agreed that homosexuals pose a danger not only to one's children through seduction/recruitment, but to society's very survival, since their tolerated presence within a community lays that community open to God's righteous wrath and a retributive judgment which will inevitably, at least to some extent, fall on just and unjust alike.

Representative Denominations and Para-Church Groups

Although traditional Roman Catholic teaching initially defined this viewpoint for Western Christendom, the Church's magisterium now articulates a significantly different perspective, as discussed in viewpoint 3, "A Call to Costly Discipleship." As a consequence, this present viewpoint is now most strongly identified with the Protestant Christian Right. For groups like the Reverend Jerry Falwell's Moral Majority, the Reverend Donald Wildmon's American Family Association and the Reverend Lou Sheldon's Traditional Values Coalition, the political agenda growing out of this conviction has become a major focus of activism. Condemnation would also be the typical viewpoint in many of the fundamentalist and conservative evangelical congregations which make up the primary support base for these national organizations, although, as noted, increasing awareness of the theories and claims of the ex-gay movement (viewpoint 2) has had a significant impact in these churches in recent years.

The largest American denomination to identify itself explicitly with this viewpoint is the Southern Baptist Convention. In 1987, that church's convention condemned homosexuality on the personal level as a manifestation of a depraved nature and on the societal level as an indication of general moral decline.

Cross-Perspective Critique

Critique

(1) It is often charged by those opposing this viewpoint that its most consistent characteristic is an attitude of contempt and hatred for the homosexual person which is completely at odds with the spirit of Christ. Whereas Jesus went out of his way to minister lovingly to the social outcasts of his own society, saving the sting of his condemnatory judgments for the hypocrisy of the conventionally pious, those holding this view—it is asserted—reverse the equation, justifying themselves in their self-righteousness by projecting all that is evil in the human heart onto the "other," the homosexual.

(2) In so doing, they demonize the gay person with little or no regard for the facts. Despite overwhelming evidence that the vast majority of child molesters are heterosexual, for example, they continue to label homosexuals as a danger to children. Even though most homosexuals lead remarkably normal lives not that dissimilar in most respects from those of their straight neighbors, spokesmen for this view consistently invoke bizarre images from the outer reaches of the gay subculture (drag queens, leather fetishists and devotees of bondage) as typical of all gay and lesbian people. Such "bearing false witness," as it is labeled by former evangelical celebrity ghostwriter Mel White, now a minister of the Metropolitan Community Church, is endemic among those in the forefront of the Christian Right and is often used with at least subconscious cynicism as an inflammatory scare tactic for fund-raising.

(3) Also often criticized is the misuse or inconsistent use of Scripture by those holding this viewpoint. As an example of the former, opponents cite the fact that the Genesis account of the infamous

sin of Sodom at most can only speak to the subject of homosexual gang rape, which has no more relevance to the question of loving, consensual homosexual partnerships than the story of the rape of Tamar by her half brother (2 Sam 13:1–20) has to heterosexual marriage.

As for inconsistencies in fidelity to Scripture by those claiming to be strictly bound in their views and practice by the inerrant teachings of the Bible, it is noted that contemporary conservative Christians ignore many explicit biblical injunctions. Few fundamentalists, for example, argue that—out of obedience to the divine command in Lev 20:9—children who curse their parents should be put to death by the state. The Holiness Code also imposes the death penalty for adultery (Lev 20:10), and Jesus specifically teaches that divorce and remarriage are adulterous (Matt 19:9; Mark 10:10–12; Luke 16:18), yet not only are no voices on the right calling for the institution of capital punishment for the divorced and remarried, many—if not most—fundamentalists now accept second marriages for divorced Christians without objection, despite this scriptural teaching.

Similarly, the consistent biblical prohibition of usury—lending of money at interest—is ignored (indeed, conservative Christian organizations are anxious to place bankers on their boards), sex during menstruation is no longer banned (some Christian marriage manuals specifically approve it), and Jesus' clear teaching that his followers should not lay up treasures for themselves on earth is, in practice if not in proclamation, dismissed as spiritual hyperbole by most conservative Christians, some of whom have gone so far as to create an entire "prosperity theology" of Christian entitlement to this world's goods.[43] As Alfred Corn notes in his contribution to *Wrestling With the Angel: Faith and Religion in the Lives of Gay Men*,[44] "Fundamentalism is strange to me, but selective fundamentalism is stranger still." Malcolm Macourt makes a similar point in *Towards a Theology of Gay Liberation*:[45]

> [F]ew other statements in the Bible have been treated as literally as those that touch on homosexuality by people who have found more flexible or non-literal interpretations for every other topic.

Conservatives on the far right of the spectrum are faulted for theological error in their claim that homosexuality is a particularly heinous class of sin that sets those who commit it apart from the rest of humanity. Ultimately, opponents argue, Christianity admits to no sin being "worse" than any other.[46] It is a consistent scriptural principle that *all* sin separates us from the Holy God. Every human being stands equally in need of God's grace and one can damn oneself just as thoroughly by backbiting or resentment as by fornication. Indeed, as already noted, Jesus himself saved his hard sayings not for the sexually reprobate but the self-righteous and judgmental.

Further, even many Christians who would see all homosexual acts as inherently sinful would nevertheless insist that to argue that homosexual desire is in itself culpable does violence to a fundamental Christian principle, that being: temptation alone is never sinful, since Jesus himself was tempted "in every way as we are, yet without sin" (Heb 4:15).

The assertion that homosexuality is "contrary to nature" is also contested. While admitting this charge has a venerable history (both Josephus and Philo make it, as does Paul in his Epistle to the Romans),[47] critics challenge it on two grounds. The first is that the term "nature" is itself problematical due to its having more than one meaning. The ancient and medieval understanding was that "nature" is *normative*; it references what "should be." What "should be" was deduced from biological data (human anatomy, the procreative process) and majority experience (the fact that most people are erotically drawn to members of the opposite sex)[48] and was interpreted generically; that is, was assumed to be applicable to all human beings equally. Under this definition, homosexual inclination or acts were deemed "unnatural." The modern, "scientific" definition of "nature," on the other hand, is *descriptive*; it references what "is"—the "sum total of things which can be observed."[49] Since homosexual attraction and behavior are an observable phenomenon within human experience, they are part of "nature," part of the multifaceted reality of human experience. From the perspective of contemporary understanding, to call them "unnatural" is therefore inaccurate empirically and meaningless morally. The second ground for challenge lies in what is taken to be a logical flaw in the traditional understanding of nature as normative, this flaw being its "naturalistic fallacy" that one can derive a prescriptive norm (e.g., it is "unnatural" and consequently immoral for male to have sex with male) from a statement of

"what is" is not necessarily
"what ought to be"

observation (e.g., male has sex with female and the result is a child). This, Pronk insists, is "logically impossible," since "no 'ought' can follow from an 'is.'"[50]

Adherents of this viewpoint are also faulted for their stubborn rejection of what more liberal critics assert is scientific fact—the existence of a homosexual orientation, the general mental health of gay men and lesbians—when such fact contradicts their prejudices. It is noted as well that clinging to an experience/addiction/identity etiological model or insisting that homosexual inclination is "chosen" or "learned"—in the face of extensive evidence that the majority of homosexuals are to at least some extent aware of their condition long before they have any homosexual experience or have made any conscious "choice" as to sexual orientation—constitutes nothing more than willful and obstinate intellectual dishonesty.

As for the claim that Christians must oppose any decriminalization of homosexuality and support discriminatory measures against gays and lesbians in the name of protecting the innocent, critics note that conservatives have completely failed to prove their case on the issue of homosexuals posing a threat to children either through "recruitment" or unwholesome example.[51] On the matter of opposing tolerance or legal equality for homosexuals so as to preserve social righteousness, opponents argue that an essential element of the social contract in a diverse, democratic society is the refusal to discriminate in law against any individual over private opinion or behavior that does not involve violation of the rights of another. Thus, a basic tenet of that American system which most fundamentalists claim to hold so dear is the primacy of personal freedom within the private sphere and that freedom is equally the right of all citizens, not just heterosexuals.

The Viewpoint Responds

"stakes are too high"

What sort of "compassion" is it, those holding this viewpoint ask, that would rather encourage grievous sinners to remain in their sin and be eternally cut off from the presence of God than accept the Christian's obligation to speak God's truth, even when that obligation entails forthrightly condemning sin in the hope that some will repent, turn from their wickedness and live? What sort of "love" does it show for the impressionable young (whose temporal and eternal happiness are at stake) to imply even by social "tolerance," much less positive affirmation, that a homosexual lifestyle is a morally acceptable alternative to God's created heterosexual order—and, worse, to allow these children to become potential victims of predatory homosexuals? What sort of Christian responsibility is it that would put one's neighbors at risk of inadvertently sharing in the outpouring of divine wrath against a society that protects and promotes the most depraved forms of human godlessness, rather than take on the admittedly often thankless task of standing against the spirit of the times and fighting for a return to civic righteousness?

As for appeals to the "love of God" as a basis for changing the church's longstanding condemnation of homosexuality, while it is certainly true that God is—as Scripture makes clear—love, that is not all God has revealed Himself to be. The God proclaimed in Scripture is a holy God as well, a God who, when confronted with evil, exercises that fearful holiness through retributive wrath— both within history and finally at a judgment which, as Jesus' own teaching makes clear, will result in those who reject God's law and grace being cast into the hell "prepared for the devil and his angels" for eternity. Unlike contemporary religious liberalism, the Bible does not teach an accommodating, domesticated God of undemanding, permissive "love" who is ultimately far too kindhearted to take our human rebelliousness all that seriously. On the issue of homosexuality, as on other vital moral questions, the stakes—both for individuals and nations—are simply too high to allow a sentimental, enfeebled notion of the "love" of God for sinners to become the basis for rejection of the clear scriptural teaching as to the inescapable consequences of unrepented human sin.

For those holding this viewpoint, the biblical message could not be more forthright: "homosexuality . . . both in practice and desire—is a grave sin in the sight of the Lord." Furthermore, the homosexual "is morally responsible for his attraction to, and sexual relations with, members of the same sex."[52] This explicit biblical message—which states the changeless, universally binding judgment of God—carries with it a series of imperatives: "Individuals should disapprove of and oppose homosexuality as immoral. Churches should decline membership and office to unrepentant homosexuals. States should restrain homosexuality rather than making it a civil right."

What is ultimately at issue in the current debate is a fundamental truth on which Christians can brook no compromise—the trustworthiness of God's holy and inspired Word. The Bible makes it unarguably clear, both in the Old Testament and the New, that homosexuality is sin. The negative scriptural statements could not be more straightforward or explicit. No qualification on this judgment is made anywhere in the sacred pages of Holy Writ. Thus, when it comes to the matter of homosexuality, there is only one simple question that matters: shall we believe God, speaking through His Word, or men? For any believer worthy of the name, the answer is evident. As Harold Lindsell writes:

> The final and conclusive argument against homosexuality does not come from the sociologists, the secularists, or the humanists. It comes from God, who has spoken His word against it and has never stuttered in His speech.[53]

For the true Christian, therefore, the matter is settled. Even to suggest any alternative viewpoint is to manifest that rebellion against God's sovereign and rightful authority over his creation which was the essential spiritual element in the original fall of mankind.

A PROMISE OF HEALING

While sharing a number of convictions with the previous viewpoint, this second position differs from it significantly both in its more pastoral tone and in its confident proclamation of "hope for the homosexual" through a psychological and spiritual process of "recovery" by which the gay man or lesbian is promised healing of homosexual "brokenness." Achieving this recovery generally involves a combination of prayer for inner healing, ongoing discipling fellowship and some form of reparative therapy.[1]

Whatever the specific methods utilized, however, the psychospiritual reordering they are believed to effect means that men and women caught in an unfulfilling and ultimately destructive "homosexual lifestyle" can find freedom and restoration; they can put homosexual sin behind them and become "ex-gay." This assurance is based on nothing less than the pledge of Jesus Christ himself, in whom we are reborn as "a new creation" for whom, truly, "everything old has passed away; see, everything has become new!" (2 Cor 5:17).

Question 1:

What is the ultimate authority upon which any moral judgment regarding homosexuals and/or homosexual acts is to be based? BIBLE

In agreement with the view of Condemnation on this question, those holding this viewpoint insist there is only one final authority for authentically Christian moral conviction: the revealed Scriptures, which are understood to speak an unqualifiedly negative judgment upon homosexual acts. This judgment is evidenced both in the positive statements of male-female complementarity set forth in the creation accounts (Genesis 1 & 2) and affirmed by Jesus himself (Matt 19:4–6; Mark 10:1–10), and in the negative proscriptions of both the Old Testament (Lev 18:22; 20:13) and the New (Rom 1:18, 24–28; 1 Cor 6:9–11; 1 Tim 1:8–11).

Question 2:

What is the God-given intent or design for human sexuality?

Human sexuality has four fundamental purposes. The first is biological: procreation. The second is psychological: the uniting of man and woman in intimate, committed community, which purpose includes the love, society, pleasure, mutual aid, and comfort such a union provides. The third is spiritual, or what those of a Catholic perspective would term "sacramental"—mediated to husband and wife through their physical bond and the common life that grows from it in marriage, it is a particular form of the sanctifying grace of God.[2] The last is symbolic: in the sexual union of male and female—so similar in their common humanity and yet so distinct, both physically and psychologically, in their genders—is enacted a profound mystery which flows through all of creation and back into the very nature of the Creator himself.

Each of these elements—reproduction, familial solidarity, imparted grace and archetypal significance—plays a part in what Scripture speaks of as the "one flesh" union between a man and a woman which is intended by God to be both the consequence of and the context for human sexual expression. If conception results, the partners quite literally become "one flesh" in their child, who will share the genes of each. Even absent procreation, if sexual relations take place within the marital commitment, man and woman become one in intimate solidarity, shared fate and mutual spiritual growth. Moreover, they become a living icon of an essential aspect of reality: the never-ceasing drive to wholeness.

St. Paul goes still further, affirming that, in the fallen state of the world, a debased form of the one flesh union is effected even by sexual congress *outside* the divinely ordained parameters of committed partnership: intercourse with a prostitute binds a man to her as one flesh (1 Cor 6:15–16). This leads C. S. Lewis to argue—specifically citing Paul—that, for better or worse, an eternal spiritual connection is made between a man and a woman simply by the sexual act alone, irrespective of its context. As he writes through his "Senior Devil," Screwtape: "The truth is that, wherever a man lies with a woman, there, whether they like it or not, a transcendental relation is set up between them which must be eternally enjoyed or eternally endured."[3] Similarly, Andrew Comiskey—founder of the Vineyard Christian Fellowship's Desert Stream Ministry and a "homosexual struggler" (his term) who is now married and the father of four—states that, in heterosexual intercourse, "souls and spirits" are united as well as bodies.[4]

This profound and inescapable coupling gains still greater import from the fact that the gender differentiation which is the ground of human sexuality is itself a reflection of a larger, indeed a fundamental, principle built into the universe, which principle Karl Stern has termed "polarity in unity."[5] All things, it is argued, in ways we cannot always fully apprehend, are what they are in terms of the balance of opposites. These opposites, moreover, exist in a perpetual tension resulting from the fact that they are also, on some fundamental level, similar, and thus complementary. As regards gender, this means masculine and feminine can ultimately be understood "only in terms of each other; basically they are opposite and complementary qualities."[6] That being the case, it is argued, gender differentiation is much more than an incidental, random or malleable fact of biological nature. It is a transcendent reality; it has, in Leanne Payne's words, "cosmic meaning."[7] As C. S. Lewis puts it in his metaphysical fantasy novel *That Hideous Strength*:

> Gender is a reality and a more fundamental reality than sex. Sex is, in fact, merely the adaptation to organic life of a fundamental polarity which divides all created beings. Female sex is simply one of the things which has feminine gender; there are many others and Masculine and Feminine meet us on planes of reality where male and female would be simply meaningless.[8]

Stern, in fact, sees polarity in unity not as a created phenomenon but rather as an eternal, ontological reality existing within the very nature of God, which reality is then reproduced in creation. Payne makes the same point in her preface to Andy Comiskey's

Pursuing Sexual Wholeness[9] when she writes: "gender . . . is rooted in God Himself."

Neoorthodox titan Karl Barth argues similarly when he states that a fundamental element of mankind's being made in the image of God, and therefore a vital component of our essential humanity, is the defining fact of male-female complementarity.

> . . . the male is a male . . . to the extent that he is with the female, and the female likewise . . . [T]hey have their essence in the fact that they are directed to be in fellowship . . . [T]heir humanity can consist concretely only in the fact that they live in fellow-humanity, male with female, and female with male.[10]

Barth acknowledges that those who are single can express this divinely ordered fellowship through relationships other than the marriage bond (parent/child or sibling kinship, acquaintance, friendship or shared vocation). But, whether married or not, every human being should be "committed to liv[*ing*] consciously and willingly in this interrelationship, not regarding his being abstractly as his own but as being in fellowship [*with the opposite sex*], and shaping it accordingly." "The command of God shows irrefutably" Barth concludes, that human beings "can only be genuinely human [*as man*] with woman, or as . . . woman with man."[11]

Comiskey is clearly echoing Barth when he refers to God's image in humankind being, at least in significant part, "male and female in heterosexual covenant." Expanding on this idea, he writes:

> God [*in Genesis*] tells us that to discover our true humanity, we must be known by the opposite sex. A fundamental part of our bearing the divine image is its heterosexual reflection . . . Adam knew his maleness in the gaze of Eve's distinct femaleness and vice-versa. The uniqueness of each was realized in the other's difference. The dynamic sense of dissimilarity and similarity drew them into an adventure of self-discovery.[12]

The specifics of this "dynamic dissimilarity and similarity"—that is, of gender differentiation and complementarity—are foundational to this viewpoint's understanding of the causes of homosexuality, the nature of homosexual desire and the appropriate treatment for effecting recovery and restoration to God's intended heterosexual order. As Payne, Comiskey and others insist repeatedly and at considerable length, gender differentiation and complementarity are not merely matters of biology.[13] In man and woman, gender polarity is evidenced in ways of *being*, even ways of *knowing*.

On the level of being, those holding this view contend, the essence of the masculine principle—expressed, as it were, through a fundamental "stance" toward all of life—is initiation. The essence of the feminine principle is response.[14] While every human person, male or female, must to some extent incorporate both masculine and feminine elements into the personality (with the different balance of these two components appropriate to each) the divine intent—indeed, the fundamental nature of reality—is best expressed when, both in the family and society, males predominantly embody and pass on to their sons the masculine principles of leadership, authority and protection of the dependent, while females primarily express and engender in their daughters the complementary feminine principles of receptivity, nurturing and sacrificial love.[15]

[margin note: con sound like sexism]

On the level of modes of perception, a similar polarity is perceived: discursive reason is a masculine principle; intuition a feminine mode. Men typically see in straight lines, step leading to step. Women more naturally perceive wholes and the overlapping embrace of the circle. This is not to say that females are incapable of linear logic, or that males should not be expected to exhibit some measure of empathic or holistic sensitivity. Again, both men and women are intended to embody a balance of masculine and feminine—but not an *equal* balance.

Furthermore, each of the two gender identities has its own fundamental "drive" (as Payne terms it) which is intended to express itself in all aspects of the personality—the erotic, the intellectual, the spiritual—and which has its logical consequence in naturally appropriate spheres of activity. The divinely appointed masculine drive is a "drive toward power." On this point, Payne quotes Stern approvingly in his comparison of the spermatozoon's "attack" and "penetration" of the ovum to the male's aggressive, masterful place in the natural order: digging up stones and trees to plow, damming rivers, overcoming the laws of nature and, even in intellectual pursuits, "pierc[ing]" the "nature of things."[16] The female gender drive, on the other hand, is fundamentally "to respond to and to receive the male." It is a drive toward "receiving, keeping and nourishing—woman's specific form of creativeness . . . [is] . . . motherhood."[17]

[margin note: this seems very manipulative (using evidence that is open to interp]

Thus, on the symbolic level, human sexuality properly employed is a living sign of that complementary polarity which is creation's reflection of the nature of its source. In the glorious mystery of sexual union, the differentiated similarity of male and female is subsumed into a higher unity in which the two partners, without losing their individuality, become something more than the sum of their parts. As Episcopalian seminary professor and psychiatrist Ruth Tiffany Barnhouse writes: "The true religious goal of human sexuality can be seen not as satisfaction but as *completeness*."[18] Such completeness is, as Barnhouse quotes John Dixon,[19] by its very nature "the coming together of differences" which symbolizes on the human level what Barnhouse calls the "wholeness of the sacred order." That this symbolic aspect of human sexuality is of the most profound significance is evidenced by the fact that St. Paul finds it a fitting symbol for the relationship between Christ and his Body, the church—the form in time of that reality outside of time which is the destiny of all creation remade and redeemed in the new heaven and earth.

Question 3:

What are the necessary criteria for morally legitimate sexual expression?

Sexual acts are only licit when they take place within heterosexual marriage. Any other use of human sexuality is by definition an abuse of this great gift and therefore sin.

Not every sexual act between spouses need be open to conception in order to be acceptable, since the defining moral issue is male-female complementarity within the marriage covenant, but neither is sex between married partners to be pursued selfishly by either partner or—within the larger framework of the marital relationship—strictly for its own sake. While married partners should feel free to fully enjoy the gift of their sexuality without shame, they should also always be mindful of those deeper meanings and purposes of their sexual union which go far beyond mere physical pleasure.

Question 4:

Is there a "homosexual condition" (orientation) and, if so, what is its cause or origin?

No

Leanne Payne, whose books have had considerable influence in the ex-gay movement, explicitly denies the existence of what is generally meant by the homosexual orientation. In *Crisis in Masculinity*,[20] she states flatly that "[t]here [*is*] no such thing, strictly speaking, as a lesbian or homosexual . . . there are only those who are separated from some valid though *unaffirmed* part of themselves," and in *The Broken Image: Restoring Personal Wholeness Through Healing Prayer*,[21] she writes:

> There is no such thing as a "homosexual person." There are only those who need healing of old rejections and deprivations, deliverance from the wrong kind of self love and the actions that issue from it, and—along with that—the knowledge of their own higher selves in Christ.

In a similar vein, Joanne Highley of L.I.F.E. ("Living in Freedom Eternally") Ministry in New York City insists that Christians must recognize the notion of "homosexual orientation for what it is—a lie." We are all, Highley contends, "truly heterosexual."[22] Andy Comiskey, while speaking less absolutely, prefers "person with homosexual tendencies" or "homosexual struggler" to "homosexual." "I hesitate . . . to label . . . anyone . . . as homosexual," he writes. "Gay feelings are part of his personhood but need not be *the*, or even *a*, primary reference point."[23]

Dr. Elizabeth Moberly, on the other hand, whose *Homosexuality: A New Christian Ethic*[24] outstrips even Payne's work in its impact within ex-gay circles,[25] does appear to believe that there is such a thing as a homosexual orientation. Holding with mainstream therapeutic opinion, Moberly contends that human persons are born neither homosexual or heterosexual, but rather that sexual orientation is formed through a psychodynamic developmental process involving, in particular, one's relationship with the same-sex parent. The divinely intended goal of this process is mature heterosexuality, to be sure, but that goal is not always achieved. When it is not, the affectional and erotic attractions of the homosexual can "exist independently of sexual expression."

Despite such unequivocal statements as those of Payne and Highley noted above, the reality is that even ex-gay advocates who make a point of denying the existence of a homosexual condition or orientation tend to write and minister from a presumption that such a phenomenon does, in fact, exist. After insisting that the notion of homosexual orientation is "a lie," for example, Highley goes on to promise a "transformation of one's orientation." Similarly, Payne, throughout her works, consistently uses "homosexual" in the commonly understood sense of a person with same sex erotic and emotional attraction (as in the title of her *The Healing of the Homosexual*).[26] Generally, however, what would commonly be called homosexual orientation is given other names in ex-gay literature: "homosexual compulsion," "homosexual identity crisis," "homosexual tendencies," "gender identity deficit."[27]

Opinions vary among ex-gay theorists and therapists as to the etiology of same-sex emotional/erotic drives, whatever the name by which one chooses to refer to them. For Leanne Payne—whose literary method is highly anecdotal, with the theories of causality underlying her treatment emerging somewhat piecemeal from the personal stories of those who have come to her for healing prayer—what she often terms the "homosexual identity crisis" is always the result of some form of psychological injury.[28] Beyond that, and whatever the etiology of a particular case, Payne detects in both male homosexuality and lesbianism strong elements of what she dubs the "cannibal compulsion"—same-sex erotic attractions as a confused attempt to reach out and incorporate from another person a part of the self which has been cut off, alienated or not properly integrated. Gays and lesbians, Payne argues, *unaffirmed in their own gender identity*, eroticize the aspects of themselves to which they have been denied access and seek out those things in same sex partners.[29]

Contrary to the vast majority of therapeutic professionals, Payne places the critical point for establishing gender identity not in the first years of development (before five or six), but rather at puberty and immediately thereafter in adolescence. For both boys and girls, the crucial figure in this portentous moment of self-definition (or failure thereof) is the father. As for boys, Payne writes, "Men . . . in possession of their masculine identity, are on the natural plane the chief channels God has ordained for passing manhood on to man."[30] Men who are unaffirmed in their masculine identity by their fathers, therefore, cannot accept themselves as men, and consequently seek out their lost or unintegrated male self erotically in other males. Similarly, girls who are not validated as feminine by their fathers at this crucial moment of transition will be uncertain in their own femaleness and will recoil from that response to the male which should naturally be theirs, eroticizing a child's need for the safety of mother love and turning to other women to meet that need.[31]

Elizabeth Moberly's etiological model, which is in its broader outline consistent with the paradigm argued by reparative therapy proponents, is considerably more systematic than Payne's. According to Moberly, the homosexual condition "involves legitimate developmental needs, the fulfillment of which has been blocked by an underlying ambivalence to members of the same sex."[32] This same-sex ambivalence, Moberly contends, is rooted in "difficulties in the parent-child relationship, especially in the earlier years of life." Thus, the defining common factor for all homosexuals, male or female, is the same: "The homosexual . . . has suffered from some deficit in the relationship with the parent of the same sex . . . there is a corresponding drive to make good this deficit—through the medium of . . . homosexual . . . relationships."[33]

While this "deficit" can be caused by deliberate ill-treatment, abuse, rejection or neglect, it can also be the result of some inadvertent situation: illness and consequent hospitalization on the part of the parent or the child, death or necessary absence. The point, in some ways, is not so much the intention of the parent as the perception of the child. That is to say, this disruption in the normal psychological process of attachment to the same-sex parent is experienced as hurtful by the child, who reacts to the pain of the disruption "by an unwillingness to relate any longer to the love-source that has been experienced as hurtful." This unwillingness is termed "defensive detachment." In such detachment, the child (and later, the adult, subconsciously) says, in effect, "I sought love and affirmation from you and you failed me. I won't let myself be hurt like that again." As a result the child resists the same-sex parent as a love-source.[34]

This resistance leads to two things: (1) a "disidentification" with the child's own gender (which is not just an absence of same-gender identification but an active reaction *against* such identification) and (2) an abiding deficit in the ability to relate to members of the child's own sex in general. In the truest sense of the term, this situation creates a vicious cycle: the disidentification feeds the deficit in relational ability, the relational handicap leads to rejection by same-sex peers (both because the gender-identity deficient child is perceived as "different" and because he or she probably expresses some level of aversion to children of the same sex), this peer rejection reinforces the existing disidentification, and so on in an escalating spiral.

Yet the God-given need for same-sex parental bonding still exists, so, in opposition to the energy for disidentification, there is in the homosexual an equivalent ongoing psychological drive to undo this detachment and meet the unfulfilled same-sex attachment needs—the "reparative drive." This reparative drive, in and of itself, is not a bad thing. It is the natural tendency of the psyche to attempt to make up for what it needs and has been denied—in this case a strong same-sex attachment which can be the ground of a stable gender identity.

Clearly, these factors, taken together, create a classic approach/avoidance conflict. Members of the same sex are rejected (along with the gender identification of that sex) out of fear of further wounding. Yet, at the same time, members of the same sex are desired as a love-source to make up for the missing love of the same-sex parent, the need for which was never met at the appropriate developmental stage. This conflict is the essence of "same-sex ambivalence" and its result is an unstable or weak gender identity.

Under the overwhelming force of exploding sexual drives at puberty, Moberly argues, same-sex ambivalence and the lack of strong gender identification are eroticized in both male and female homosexuals. But what the homosexual experiences as sexual desire for or romantic attachment to members of the same sex is, in reality, a desire to heal the wound created by unfulfilled same-sex parental attachment needs. "Homosexual love need is essentially a search for parenting," Moberly writes, and therefore homosexuality is always "a problem of gender identity."[35]

Comiskey[36] acknowledges his indebtedness to both Payne and Moberly (and does not address the fact that they disagree on certain points). Given the significance fatherhood appears to hold for him personally,[37] as well as the repercussions of that significance upon his theological understanding of familial relationships, it is not surprising that Comiskey shares Payne's conviction as to the vital importance of the father in forming strong, stable gender identity in both boys and girls. It is the father who must "bless" or "cover" his children in their gender self-perception,[38] Comiskey argues, and most gay men have been (or at least have *felt*) rejected by their fathers, just as a great many lesbians have been either sexually abused or belittled by their fathers. These failures in fatherly covering result in a boy "at odds with his 'boyness,'" a girl "at odds with her 'girlness.'" Such children, Comiskey contends, are vulnerable to an "intensifying identity crisis" which can erupt in homoerotic feelings in adolescence.

Both the importance of the father's role in forming gender identity and Comiskey's opinion (with Payne and *contra* Moberly) that the direction of one's sexual desires takes its form not just in the first five or six years of life but throughout childhood and adolescence are made clear in the following description of Comiskey's own childhood struggles:

> Much of my early sexual development was marked by alienation from my own masculinity . . . A lot of that stemmed from emotional detachment from my father . . . This dissociation was strengthened by cyclical rejections from male peers, beginning in grade school and continuing throughout adolescence.[39]

Yet despite the fact that he shares Payne's perspective on the centrality of paternal affirmation to gender wholeness for both boys and girls, Comiskey relies more on the model proposed by reparative therapy for his overall etiological paradigm. As he states: "The same sex parent provides the main source of gender identification."[40] Explicating reparative therapy's concept of defensive detachment, he writes:

> [D]efensive detachment pollutes the child's response to his own gender. Not only does he distrust the [*same-sex*] parent, but he also comes to distrust his own adequacy [*as a member of his gender*] . . . Positive aspects of masculinity and femininity are rejected due to their association with the troubled [*same-sex*] parental relationship.
>
> . . . masculine strength is written off as abusive, feminine vulnerability as weak and helpless. The child grows up timid and defensive with same-sex peers, preferring isolation to healthy engagement.[41]

As such a child moves into adolescence and adulthood, his or her insecure, incomplete gender identity seeks to perfect itself through eroticized fulfillment of same-sex attachment needs that should have been met nonsexually years before in childhood. As Comiskey quotes "Jim," one of the case studies in his book:

> *. . . what's really going on in me is some kind of struggle to become a man . . . I don't need *a* man. I need to become one.*

Question 5:

Can a legitimate moral distinction be made between a homosexual condition (orientation) and homosexual acts?

Aside from a reluctance to term same-sex erotic and emotional attractions a homosexual "condition" or "orientation," those holding this viewpoint generally tend to view homosexual desires as partaking of sinfulness in some manner, but not as specifically culpable in and of themselves, so long as they are resisted and submitted to the healing work of the Spirit. While Payne is somewhat ambiguous on this point,[42] Comiskey insists that the homosexual struggler can no more "choose not to have homosexual feelings . . . than heterosexuals can deny their impulse for the opposite sex." Therefore, "the presence of homosexual tendencies doesn't necessarily imply wilful sin. Homosexual impulses in and of themselves do not constitute wilful sin." Nonetheless, as part of their healing process, homosexual strugglers must confess the fact of "sexual disorder" in their natures.[43]

Moberly states explicitly that the unmet needs for same-sex love which are the source of homosexual desires are not only *not* sinful but that they are a God-given good, albeit a good that should have been met through nonsexual bonding with a same-sex parent in early childhood. Homosexuals are not experiencing "abnormal needs," she writes, but rather unmet *normal* needs which they are seeking to meet inappropriately. Attachment to the same sex is not wrong (at the proper developmental level), it is the eroticization of same-sex attachments which is wrong. Indeed, "legitimate [*same-sex attachment*] needs are to be met in legitimate ways, that is to say, non-sexually."[44] In this observation, Moberly would seem to make a clear moral distinction between homosexual feelings (even though they represent a disordered misdirection of legitimate desire) and acting upon such feelings sexually.

Thus, according to this viewpoint, the mere presence of homosexual urges is not "damning to the soul"—to use the phrase employed by Payne in reference to homosexual acts.[45] All wounds of the "deep heart" (again, the term is Payne's) involve both sinning and being sinned against. Not all such wounds are healed at conversion, and their continuing presence—including the reality of unforgiven sin within them—does not separate one from salvation. They do, however, pose significant obstacles to the full freedom and wholeness which God desires—indeed, *promises*—for all His children.

Question 6:

What is the psychological significance of homosexuality? *impaired psyche*

Since, according to this view, homosexual attractions are always indicators of deficient gender identity, it follows that homosexuality is a matter of psychological impairment in every instance.

Moberly states repeatedly that, since the homosexual has not met the normal needs for same-sex attachment at the appropriate developmental level, he or she is by definition immature. Homosexuality is intrinsically a state of psychological incompletion and a corresponding (albeit misdirected) striving for completion. It is a matter, in simple terms, of blocked psychological growth. Indeed, the fundamental issue for the homosexual is not really sexual at all but rather psychological immaturity in terms of same-sex gender identity. Homosexuals relate to both their own and the opposite sex as "incomplete members of their own sex."[46]

Moberly does not appear to globalize homosexual "arrested development" in the manner of many mid-century clinicians who viewed the homosexual's entire personality as "sick" or "immature." In fact, at one point she states that, in the homosexual, psychological needs that are essentially pre-adult remain in a person who is, in other respects, adult.[47] Her judgment upon gay relationships, on the other hand, is uniformly and extremely negative— and logically so, given her theory. Since both partners in a gay couple are seeking to resolve unmet same-sex attachment needs, she argues, they are ultimately unable to satisfy each other. This inevitably leads to instability in the relationship. Further, defensive detachment from one's own sex will often reemerge under the pressure of ongoing intimacy and disrupt whatever commitment may exist between the partners.

For Moberly, even long-term, monogamous homosexual relationships are "inherently self-limiting" because they are, in fact, misdirected attempts to meet deficits which—once met—would abrogate the need for such a relationship. Indeed, the more successful a gay relationship is in meeting the needs for same-sex attachment, the more effectively it will work itself out of a job, just as a healthy parent-child relationship should do. And the parent-child analogy is precisely appropriate since, according to Moberly, the accurate paradigm for homosexual pair-bonding is not heterosexual marriage but rather *the same-sex parent-child relationship*. That being the case, homosexual "love," no matter how strongly felt or faithfully lived out, can never be real, adult love, because it is by its very nature a search for fulfillment of immature needs.

Payne agrees that gender identity problems bind the homosexual in varying degrees of immaturity and she considers homosexuality a form of "sexual neurosis." Every homosexual, she avers, suffers from "arrested growth" in at least a part of the personality. Indeed, since all homosexuals are characterized by a failure to mature past adolescent narcissism, every homosexual is a "study in immaturity."[48]

Question 7:

What is the spiritual significance of homosexuality?

Most holding this viewpoint would agree with Payne when she writes: "Homosexual behavior is merely one of the twisted paths the basic fallen condition of man takes."[49] That is, while it is serious sin, it is not qualitatively different from any other serious sin. Homosexuals stand in the same position before God as their fallen heterosexual neighbors. Comiskey, in fact, makes precisely this point: "People with a heterosexual orientation are no less fallen than those with homosexual tendencies."[50] The church should not express greater moral concern over homosexual acts than it does over heterosexual acts outside of marriage simply because heterosexuality seems more "normal," he adds.[51]

Having established that straight and gay sinners stand equally condemned before the righteousness of God, however, proponents of this viewpoint insist that homosexuality is always evidence of profound spiritual need. This is because the "false self"—the "old man" or the "flesh" that is the primary agent of resistance to the redeemed "true self" awaiting one in Christ—is, for the homosexual, particularly and specifically expressed through the perceived gay identity. So long as the homosexual insists on defining himself or herself as gay, therefore, the false self is ascendant, effectively blocking God's redemptive work of gathering together the scattered parts of the personality into the new, higher integration of the true self.

According to Payne, fundamental to this false self in the homosexual is a lack of appropriate self-love, that is, a failure to accept the true self (which would include a healthy heterosexual orientation). This lack of proper self-love leaves the homosexual floundering in *improper* self-love: egoism, self-centeredness, narcissism and a hysterical searching for the self in others (rather than God) through homosexual acts. Homosexuality, therefore, is a form of "sexual idolatry." Further, when it reaches the point of overt behavior, either in thought or deed, it always involves the "animal self" (through lust) and the "diabolical self" (through rebellion against God's rightful sovereignty).[52]

Nonetheless, Payne writes of authentic Christians who come to her for healing of homosexual impulses and behavior. Thus, she would reject Bahnsen's contention that anyone experiencing either could not properly be called a Christian.[53] Rather, Payne argues, such a person would be a Christian still acting as a child "under the law" rather than as an adult son or daughter of God living "under grace" in a process of emergence from bondage to the false self and into the wholeness and integration of the true self.

Moberly agrees with Payne that homosexuality exists as a result of the Fall. In one of the more unique elements of her argument, however, she rejects the idea that homosexual urges in and of themselves represent a repudiation of the created order or some sort of "symbolic dissonance."[54] Rather, she contends, the reparative drive which is at work in homosexual desire paradoxically *confirms* the primacy of God's created order by expressing (in a distorted fashion, to be sure) the continuing vigor of the psyche's impulse to gender wholeness through the divinely appointed means of same-sex attachment.[55]

Like Payne, Moberly recognizes the possibility of a true Christian having homosexual desires. To act on these desires would unquestionably be sin, but their mere existence does not necessarily imply global spiritual immaturity or lack of sincere commitment to Christian discipleship. This is not to say that the gay or lesbian may treat his or her homosexual feelings as morally neutral, however, so long as they are not acted upon either in fantasy or fact. Simply attempting to stop homosexual acts (or even succeeding at stopping them) does not resolve the very real problem which underlies homosexual desire—legitimate, God-given needs which must be met as part of the necessary process of maturation.

As human beings, we are called by our Creator to strive for wholeness both spiritually and psychologically. There is then, for the homosexual, a moral imperative. God does not intend homosexuals to remain as they are. "The possibility of healing," as Moberly puts it, "is meant to be actualized."[56]

Question 8:

Can a homosexual become heterosexual (the question of "cure")?

While the phrasing of the question might be debated by some, the answer is unambiguously affirmative. Indeed, the conviction that recovery from homosexuality is possible is the defining distinctive of this viewpoint.

In an interview filmed in 1990,[57] Sy Rogers, then president of Exodus International, states that the "good news" is that there is a "very high recovery rate" from "homosexual brokenness" for those having a genuine motivation to change and the appropriate support. Citing a Masters & Johnson study[58] which claimed a 71.6 percent recovery rate, Rogers notes that such results can be achieved "with or without God." He adds, however, that a desire to obey God is the greatest motivator possible and that the fellowship of God's people is the very best support for change.[59]

Elizabeth Moberly agrees. In an interview in the same film, Moberly asserts that the "gender specific therapy" she has pioneered—"which is the new reparative therapy"—helps build a more "secure masculine identity" in the male homosexual and a "more secure feminine identity" in the lesbian. With this newly established gender identity in place, Moberly continues, homosexuals can be confident that "later on, down the line, they are going to be able to choose heterosexual relations."

Leanne Payne is equally positive regarding the possibility of change for homosexuals. "As a condition for God to heal, [*homosexuality*] is . . . remarkably simple," she writes.[60] Citing Paul's "such were some of you" (1 Cor 6:11) as biblical confirmation of God's promise of recovery for the homosexual, she insists that prayer for inner healing "always works." In a number of the composite case histories recounted in Payne's books, a single session of "healing of memories" is sufficient to end "homosexual compulsion" forever, though at other points she does admit that changing one's "attitudinal life" and the "thought habits" of years "will require some time." Nevertheless, while coming into the fullness of the true (heterosexual) self does not always "happen overnight," it "can and does take place so much more quickly than is ordinarily supposed"— within two to three weeks, she suggests at one point, as opposed to the years required for substantive change through traditional therapy.

While Payne argues in *The Broken Image* that no two healings are alike and that therefore she has no set "method" as she follows the Spirit's lead in each individual case, a certain methodological framework does, in fact, emerge from her published work.

As is true with any other form of inner brokenness or immaturity, homosexuality, according to Payne, requires that three psychological "barriers" be overcome in order for one to reach wholeness: (1) failure to forgive others their sins against us; (2) failure to repent of and receive forgiveness for our own refusals to forgive those who have wounded us; and (3) failure to accept our true selves and love ourselves "aright."

The first two barriers, Payne asserts, are always and instantly overcome through prayer for healing of memories. What distinguishes such prayer from traditional psychological techniques focusing on analysis of past trauma is the fact that healing prayer places both the client and the practitioner in the living presence of Jesus for whom all time is an eternal "now." This means that the healing, forgiving work of Christ can be applied even to forgotten or repressed events long past and to people long dead. It is precisely this "mending of relationships" within the "deep heart" or "deep memories" (i.e., the subconscious), Payne explains, that allows for integration of the rejected, projected gender identity and a consequent end to the compulsive search for that identity in others through homosexual urges or acts.

The general pattern of such healing prayer runs along the following lines. Payne and the client place themselves in the "Presence," with Payne often using various sacramentals (oil of chrism, holy water) for blessing upon the petitioner. They then practice what she refers to as "listening prayer," through which God brings to conscious awareness those traumatic events and relationships in the past, and the reactions to them on the part of the client, which need to be forgiven and healed. Sometimes these incidents are already known to the seeker; often they have been completely repressed.[61] Payne's own role as facilitator in this uncovering of deeply buried pain is considerable, in that she has, she attests, a "knowing that is a gift from God," so that she is able to discern what such traumas and wounds are in each particular case.

As these determinative injuries are uncovered by the Spirit, healing can begin through naming these bitter realities for what they are, forgiving the sins of others and asking for forgiveness for one's own sins. What is commonly referred to as visualization (Payne prefers the terms "faith pictures" or "seeing with the eyes of the heart") is a key tool in this process. Payne encourages those to whom she ministers to picture Jesus physically present in scenes of early childhood and infancy wounding,[62] placing a healing hand upon hurts and serving as a loving bridge between the child and those who injured it. She also leads clients in visualizing the desired healing taking place, as one yields up childhood pain and all the deep-rooted rage it has created to the redemptive suffering of Jesus on the cross.[63] Also significant in the healing of memories is "claiming prayer," through which God's promised gifts of forgiveness, restoration, integration, freedom and wholeness are affirmed as granted and received. When such healing is completed, the petitioner is truly a new creation. "We no longer define ourselves by our sins, neuroses and deprivations, but by Him whose healing life cleanses and indwells us."

The final step in recovery, which involves overcoming the third "barrier" of failures in self-acceptance and appropriate self-love, begins in the healing of memories itself, as one sees oneself for the first time through the loving, accepting eyes of Christ. It continues in a consciously practiced process of choosing, again and again, to hold on to the truth of who one is and the healing which has been given in Christ, even in the face of old doubts, fears and neurotic responses. This last step in healing can take time and a "good bit" of "wrestling" in prayer against habituated attitudes and responses, Payne notes. Further, during this period of coming into self-acceptance, some who "*are* freed" (*emphasis added*) from "severe" lesbian or homosexual neurosis may find themselves "swiftly and powerfully" overtaken by renewed temptation. Such temptation in no way compromises the absolute fact that healing change has occurred, however. It is merely evidence that, in the process of accepting their true selves, their "deprivational neurosis" is expressing itself through a longing for same-sex arms around them and the "gift of well-being" such an embrace would seem to afford. As various testimonials from Payne's former clients attest, in relatively short time the healing will be fully realized and the restored identity functional and complete.

As unfamiliar as such life-changing deep healing may seem in the church today,[64] Payne insists it is available to any who will seek it, since it is based in the explicit promise and power of God. There is indeed "hope for the homosexual." As she approvingly notes of one of her clients:

> He knows beyond all shadow of doubt that if God could and would heal him, He can and will heal anyone.

Moberly not only agrees that healing for the homosexual is "entirely possible," she shares Payne's certainty as to the efficacy of healing prayer. In fact, she writes,[65] since the "decision" to turn away from the same-sex parent as a love source was made "very early," on a subconscious and—at least to some extent—involuntary level, that decision cannot be reversed by conscious choice or willpower; it can *only* be healed. And until it is healed, defensive detachment, same-sex ambivalence and eroticization of same-sex attachment needs cannot begin to be resolved.

"Deep forgiveness," as Moberly terms it, will be required toward the same-sex parent and, depending on the severity of the injury done by that parent, prayer may need to begin not with forgiveness as such but with a petition for the ability to forgive. If, even then, forgiveness seems beyond the capacities of the client, there may be need to ask for Christ's love to make up what is lacking. The homosexual must also seek forgiveness for his or her own unforgiving attitudes toward those who caused grievous wounding. Finally, not only must traumatic memories themselves be healed, but the emotions, attitudes and judgments attached to these painful memories as well.

Contrary to Payne's assertion that prayer for healing of memories does its work immediately and completely, however, Moberly counsels against expecting one ministry of prayer, no matter how powerful, to bring complete healing all at once. Further, in Moberly's approach, healing prayer—while essential—is not enough in and of itself. Paired with such prayer must be a complementary therapeutic process involving a same-sex counselor or a "deep friend" through whom unmet but legitimate developmental needs can finally be fulfilled nonerotically. Such a deep same-sex relationship is "essential, central" to full healing for the homosexual because, whatever the salutary effects of healing prayer, a good relationship with people of the same sex "remains the primary need of the homosexual." Until this legitimate same-sex attachment need is met, the gay or lesbian person is "stuck" in immaturity. Since "God does not 'cure' people of legitimate needs," it is fruitless to pray that a gay or lesbian person will be "delivered" from homosexual feelings when the *satisfaction* of those feelings (nonsexually, of course) is exactly what is required for him or her to move on to heterosexual maturity. Just as the child cannot skip the normal route to adult heterosexuality, that route being the meeting of same-sex attachment needs, so the adult homosexual cannot circumvent this step in maturation either.

For Moberly, the ultimate goal of true healing cannot simply be stopping homosexual behavior (which is only a symptom of a deeper gender identity deficit). The goal must be undoing defensive detachment by creating a strong same-sex attachment that is not erotic, thereby fulfilling previously unmet needs for same-sex bonding and moving the client on to complete, solid gender identity. Once this process is complete, the "presenting symptom"— homosexual desires or behavior—will be eliminated, as it were, automatically, since the needs such desires and behavior are attempting to meet inappropriately will have been met appropriately.

That is not to say that healing is necessarily easy. There are few quick fixes in Moberly's view. "It is often difficult for a homosexual to change," she notes. Sometimes, depending on the extent of deficits and the strength of the defensive detachment, the reparative process may take years. Nevertheless, the certain promise of genuine change is the good news Christians are privileged to proclaim to the homosexual:

> Where a psychological deficit is marked, healing may be neither rapid nor easy. But in principle, healing is possible for all . . . Healing is the general human . . . capacity.[66]

Just how difficult such change can be is made clear by Andy Comiskey in his *Pursuing Sexual Wholeness,*[67] which closes with a ringing affirmation:

> [*Jesus*] will heal wounds incurred by homosexuality; He will be glorified in the honest testimony of His healing authority. Through the [*homosexual*] struggler's restoration and resulting ministry, the church and the world will be awakened to His powerful love.

Despite this triumphant summation, Comiskey is painfully open throughout his book regarding the ongoing struggle that healing represents for the person seeking recovery from homosexual tendencies. Although now married, the father of four and leader of one of the most respected of ex-gay ministries, Comiskey writes candidly of the fact that he still must contend with "homosexual feelings."[68] As he writes:

> [W]e cannot expect to experience a complete absence of sexual struggles in this lifetime . . . the homosexual struggler may still experience homosexual temptations. [*This does not*] minimize . . . God's healing power. It simply places that healing in the dynamic process of *becoming* whole, a process that will never end until we see Jesus in heaven.

What the homosexual struggler *can* hope for is "to become *whole enough* in this lifetime to sustain fulfilling, heterosexual relationships . . . [*to*] encounter the opposite sex as a desired counterpart—with interest, not fear or distaste." As for himself, Comiskey testifies that "Jesus has granted me enough heterosexual desire and personal maturity to love a woman, take her as my wife, and oversee a household and growing family."

Comiskey's method of healing and restoration for the homosexual does not, in fact, start with an address of the "problem" of homosexuality at all, but rather with spiritual renewal. Most homosexual strugglers should first "become rooted in Jesus and His community," Comiskey insists, before tackling the specifics of their need for sexual healing.

After a time, however, particularly within the worship context, the "Father's supportive love" creates an understanding of the fact that God's image is particularly expressed through "mankind as male and female." This realization in turn leads to a desire for personal faithfulness to that divine order. Such recognition of the transcendent nature of gender is vital to the healing process, Comiskey notes. Without it, the individual struggler can get bogged down in the specifics of his or her needs and temptations and lose sight of the "big picture" of "God's powerful love [and] the powerful image of sexual wholeness" that is held out in the mystery of male-female complementarity as an image of God.[69] But once the Spirit begins to move upon the struggler's heart with conviction of the sinfulness of his or her homosexual tendencies and acts and the need for change, then the specific healing work can begin.

The first necessary condition for such healing is an unflinching recognition by the struggler of the "sexual disorder" homosexual desires represent in his or her personality and a genuine desire to change so as to conform to God's intended design for His creation. This desire must be so fervent that one is ready to say to God in all sincerity, "Do what you need to do to help me get free." Without such an earnest desire, the struggler will not be ready to accept the pain which is an inevitable part of the process of healing—inevitable because inner healing is by definition a matter of opening up and getting in touch with old experiences of rejection, deprivation, abuse and estrangement which were so deeply hurtful that the psyche repressed or blunted them at the time they occurred in order to allow the struggler to function at all, however imperfectly.[70]

Along with a willingness to embrace the pain that healing necessarily entails, there must be genuine repentance as well. This repentance involves not only a thorough confession of homosexual sin (generally in the context of group prayer and ministry) but also a conscious "laying down" before God of homosexual acts, same-sex relationships that generate a homosexual bonding even if they are not genitalized, addictions to pornography or masturbation, homoerotic fantasies, and sentimentalized romantic notions of homosexual love. All these are to be named and rejected as the deadly deviations from the divine will that they truly are. Then the struggler must align himself or herself with the Lord, holding fast to God—even when doing so seems like a kind of death—and seeking his or her identity in the wholeness of Christ rather than in the broken and defensive palliatives of a perceived homosexual identity. Such thoroughgoing repentance finally turns upon one very clear, but agonizing decision, Comiskey writes: "Whom will we serve, Jesus or the powerful lure of homosexual desire?"

The choice to serve the risen Lord brings one to readiness for prayer for inner healing; but for Comiskey, as for Moberly, such prayer is no one-shot cure. Healing prayer is a continuing process which takes place both in corporate worship and small group ministry, and it may well extend over a period of years. Moreover, such healing prayer must be grounded in the ongoing fellowship of a Christian community that is aware of the struggler's need and can offer support and require accountability through the lengthy and often "painful and uncertain season of healing."[71]

Through such healing prayer and the forgiveness it entails of injuries done both by parents and same-sex peers, the gender identity deficit that is the ground of homoerotic desire begins to be righted.[72] While this does not mean that all homosexual urges will immediately disappear, Jesus now becomes the "bridge" between "whole heterosexuality" and "the struggles at hand." As strugglers make the decision to respond to Jesus' love by "pledging allegiance" to him, "we are delivered. By deliverance I don't mean being rid altogether of homosexual feelings . . . but deliverance defined as the power of love purging the power of perversion." *def*

For Comiskey, as powerful as such ongoing healing prayer is for the restoration of the homosexual struggler, it is not enough by itself. Following Moberly on this point, Comiskey insists that "making whole relationships in the present" is also required—that is, the creation of healthy, nonerotic same-sex relationships that will help strugglers "secure their true identities as gender persons." The same-sex intimacy and appropriate affection such relationships will provide can serve as a much-needed balm for years of same-sex deprivation and rejection. Comiskey candidly admits the treacherous nature of such necessary intimacy: it will often "stir up the old homosexual yearnings. Strugglers will be sorely tempted to eroticize the other . . ." When this occurs, strugglers must be honest with God about such infatuation, confess it to others to whom they are accountable and forsake it so that the way is cleared for whole, "de-eroticized" same-sex attachment to occur. Then, over time, not only will strugglers find the ability to relate as a man to other men, a woman to other women, but also as a man to woman, a woman to man. Healing, while in some sense never "complete," will be sufficient for the struggler to begin exploring heterosexual options: dating, engagement and marriage.[73]

As Comiskey writes: "resolving who we are in relation to our gender must occur in order to press on into heterosexuality. And press on we must." The promise, after all, as was already noted, is that the homosexual struggler can "become whole enough in this lifetime to sustain fulfilling, heterosexual relationships," despite the fact that, "even with the help of fellow believers, the struggle continues."[74]

Even in the midst of this ongoing struggle, however, the ex-gay can confidently affirm that he or she *has been* healed. This is possible because—just as every redeemed sinner, justified by faith, still struggles with sin from the human perspective, but is at the same time "viewed" by God as sinless *through* the imputed righteousness of Christ—so the ex-gay *chooses* to view himself or herself from the divine viewpoint of his or her higher, true identity in Christ (which identity is heterosexual), even though certain aspects of the false homosexual identity may continue to exist within the personality as a source of temptation. As Jack Hickey writes in the *Exodus Standard*: "Heterosexuality is our God-given identity, not what we feel."[75] Or, as another ex-gay puts it:

> Truly, I was no longer a homosexual in God's eyes . . . I had a new identity . . . All this was certain in spite of what temptations from my lower carnal nature might still remain to plague me.[76]

Question 9:

What is the moral opinion arrived at, given the responses to Questions 1 through 8?

There is no such thing as a moral homosexual act under any circumstance.[77] Practicing homosexuals unwilling to renounce their sin and seek healing are living in a state of separation from God and face the eternal consequences of that estrangement. Nonpracticing homosexuals can be Christians, but until they receive the recovery available to them, they cannot help but be immature Christians, profoundly hobbled in their discipleship and ability to minister. Yet homosexuality is ultimately no different than any other sin; it can be forgiven and the homosexual can be healed.

Question 10:

What is the personal call of Christ for the gay man or lesbian?

The homosexual must repent and seek recovery through the ministry of a community of God's people that understands the true nature of homosexual brokenness and practices inner healing, appropriate gender wholeness counseling and long-term supportive fellowship. The goal of such ministry is not necessarily a heterosexual marriage in all cases, but rather the freedom to choose either marriage or celibacy from a position of restored gender identity.

Question 11:

What is the pastoral call of Christ to the church on the issue?

The church must proclaim not only God's unequivocal judgment on homosexual acts, but also God's loving promise of hope and healing for the homosexual person.

As Moberly notes, since homosexuality is evidence of an "intrapsychic wound" based in very real childhood suffering, the attitude of the church toward the homosexual must be one of compassion, not hostility, disgust or fear. Homophobia is always "unjustified" and the homosexual condition (as opposed to homosexual acts) is "not reprehensible." Indeed, the church has a special calling to minister to homosexuals: since gay people need to fulfill their same-sex attachment needs by means of strong, nonerotic bonding with same-sex friends and mentors, the church needs to "get involved . . . hands on" in providing a context for such healing relationships.[78]

Payne speaks less directly to the question of the church's call, but she clearly believes it to be imperative that Christians revive the neglected spiritual gifts of inner healing that are a part of the church's birthright and calling, not only for ministry to homosexuals but to all who are broken and wounded by sin. While such ministry must be grounded in compassion for the person struggling with homosexual issues, to be sure, Payne does issue a caution:

> Since many [today] seek to justify homosexual activity, we need to stress the fact that it is sinful, and that obedience to God's revealed will is indeed a happy thing.[79]

Homosexuals within the Christian community who attempt to justify their brokenness should be pastorally counseled both as to God's will for sexual wholeness and God's promise of healing for all who are willing to seek his will and follow it. Comiskey, however, appears willing to tolerate the presence of what might be termed "unreconstructed" homosexual strugglers within the Christian fellowship, at least so long as they are in some sort of process *toward* openness to God's calling to be made whole, although he insists that homosexual strugglers should be barred from any responsible position of Christian leadership until they have renounced homosexual practices and sought accountability, counseling and healing prayer from the body.

Question 12:
What is the political call of Christ to society on the issue?

As Sy Rogers puts it in *One Nation under God*, the ex-gay movement does not see itself, or wish to be perceived, as an "enemy of the homosexual community." Exodus recognizes, he continues, that "in a pluralistic society," if people wish to "pursue a homosexual inclination," they have the "prerogative" of doing so. This does not mean, however, that homosexuals should be offered "social legitimization."[80] Consequently, while those who identify themselves as gay and lesbian should not be persecuted, neither should their sinful lifestyle choices be affirmed by society as a viable alternative to heterosexuality.

Colorado-based Focus on the Family,[81] which has for some years been in the forefront of advocacy for ex-gay claims[82] and opposition to "gay rights" legislation, on October 1, 1998 issued two position papers on "Homosexual Rights" and "Violence Against Homosexuals." These documents well articulate this viewpoint's understanding of the practical political implications of its position. While affirming that "homosexuals are entitled to the same basic rights as other citizens," the statement on homosexual rights goes on to insist that "there are substantial reasons for opposing current attempts to grant gays, lesbians and bisexuals the *special rights* which they are seeking."[83] Included among these "special rights" are passage of a lesbian, gay, bisexual and transgender civil rights bill; an end to discrimination on the basis of sexual orientation by state and federal governments (including the military); and repeal of all state sodomy laws and other laws that criminalize private sexual behavior by consenting adults. Focus on the Family, the statement continues, believes that "grave personal and social consequences" would follow upon the granting of these special rights.

The position paper then lays out a three-point legal challenge to the claim that homosexuals as a class are entitled to civil rights protections:[84] (1) homosexuals "are not discriminated against in any of the key areas considered essential [*for creation of a protected class*] by the courts: economical [sic] status, educational opportunity or political representation"; (2) homosexuals do not share any "innate" or "immutable" distinguishing characteristic as a class (since, according to those of this viewpoint, homosexual orientation, if it exists at all, is a result of conditioning and can be changed); and (3) the courts have consistently held that "there is such a thing as legitimate discrimination." In the case of homosexuals, the document continues, certain forms of discrimination are justified because, "[w]hile discrimination on the basis of race or gender have [sic] no rational defense, the same does not hold for homosexual behavior, which demonstrates serious harmful personal and social consequences." Given these contentions, the statement concludes that "[c]urrent criminal and civil law, along with the basic rights accorded by the Constitution, are clearly sufficient for the protection of individual homosexuals. There is, therefore, no socially compelling reason to grant special 'protected class' status to homosexuals, while there are strong reasons to withhold such rights."

The concurrently released statement on violence against homosexuals sets out a vigorous defense of anti-"gay rights" activism, reading in part:

While echoing the biblical message of compassion and forgiveness and redemption for individuals, we nonetheless stand firm in our objection to social policies that have the effect of legitimizing homosexual behavior. We reject and oppose the attempts of pro-homosexual activists to legitimize homosexuality through such matters as the redefinition of the family, the legalization of same-sex marriages, and the instruction of children and youth that homosexuality and bisexuality are morally equivalent to heterosexuality. We believe such policies are detrimental to individuals and families, and undermine the welfare of society. Therefore, as citizens we speak and act to block the political agenda of [the] pro-homosexual movement, but we harbor no ill will toward individuals, even those who disagree with us concerning the morality of homosexuality.[85]

Representative Denominations and Para-Church Groups

From its inception, the strongest support for the ex-gay movement has come from the charismatic and evangelical churches, although representatives of other denominations (including at least one Episcopal bishop)[86] have given public endorsement to particular ex-gay ministries.

As already noted, Exodus International serves as an international umbrella organization for ex-gay programs, while Dr. James Dobson's Focus on the Family multimedia enterprise has been in the forefront of promoting ex-gay arguments and claims. Among the longest-lasting and most respected (by ex-gay supporters) of the ex-gay ministries are Love in Action, an independent evangelical organization which was for many years located in San Rafael, California, but which recently moved its operations to Memphis, Tennessee,[87] and the Desert Stream ministry founded by Andy Comiskey under the auspices of the charismatic Vineyard Christian Fellowship.

Cross-Perspective Critique

Since promises of "recovery" from homosexuality are the uniquely distinguishing mark of this particular viewpoint, it is not surprising that most criticism of the viewpoint focuses on these claims, with critics asserting that there is overwhelming and irrefutable evidence that attempts to change sexual orientation—whether by psychological means, spiritual means or some combination of the two—simply do not work. This being so, it is argued, assurances of the possibility of "healing" being made by the "ex-gay" movement and its supporters do nothing but raise cruel and deeply damaging false hopes.

Evidence for what critics contend is a striking history of failure by the "ex-gay" movement to live up to its self-promotion generally falls into one of three categories: continued covert homosexual "acting out" by purportedly healed "ex-gays";[88] recantations of "ex-gay" testimonies by former movement members now asserting they never, in fact, ceased being homosexuals;[89] and indications from the writings and witness of those still claiming to be "ex-gay" that their erotic and affectional urges remain homosexual.

While documentation of "moral lapses" and reversions to a "homosexual lifestyle" among movement leaders are often cited, for many critics the most compelling case against "ex-gay" claims of "healing" or "recovery" is to be found not in scandals or recantations, but rather in the words of those within the movement who continue to stoutly affirm they have been healed. Leanne Payne seems to lay the issue out clearly enough:

> When people suffering severe gender confusion find healing, it's evident to everyone. Such people are either being made whole or they aren't.[90]

Critics argue that this is precisely the problem: when the claims made by "ex-gays" of having been "healed" or "changed" are looked at objectively, it is far from "evident to everyone" that genuine change in orientation has taken place. In fact, quite the opposite is "evident" to all but those who are committed to believing that such change "must" be possible. As Blair comments in the film *One Nation under God*, it is significant that "the only people who are saying that change happens are the people who believe change *should* happen."[91]

Discussion on this point is made particularly difficult by the fact that, for most people, to say one is "healed" of something implies a complete and unequivocal change from a diseased condition to a condition of health. Lepers who came to Jesus for healing no longer had the sores and deformation of their disease. The lame took up their beds and walked; the blind saw. By analogy, to be "healed" of homosexuality is generally taken to mean to become heterosexual. And this is, in fact, exactly how "ex-gay" claims for healing are often presented.[92]

Given this common understanding as to what constitutes healing, most evangelicals—and, perhaps more importantly, most gays and lesbians presenting themselves to "ex-gay" ministries for help—no doubt believe that what is being offered is a genuine change from homosexual to heterosexual orientation.[93] For the "ex-gay" movement, however, it turns out that "healing" for the homosexual does not mean precisely what it sounds like to the uninitiated. As movement leader Robbi Kenney, herself always a heterosexual (or "everstraight" in the language of some in the movement), states bluntly in one mailing: "Know what you are offering . . . You are NOT offering heterosexuality."[94]

In fact, any serious perusal of "ex-gay" materials and testimonies makes clear the highly ambiguous meanings attached to "healing" or "change" within the movement.[95] Andy Comiskey is perhaps more open than any other "ex-gay" leader about the continuing difficulties faced by the healed "homosexual struggler." Despite claims on the back cover of his *Pursuing Sexual Wholeness* that "sixty-five percent or more of those who complete [*Comiskey's Living Waters program*] find freedom from homosexuality," Comiskey himself, as already noted, is very open about the fact that former gays "cannot expect to experience a complete absence of sexual struggles in this lifetime" and writes of a "process" and a "journey" that is still incomplete in him:

> Problems related to sexuality are deep-seated and powerful. They take time to be resolved. And that process of change is . . . subject to fits and starts . . . God has wonderfully freed me to love as He wills, but He isn't finished, nor am I. Troublesome, immature tendencies remain in me . . .

As for the former gay "never hav[ing] a homosexual thought again," his terse response is: "Welcome to reality."[96]

Heterosexual "ex-gay" supporters likewise undercut the movement's claims, it is asserted. For example, while psychotherapist Joseph Nicolosi, in his *Reparative Therapy of Male Homosexuals: A New Clinical Approach*,[97] speaks highly of religiously-based "ex-gay" efforts, Nicolosi himself admits that "the treatment of homosexuality" is "a lifetime process." Blair also quotes Nicolosi in a 1991 review[98] to the effect that "[r]eparative therapy is not a 'cure' in the sense of erasing all homosexual feelings" and that, in such therapy, the client "commits himself to treatment with the belief that 'irrespective of how I feel, I am a latent heterosexual.'"

To critics of the movement's claims, such statements make it irrefutably clear that homosexual orientation (the *definition* of which is erotic and emotional attraction to the same sex) continues unchanged in purportedly "ex-gay" men and women. Therefore, they are not, by any reasonable understanding of the word, being "healed" and such language is nothing more than convoluted psychospiritual double-talk which leads to profound cognitive dissonance among homosexual participants in "ex-gay" ministries, as they must every day affirm that who they experience themselves to be is not, in fact, who they are.

"Ex-gay" critics also question the movement's often slippery handling of the question of homosexual orientation itself. As already noted, many "ex-gay" theorists flatly deny that there *is* such a thing as a homosexual or a homosexual orientation, although they will often use these terms themselves in ways that clearly assume their commonly accepted meanings. Even the usually straightforward Andy Comiskey falls into this sort of equivocation, it is argued, when he subtitles his book "*How Jesus Heals the Homosexual*," but then states within the covers of that book that he "hesitate[s] . . . to label . . . anyone . . . as homosexual."

Comiskey's rational for this reluctance may sound reasonable, even charitable, at first glance: "Gay feelings are part of his personhood, but need not be *the*, or even *a*, primary reference point."[99] On closer consideration, however, Comiskey's reasoning quickly crumbles, critics charge. In point of fact, the designation "homosexual" has not held the globally descriptive connotation Comiskey would give it for at least twenty-five years, whether in clinical or ordinary usage. While a few radical queer theorists and archconservatives may insist that the gay or lesbian person is somehow fundamentally different from the straight man or woman, it is generally understood that to call a person a homosexual is simply to describe the direction of his or her emotional and erotic energies. That this is far from a complete definition—or even necessarily a "primary reference point"—of the homosexual's personhood goes without saying.[100]

In fact, critics contend, the refusal of "ex-gay" proponents to acknowledge the commonly accepted descriptive is simply intellectual dishonesty; and, they add, it is intellectual dishonesty with a very clear purpose. "Ex-gays" claim to effect substantive change, to "heal" the homosexual. By common definition, a homosexual is someone who is emotionally and erotically attracted to people of the same sex. Yet, as countless "ex-gays" themselves admit, "ex-gays" still feel emotionally and erotically attracted to others of their own sex and may well continue to do so for the rest of their lives, despite their having been "healed." Given that fact, the only way to at once assert "healing" and yet be honest about the reality of "ex-gays'" daily experience is to insist that same-sex emotional and erotic attractions are not, in fact, true indicators of one's sexual orientation at all. If they were, "ex-gay" programs and their advocates would have no choice but to admit that they are not "changing" anybody from homosexual to heterosexual. Caught in this bind, it is charged, many "ex-gay" apologists have opted to redefine their dilemma out of existence: there is no such thing as a homosexual, there are only "those who are separated from some valid though unaffirmed part of themselves,"[101] or some other circumlocution, therefore the still struggling "ex-gay" can affirm in all sincerity: "I am not a homosexual."

Some have suggested that it would be far more honest if conservative Christian ministries to homosexuals simply admitted that what they are offering is not "change" at all but rather a support system for control of homosexual behavior.[102] However, critics note, there would seem to be several cogent reasons for the "ex-gay" movement's determination to cling to the ambiguity of its current vocabulary.

In the first place, movement members cannot be unaware of the widespread homophobia within the very churches from which "ex-gays" seek fellowship and support. Consequently, it is perhaps understandable that claims of "change" would seem to make the "ex-gay" more likely to find acceptance in fundamentalist/evangelical circles than would a frank admission of ongoing struggles within a basically unchangeable homosexual orientation.

As well, the charismatic theology embraced by many "ex-gay" groups assumes that part of the normative Christian experience is substantive healing of all those broken elements of the personality which create stumbling blocks to maturity in Christ. Since homosexuality is believed to be such a stumbling block, it follows logically that God should heal it.

Still others may well uphold the possibility of cure out of real (but, critics would argue, misapplied) compassion for homosexuals. If homosexual acts are believed always to be sinful and if there is not some real hope that the sexual orientation out of which such acts arise can be significantly changed, then the call of Christ to the homosexual is a life that is not only celibate, but without any hope of genuine coupled intimacy; a life that will be, at least to some extent, a never-ending battle against not only same-sex erotic activity but same-sex affections that run the risk of turning into "occasions of sin." In the face of so uncommonly bleak a prospect,[103] promises of "change" can seem the only viable solution for sensitive heterosexual Christians who are convinced of the sinfulness of homosexual acts but who also flinch at the idea of imposing on the gay or lesbian a life of emotional and sexual austerity from which they themselves would shrink.

Finally, ex-gay programs are certainly cognizant of the fact that their financial survival depends upon contributions from conservative Christians who want to believe that real change is possible—and sometimes upon fees from program participants seeking such change. It would seem likely that far fewer troubled gays and lesbians would seek the help of ministries offering nothing more than support in a lifelong struggle to control homosexual urges, and conservative Christians most certainly would be far less generous in their contributions to such organizations.[104]

While claims of "recovery," "cure" or "healing" for the homosexual are the most common focus for criticism of this viewpoint, other challenges are made to it as well. These generally fall into one of two general categories: allegations of theoretical fallacy and charges of theological error.

As for alleged theoretical failings, it is often pointed out that the "ex-gay" movement, despite its repeated proclamations of a "new" approach to the treatment of homosexuality, in reality is simply reasserting old, already discredited psychological theories.[105] Moberly, for example, while admitting the failures of traditional therapy in effecting real change in the homosexual, argues that her own "gender specific therapy," which is "the new reparative therapy," is different because it is based on a new under-standing of the causes and significance of homosexual love-needs.[106] Yet, as is documented in *One Nation under God* through cross-cutting between one of Moberly's presentations at an Exodus convention and clips from forty-year-old lecture films by traditional therapists, the basic points of Moberly's theory have been in circulation since at least the 1950s, if not before.

Also disputed is the idea, widely promoted in "ex-gay" circles, that homosexual desire is always a result of an insecure or incom-plete same-sex gender identification, a "gender identity deficit" as it is often termed. Despite ex-gays' absolutism on this point, Blair notes that even Nicolosi admits that some homosexuals, while wishing to change, "are inappropriate for reparative therapy because they show no signs of gender identity deficit and do not match our developmental model."[107] In fact, Blair contends in a review of Nicolosi's book, "clinical and social psychological research" has found that "arrested gender identity . . . is not, as such, associated with homosexual orientation." Further, research does not support claims that a failed relationship with the father always underlies homosexual orientation in males.[108]

"Ex-gay" theories of "gender identity deficit" are held to be flawed as well in their assertions as to what constitutes appropriate gender behavior to begin with. Indeed, many critics see in the models of masculinity and femininity held up by "ex-gay" propo-nents and the theorists upon which they rely the very worst extremes of sexist gender stereotyping. Roman Catholic feminist theologian Rosemary Radford Ruether writes scathingly of the notion that "those [*traits*] traditionally called masculine and those called feminine . . . define the unchangeable natures of men and women. Men are actors, thinkers, doers who protect and act upon others. Women are passive, dependent, weak in their ability to take care of themselves, emotional, lacking full rationality, per-haps more 'spiritual' and 'intuitive.'"[109] The fact is, critics argue, gender attributes are not a fixed, immutable given. Rather, they represent the highly fluid convergence of the enormous variety of human personality configurations possible, the varied gender expectations assigned by given cultures, and the disparate mean-ings of particular traits created by changing circumstances and evolving social needs.

If, for example—as Comiskey argues—the properly gender-identified male will relish competition in which he is challenged to "fight and lose and fight again . . . to push through every resistance until [*victory is*] achieved,"[110] how is one to explain fully heterosexual men who are nonetheless more supportive behind-the-scenes players than dynamic leaders, more detail men than visionaries, more quiet scholars than bold adventurers? Have all these men in some way failed in their calling to embody the "masculine principle?" Conversely, are women who have acted upon their strong leadership abilities (a Golda Meir, a Margaret Thatcher or a Mother Teresa) to be condemned as lacking in suitable gender credentials and suspected of latent lesbianism? In reality, critics allege, "ex-gay" arguments regarding gender identity are simply gross reductionism.

Many also question what is seen as the presumption inherent in labeling all homosexual love as qualitatively different from the love experienced by heterosexual partners. While Barnhouse insists that homosexual love, even within a committed relationship, is more or less "immature"[111] and Moberly contends that the love shared by a gay or lesbian couple can never be "real, adult" love since it is actually a species of parent-child attachment, critics respond that since mature homosexual partnership love can evince exactly the same "marks" as heterosexual spousal love—affection, mutuality, passion, commitment and self-sacrifice—to maintain that it is nevertheless a qualitatively different phenomenon is nothing more than arbitrary prejudice expressing itself through pseudo-scientific jargon. As gay author Ron Caldwell has written:

> Love is generic, I think . . . no matter who the lovers are. And life for [*homosexual partners*] is not bizarre—it's fairly calm and domestic. For men in love the major difference is that the rules for taking care of each other are not always apparent. Decency, respect, attention and devotion are still the operative words, though. We just don't seem to have too many models for the way we conduct our lives.[112]

Turning to theological objections to this viewpoint, the most fundamental of these focuses on claims by Payne, Comiskey and others that gender differentiation is "transcendent," rooted in the reality of God's own being, and that male-female complementarity is therefore an essential element of the image of God in humankind. Neither of these doctrines, it is charged, has any real foundation either in Scripture or in historic Christian tradition.

As for gender differentiation being a "transcendent reality" having its source in some sort of "polarity in unity" eternally existing in the Godhead (so that such differentiation is more than a created thing like time or space), critics contend that it is clear such an idea would be entirely foreign (indeed repugnant) to Old Testament sensibilities. The great prayer and rallying cry of the Hebrews was, after all, the *Shema*: "Hear O Israel, The Lord our God, The Lord is One." (Deut 6:4, NRSV alternative reading)

While the post-New Testament formulation of the doctrine of the Trinity might seem to provide a somewhat more congenial context for the sort of claims made by Payne and others on this point, the fact is that *never* within the development of the orthodox articulation of this mystery over several centuries was there a suggestion that the one God eternally existing in three persons (as it was termed in the West) or three *hypostases* (as the Eastern church put it) had anything at all to do with some sort of bipolar complementarity analogous to the two genders found in organic life on earth. Indeed, some note, conceptions of a transcendent pattern of polarity with its root in the nature of ultimate reality have a great deal more in common with certain pagan mythologies than they do with orthodox Christian faith.

As for Karl Barth's assertion that a significant element of the image of God in human beings is to be found in the complementarity of male and female, opponents argue that, while Barnhouse, Payne, Comiskey and others write as though Barth's interpretation of the image of God were an undisputed biblical (and therefore Christian) given, his teaching on this point is, in fact, a recent theological *novelty*. While there is no question, these critics admit, that Christians have from the beginning seen the biological (and, at least to some extent, the psychological) differentiation of male and female as an essential component of the created order, that differentiation has not historically been understood as having anything to do with the image of God in humankind.[113] Therefore, in his assertion that male-female complementarity represents a significant part of the divine image in human beings, Barth takes a dramatic step outside the generally held "consensus of the faithful" expressed through nearly two millennia of Christian exegesis and reflection—as do Barnhouse, Payne, Comiskey, et al. after him. This fact is significant, critics insist, because "ex-gay" theorists premise much of their abhorrence of homosexuality on a claim that homosexuality specifically violates the image of God in humankind.

Also challenged by many is the assumption of the "ex-gay" movement that spiritual or "inner" healing is or should be a normative part of Christian experience. In terms of physical healing, it is uncontested that the majority of Christians suffering illness or disability are not in fact miraculously cured, despite what would seem to be scriptural promises that they should be.[114] Why, then, it is asked, should the situation be any different with "inner" healing? When Payne writes of one of those to whom she ministered that "[h]e knows beyond all shadow of doubt that if God could and would heal him, He can and will heal anyone,"[115] she is clearly going well beyond what most Christians understand to be true about the operations of God's grace in the world, a point which becomes obvious if one applies her statement to a person healed of cancer or some other physical ailment. The fact is, as Christian conviction holds generally, while God *sometimes* intervenes miraculously to heal and restore the ill and the broken, that does not mean that God *always* does so. Healing, far from being the norm, would seem to be the exception.[116]

Finally, it is asserted, ex-gay programs amount to a form of "brainwashing" in which struggling homosexuals are encouraged to have contact only with like-minded Christians, to avoid exposing themselves to any differing views and to devote themselves to an all-consuming round of Bible study, worship, fellowship and prayer. For a time, as Mel White admits, such immersion may give the fledgling "ex-gay" a sense of release and freedom.[117] But when, according to former "ex-gay" Michael Bussee, despite such an intensive program, homosexual feelings return—as critics contend (and Comiskey and others admit) they inevitably will—those who despair of being healed are then told that they themselves are the ones responsible for the failure of "ex-gay" promises of deliverance. As Blair puts it, the accusation is that "those who do not change never really tried to change."[118]

The result of being caught in such a bind is predictable, "ex-gay" opponents contend. In interviews with former movement members, the film *One Nation under God* documents anguish, guilt, abandonment of Christian belief altogether, depression, stress, psychosomatic illness, self-mutilation and even suicide among those who, for all their faith and effort, could not achieve the "recovery" the "ex-gay" movement promised them and who felt there was no one to blame but themselves.

Given such sobering data, critics argue, it is hardly surprising that Mel White should warn of the "tragic, long-term consequences of . . . false hopes and counterfeit cures"[119] or that Ralph Blair would describe the "ex-gay" phenomenon as, ultimately, a "cruel hoax."[120]

The Viewpoint Responds

The ex-gay movement is young, less than a quarter of a century old. It may well be that, especially in its earliest years, caught up in the first flush of enthusiasm and release they experienced in discovering a way out of a homosexual lifestyle they knew to be not only sinful but ultimately unfulfilling on its own terms, some ex-gay advocates underestimated the nature and cost of the journey to wholeness in Christ. To the extent that this is true, it is surely typical of any new work God undertakes among and through his still very human people. Babies stumble learning to walk; so too do those following the Lord's leading into new areas of ministry and deeper understandings of unchanging biblical truth. In short, at times ex-gay claims—in all sincerity and good faith— may have been somewhat overstated or too simplistically presented. Insofar as that is true, there is now extensive published evidence (much of which is cited by the movement's critics to condemn it) that the majority of ex-gay leaders fully recognize that the healing or recovery offered by Christ to those who identify themselves as gay and lesbian is a lengthy, ongoing struggle—not a "quick fix" but rather a process, and an often slow and painful one which will most likely be incomplete in this lifetime. Therefore, defenders of ex-gay teaching insist, critics who charge that the "healing" promised by ex-gay ministries is a lie because it is not a fast, painless and permanent switch to mature, exclusive heterosexuality are themselves being less than honest.

In fact, contrary to the argument of critics that, unless the homosexual is fully and permanently changed, no healing at all can be said to have taken place, ex-gay proponents contend that there can be *substantial* change and healing, even if such recovery is on some level never complete short of the Kingdom of God. Indeed, it should come as no surprise to Christians that such growth in grace is gradual, an incremental outworking in the particulars of the individual life of what is, at the same time—in spiritual terms—a "completed" work of redemption, accomplished and sealed by Christ through his cross and resurrection. This is, after all, the case for *every* believer, whatever the specifics of his or her brokenness. All Christians understand that, so long as they are "in the body," they must do battle with their own sin and woundedness. At the same time, they also trust that a consistent struggle for faithfulness—the daily submission of the human will to God's Spirit, a willingness to confess failures and steps backward, the determination to accept divine forgiveness and the strength to press on—can, over time, result in significant movement toward the wholeness that is ours now and forever in Christ.

In this sense, Christians live paradoxical lives, aware that what they are to be and in fact already *are* in eternity they are still in process of becoming in this present life. Paul did not hesitate to assure the men and women of the problem-ridden church he founded in Corinth that they were a new creation (2 Cor 5:17), yet we know from Paul's remonstrances in his correspondence to them that these Christians were struggling with and sometimes fell into sins of all sorts, some of them spectacular even by pagan standards (1 Cor 5:1). For someone who has been trapped in the deceptions, compulsions and disappointments of the "gay" lifestyle, the ability to move out of that life into the loving community of God's people, to be drawn to a member of the opposite sex, in many cases even to marry and build a family, is experienced as healing indeed, as glorious new life and freedom, even if temptations and painful struggles remain. Therefore, critics' insistence than promises or claims of recovery and healing are a lie unless they conform to some absolute standard—a standard which the ex-gay movement itself has made clear again and again is not, in fact, what is being offered—represents nothing less than the creation of a "straw

man." Again, it is not ex-gay proponents who are guilty of intellectual dishonesty, but their critics.

As for the widely publicized failures, "backsliding" and recantations of ex-gay testimonies, even among some in leadership posi-
tions within the gay movement, such tragedies do not, contrary to
the claims of the movement's critics, prove that the promises of
Christ to the homosexual are false. They merely make clear what
faithful Christians have always understood: that the "cost of discipleship," as Dietrich Bonhoeffer termed it, is indeed high and that,
as Jesus warned, despite the unlimited scope of God's invitation to
redemption and restoration, "The gate is narrow . . . and there are
few who find it." (Matt 7:14)

"Eastern" Orthodox[121] author and social critic Frederica
Mathewes-Green has also noted a curious double standard which
ex-gay critics seem to apply to the personal testimonies of those
bearing witness to having "come out of" homosexuality.[122] Sitting
in as an observer on several workshops relating to gay concerns
at the 1997 triennial convention of the Episcopal Church,
Mathewes-Green found that, when sharing their own stories of
self-discovery, or when asking the church's blessing on their
same-sex life commitments, gay and lesbian spokespeople took it
as a given that they were entitled to be treated as trustworthy wit-
nesses to the reality of their own experience. Yet, when ex-gay participants in the workshops attempted to share their stories, gays
and lesbians (and their heterosexual supporters) made it clear that
such testimony was by definition tainted: the "ex-gays" were either
lying or self-deluded ("in denial"); their claims of gradual change
in erotic attraction, of having been able to form stable heterosexual unions, were rejected out of hand as "internalized homophobia" or a retreat "back into the closet." In other words, just as
extreme conservatives cling to the experience/addiction/identity
model for explaining homosexual orientation despite extensive
contradictory testimony from gays and lesbians, self-affirming
gays and lesbians generally take it as a given that change in sexual
orientation is impossible and therefore dismiss the testimony of
ex-gays just as summarily as certain elements of the religious and
political right reject their own experience.

The result is the often-repeated claim by gay apologists both in
and outside the church that there exists absolutely no credible

evidence for the possibility of any real change in sexual orientation, an assertion which is made without qualification even though numerous men and women are at this very moment living lives which—as they understand them—give the lie to such a sweeping generalization. Why, Mathewes-Green asks, especially among Christians, should one category of experiential evidence be held as unimpeachable and another category, equally real to those who claim it as their own, be patronized, dismissed or—most often—simply ignored because it flies in the face of the received wisdom of the day?

As for the question of how God can be understood to offer the promise of inner healing to every person struggling with homosexuality, when it is clear that physical healing is the exception, not the rule, of Christian life, the ex-gay movement responds that physical illness and disability, although certainly results of the fallen nature of the world, do not in and of themselves partake of sin, nor is their "direction" toward sin. Indeed, physical infirmity is often the fertile soil for truly heroic sanctity. Inner brokenness of the sort represented by homosexuality, on the other hand, is a specific deforming of the personality which turns it away from the good and toward that which is sin. As such, it is not something which God's redeeming work can leave untouched. It is, in fact, the very stuff of one's movement from the old man to the new.

In the final analysis, those holding to this present viewpoint defend its inevitability in terms of what is to them a compelling logical sequence: God's revealed Word testifies that, in general, human beings are created for sexual and emotional fulfillment in union. As God comments in Genesis, "It is not good for man to be alone." Yet Scripture also makes clear that the manner in which those who define themselves as gay or lesbian seek such fulfillment is contrary to God's created order. Since God's whole redemptive relationship with his fallen creation bears witness to the fact that he is not content either simply to accommodate our brokenness or leave us helpless in our sin, it follows that God in a very real sense must provide a way out of this conundrum if He is to remain true to Himself and the purposes of His creation. And, Scripture makes clear, such a way in fact exists: our new, higher self, the restored, redeemed nature that is ours, hidden in Christ, which conforms in all its particulars, including the sexual and emotional aspects of personhood, to the divine intent for us from the beginning. The path from "here to there," the practical journey from sexual brokenness to the wholeness God offers—call it "healing," "recovery" or "transformation"—is difficult and fraught with pitfalls, to be sure. But so is every truly Christian journey. "Few," at least by the world's calculations, may find the narrow gate, but the reality of both Scripture and experience testifies that some do. However painful the struggle may be, we can be certain that God's promise is true: wholeness in every aspect of the human personality, including matters of gender identity and sexuality, is possible. For the church to believe or proclaim anything less is for it to abandon the full power of the gospel.

A CALL TO COSTLY DISCIPLESHIP

This viewpoint is determined to be at once steadfast in its commitment to revealed truth and compassionate in ministering that challenging truth to the homosexual person. While it understands that the church must clearly distinguish and articulate what God's Word does and (equally importantly) does *not* say about homosexuality, it also seeks to be both informed and honest in its understanding of the actual situation and life experience of gay and lesbian people. To that end, it generally accepts the current state of science on questions considered to be scientific in nature (etiology and the possibility of cure, for example).

The general outlines of this viewpoint have probably never been better set out than in a letter C. S. Lewis wrote to American author Sheldon Vanauken.[1] Responding to an inquiry from Vanauken on the question of homosexuality, Lewis wrote:

> First, to map out the boundaries within which all discussion must go on, I take it for certain that the *physical* satisfaction of homosexual desires is a sin. This leaves the homosexual no worse off than any normal person who is, for whatever reason, prevented from marrying. Second, our speculations on the cause of the abnormality are not what matters and we must be content with ignorance. The disciples were not told *why* (in terms of efficient cause) the man was born blind (John 9:1–3): only the final cause, that the works of God might be made manifest; i.e., that every disability conceals a vocation, if only we can find it, which will "turn the necessity to glorious gain." Of course, the first step must be to accept any privations which, if so

disabled, we can't lawfully get. The homosexual has to accept sexual abstinence . . . [*but* t]hat is merely a negative condition. What should the positive life of the homosexual be? . . . Perhaps any homosexual who humbly accepts his cross and puts himself under Divine guidance will . . . be shown the way . . . [L]ike all other tribulations, it must be offered to God and His guidance how to use it must be sought.

Question 1:

What is the ultimate authority upon which any moral judgment regarding homosexuals and/or homosexual acts is to be based?

As is the case with the previous two viewpoints, those holding this viewpoint affirm that the only authoritative basis for moral judgment is the revealed will of God. If they are Protestants, they limit that revelation to its expression in Scripture, at least in theory. Catholic Christians—Orthodox, Romans and Anglicans—look both to Scripture and the teaching of the church. All would agree, however, that the application of that revelation to particular moral questions must involve a dialogue with reason, in particular as that reason is expressed through genuine scientific knowledge.

This is not to say that science or reason can ever legitimately make moral judgments on their own authority, independently of or contrary to revelation. Indeed, as for science, it is not—correctly understood—a mechanism for the address of moral questions in the first place. Science determines facts. Moral questions are matters, ultimately, not of fact, but of value—of the meaning and consequence of fact.

Whether homosexual acts conform to the will of God, for example, is not properly a scientific question. On the other hand, whether or not a homosexual orientation is consciously chosen *is* a scientific question. If the answer to this question is—as was once thought—that the homosexual deliberately chooses his or her bent, then the church might well apply its moral understanding to the facts at its disposal and conclude that a homosexual inclination is culpably sinful. If, on the other hand, science can demonstrate that homosexual orientation is *not* a matter of conscious choice, then the church, without in any way altering its commitment to the authority of revelation or its own moral precepts, must recognize its error of fact and adjust its judgment of homosexual orientation according to the enduring moral principle that one is not culpable for something over which one exercises no control or in which one has no free choice. The result of such a reevaluation would most likely be a judgment that homosexual orientation is not, in and of itself, culpable. It is important to emphasize that such a shift does not represent a change in moral principles. It is merely a differing application of those unchanging principles to a more accurate set of facts.[3]

Given this perspective, those holding this viewpoint welcome not only scientific research into the psychological aspects of sexual orientation but also biblical scholarship that can clarify the actual revelatory Word which addresses the church from the sacred text. Where that text can be shown to speak to (or out of) limited cultural contexts and meanings, it is understood that the church's obligation is to search out the revealed message that is, as it were, imbedded within those specifics and reaches beyond them as universal and binding truth. To accomplish such discernment, Christians must employ both rigorous scholarship and prayerful reflection so as to avoid, on the one hand, reading anachronistic contemporary attitudes or situations back into Scripture or, on the other, misapplying temporally or culturally bound biblical materials to current issues to which they are not in fact applicable.

Having said this, it is agreed that—whatever the status of certain texts traditionally and perhaps mistakenly held to speak to the question of homosexuality—there is unequivocal scriptural witness to the fact that all homosexual acts are sin. Further, it is held, such a judgment has been the teaching of the universal church from the beginning.

Question 2:

What is the God-given intent or design for human sexuality?

Those holding this view share the conviction of the previous viewpoints that the divinely appointed purpose for human sexuality encompasses both reproduction and the binding together of husband and wife in the one-flesh union of marriage. Unlike those affirming viewpoint 2, however, they tend to view absolutism regarding the metaphysical significance of gender complementarity with caution.[4] They differ from proponents of viewpoint 1, as well, in that they do not understand the unitive end[5] of sexuality to be always and in every circumstance secondary to the procreative end.[6] Rather, both the procreative and the unitive ends of human sexuality are seen as divinely ordained goods to be received and celebrated as gifts from the loving hand of the Creator. At differing points in a particular marital relationship or under varying personal situations, one or the other of these ends may more properly be the primary "moral element," as it were, which is expressed through spousal intimacy. Any attempt to prioritize definitively the elements of so subtle a mystery, it is held, has more to do with the arbitrary requirements of systematic theological categorization than it does with the complex realities of human experience.

Question 3:
What are the necessary criteria for morally legitimate sexual expression?

With the previous two viewpoints, this viewpoint affirms that the only legitimate context for the sexual act is heterosexual marriage. When consummated under any other circumstances, heterosexual or homosexual, the fundamental integrity of the act is violated and it therefore becomes culpably sinful.

Given sexuality's divinely ordained procreative and unitive ends, sexual relations between spouses should be enjoyed within a general relational framework which is generative. This does not mean every individual sexual act within a marriage must be potentially procreative, although the marital relationship as a whole should be open to the conception of children, absent truly extraordinary circumstances.

Ideally, taking into account the capacities of the individuals involved and the expectations of their time and culture, conjugal relations should also fulfill their intended unitive function. That does not mean that the presence of strong romantic love (the urge toward fulfillment of the unitive drive) justifies sexual activity before or outside of marriage, nor that the lack of such love renders sexual acts within marriage in some sense open to reproach. The passionate, consuming romantic love (what some psychologists term "cathexis") which our culture—through its literature, films and popular songs—makes such a primary value may or may not accompany the commitment "till death us do part" which is the sole necessary condition for legitimate sexual expression; likewise, it may or may not be the eventual result of such expression.

For the Christian, the single moral requirement for sexual intercourse is a pledge of lifelong, monogamous partnership as husband and wife. This may strike contemporary culture as contemptibly prosaic, but that has nothing to do with the truth of the matter. To be sure, spouses may sin against charity through selfish or manipulative uses of their sexual relationship, but there is no inherent misuse of the gift of sexuality when it is exercised by partners who are brought together in arranged marriages—as were so many of our ancestors—or who marry for reasons other than "falling in love." As C. S. Lewis writes through his senior fiend Screwtape:

> The Enemy described a married couple as "one flesh." He did not say "a happily married couple" or "a couple who married because they were in love," but you can make the humans ignore that . . . [H]umans can be made to [accept] the false belief that the blend of affection, fear and desire which they call "being in love" is the only thing that makes marriage either happy or holy . . .[and that] the idea of marrying with any other motive [is] low and cynical . . . They regard the intention of loyalty to a partnership for mutual help, for the preservation of chastity, and for the transmission of life, as something lower than a storm of emotion.[7]

Thus, those who hold this view argue, while "being in love" is, in and of itself and without consideration of context, at least a morally neutral thing, and often a very good thing, it is not the essential element of the Creator's intent for sexuality, either as a condition for marriage (and therefore licit sexual expression) or as a necessary component of a good spousal relationship. Furthermore, in even the best of marriages, "being in love" is a far more transitory phenomenon than our culture is usually ready to admit, serving in many ways as the door into the deeper and less emotionally fraught forms of stable partnered love. While, as Lewis notes through Screwtape's mordant humor, our own society teaches us to scorn God's intended ends for sexuality (which Lewis summarizes as "fidelity, fertility and goodwill") as somehow deficient or banal compared to the headier flights of passionate feeling, this is merely one of many points on which Christians' understanding of the mystery of human experience must stand in radical discontinuity with the views of the world around them.

Question 4:

Is there a "homosexual condition" (orientation) and, if so, what is its cause or origin?

The findings of science and the evidence of countless gay and lesbian lives make it clear that homosexual orientation is a reality within human experience. This orientation exists prior to and apart from homosexual activity and is "discovered" by the homosexual through the same developmental process by which heterosexuals come to understand their own sexual and emotional attractions. As is set forth unequivocally in *Life in Christ: A Catechism for Adult Catholics*:[8] "Persons who are homosexual do not choose their condition." The American Catholic bishops have spoken similarly, noting in "Always Our Children," a 1997 "message"[9] to Roman Catholic parents of lesbians and gays, that "[g]enerally, homosexual orientation is experienced as a given, not as something freely chosen." Numerous denominational statements from various mainline Protestant churches have contained nearly identical language.

The fact that Scripture never makes reference to a homosexual condition is not a basis for contending that such a condition does not exist. The Scriptures never speak of the subconscious, either, but few would argue from this omission that contemporary understandings of the human psyche are therefore erroneous.[10]

As for the etiology of homosexual orientation, most of this viewpoint—as already noted—would contend that the question is never addressed by revelation. We must turn to science for answers to such a question. If science cannot provide a definitive explanation of the source of the homosexual condition, then we can only, as Lewis wrote to Vanauken, "be content with ignorance," since how a person becomes a homosexual ultimately has no particular relevance to whether or not he or she may legitimately act upon homosexual desires. If science *can* provide such an explanation, then its findings should be accepted, insofar as science remains within its legitimate sphere of determining facts and does not attempt to draw interpretive moral judgments from these facts.[11]

Given this perspective, most holding this viewpoint accept the present state of scientific knowledge on the question of etiology: homosexual orientation would appear to be the result of a confluence of psychodynamic forces, some of which may be congenital or have a biological/genetic component and some of which may be environmental; sexual orientation, whether homosexual or hetero-sexual, is in most cases fixed by a very early age.

Question 5:

Can a legitimate moral distinction be made between a homosexual condition (orientation) and homosexual acts?

Yes. As is noted in the *HarperCollins Encyclopedia of Catholicism*,[12] it is generally agreed among Catholic moral theologians that there is no moral guilt attached to being homosexual, since the homosexual condition is not chosen. In "Always Our Children," the American bishops take the same position: "By itself, therefore, a homosexual orientation cannot be considered sinful, for morality presumes the freedom to choose."[13] The chaste homosexual (who by definition would be a celibate homosexual) is no different morally from the chaste heterosexual (celibate or monogamously married). Homosexual acts, on the other hand, are always intrinsically evil, that is, "of their very nature disordered,"[14] although "an individual's subjective culpability is [*to be*] judged with prudence" even while "the objective norm [*of heterosexual marriage*] is maintained."[15]

Question 6:

What is the psychological significance of homosexuality?

Homosexuality, in and of itself, has no psychological significance beyond the fact that homosexuals' erotic and emotional drives are same-sex directed. Since there are no wider intrinsic consequences to a homosexual orientation, homosexuals have the potential for being every bit as whole, mature and stable as heterosexuals.[16] They are capable of loving deeply, of leading highly productive lives, and of achieving profound spiritual maturity.[17]

Question 7:

What is the spiritual significance of homosexuality?

Since God's intent for humankind does not include homosexuality, the homosexual condition must be understood as being, ultimately, a consequence of the Fall, whatever its more immediate origins in a particular individual.

Given that fact, it is inaccurate to argue as some do that homosexual orientation is merely a natural variation like left-handedness. While the condition does not in any way warrant condemnation of those who "suffer" it, it does nevertheless represent—as the Vatican's 1986 document put it[18]—"a more or less strong tendency ordered toward an intrinsic moral evil." As such, it cannot be viewed by Christians as morally neutral, much less celebrated as something positive or good. It is to be understood, rather, as a "disability," analogous to some extent to various forms of physical impairment—not culpable, but not a part of the perfect will of God for creation, either.

Yet, if homosexual orientation is a disability, the Christian must always remember that, as Lewis put it, "every disability conceals a vocation." This does not mean that God "causes" a person to be homosexual—any more than it means that God "gives" a person a congenital deformity. Rather, it means that part of the mystery of redemption is that God can take any evil and turn it to greater good if it is offered up faithfully and in willingness to seek God's will over personal satisfaction or short-term gratification. Given that reality, the Christian homosexual's perspective on (and approach to) the fact of his or her condition should not be, paradoxically, entirely negative.

To be sure, the gay person must humbly recognize the brokenness inherent in disordered sexual desire and accept the often painful cost of fidelity to God's revealed will for human sexuality. Yet, at the same time, he or she must conscientiously seek to determine those unique and particular ways in which his or her homosexuality (and the constraints imposed by it on sexual and emotional expression) may be turned to greater opportunity for service, faithfulness and growth in love. If, as the Orthodox teach, everything God allows is ultimately "for our salvation," then homosexual orientation and its attendant difficulties can, like any other painful burden, become material for the higher purposes of redemption.

Question 8:

Can a homosexual become heterosexual (the question of "cure")?

Accepting the majority verdict of psychological and psychiatric professionals, and reflecting the theological judgment that spiritual healing, while possible, is not normative for the Christian life, most holding to this view are extremely cautious as to the likelihood of "healing" from the homosexual condition.

While some men and women struggling with homosexual feelings may not be constitutionally homosexual and thus may be susceptible to therapeutic intervention, the many gays and lesbians who are clearly and exclusively homosexual in emotional and erotic direction (which is not to say they cannot function sexually with an opposite sex partner) are most likely not candidates for "cure."

The fact that complete healing of a constitutional homosexual's condition is highly unlikely does not mean, however, that God's grace cannot work to effect substantive growth in self-control, victory over temptation and ability to transform the limitations imposed by a homosexual orientation into positive good.

Question 9:

What is the moral opinion arrived at, given the responses to Questions 1 through 8?

The homosexual condition is not culpably sinful, although it is one of the many manifestations of disorder and brokenness that mark God's creation after the Fall. Homosexual acts are always and without exception sinful.

Question 10:

What is the personal call of Christ for the gay man or lesbian?

Apart from the fact that, for all gays and lesbians, a fundamental requirement of Christian discipleship is complete abstinence from homosexual acts, the specifics of Christ's call to the homosexual will vary according to individual situation.

For a young person struggling with homosexual feelings, an appropriate first step would be to seek competent professional help to determine if heterosexual adjustment is possible. Some form of spiritual healing might also be explored, provided such methods are undertaken with proper pastoral supervision and a clear understanding as to the likely limits of their effect.

For adults with predominantly, but not exclusively, homosexual erotic and emotional attractions and a strong desire for children and family life, heterosexual marriage may sometimes be an option, allowing as it would for the experience of sexual intimacy and family even while an underlying bisexuality or sexual ambivalence continues to exist. In such cases (which most would admit are relatively rare), it would obviously be necessary—prior to marriage—that the intended partner be candidly apprised of the situation of his or her prospective mate and that both individuals obtain competent psychological and spiritual counsel. Furthermore, the homosexual or bisexual spouse would need to be committed to ongoing candor throughout the marriage as to his or her journey—its temptations and its ups and downs—and the heterosexual spouse would perforce be equally committed to the often painful task of bearing such knowledge and supporting his or her partner in the struggle for chastity.

While such a marriage would not conform to contemporary Western cultural notions of what constitutes a good spousal relationship (passionate romantic love on the part of both husband and wife), it would certainly conform to the Christian requirements for an authentic matrimonial covenant (those requirements being—again, as Lewis put it—intentions of "fidelity, fertility and goodwill").[19] That such a marriage would be uniquely challenging goes without saying, but, proponents argue, it could also, like many other good things that come at great cost, be profoundly holy and ultimately more Christlike in its commitment and mutual submission than many more conventional unions.

 For the vast majority of homosexuals, however, faithful discipleship most likely means a commitment to lifelong celibacy. That this is no easy calling is acknowledged by a number of authors representative of this viewpoint. David Field,[20] for example, writes that such a demand—while necessary—not only sounds harsh but "is harsh." Field admits that the homosexual Christian may well face a "very cold and grey" emotional life, adding that "loneliness can be something particularly hard to bear." Evangelical psychiatrist John White[21] is equally candid: the lifelong struggle against yearnings for emotional and erotic intimacy will often produce "pain" and even "profound depression." But, he adds, "Would you despise intimacy with the Almighty in insisting on more of human intimacy?"

Those coming to faith when already in a committed homosexual relationship confront a particularly difficult challenge. They must recognize that, no matter how loving and mutually supportive that relationship may be, or how long-standing, it must be ended if they are to follow Christ. Furthermore, gay Christians must face the fact that few of their heterosexual brothers and sisters in the church are likely to appreciate just how painful such renunciation can be: "straight friends may find it hard to understand that you may deeply love someone of your own sex and that to break up with your lover will wound you," White writes.[22] Despite the profound emotional cost of leaving a beloved partner, however, separation is absolutely necessary for the Christian.

To the many who argue that such a demand is simply "too hard" and that no one can reasonably be asked to give up sexual expression and familial, partnered intimacy permanently absent a very particular "gift" of celibacy,[23] those of this viewpoint respond that it is a peculiarity of our present time and culture to assume that Christianity promises or exists to provide emotional fulfillment in this life or some temporal form of "happiness." Indeed, when we look to the gospels, quite the opposite is found to be true:

> Whoever comes to me and does not hate father and mother, wife and children, brothers and sisters, yes, and even life itself, cannot be my disciple. Whoever does not carry the cross and follow me cannot be my disciple (Luke 14:26–27).

If even legitimate forms of familial and partnered love may need to be sacrificed to follow Christ, how, it is asked, can the homosexual complain that he or she is being called to something too rigorous when asked to reject *illegitimate* forms of sexual and romantic expression in the name of faithfulness to God's will? Such renunciation may be painful, but then the "cross" each of us is asked to carry is always painful—if it were not, it could hardly be called a "cross" in the first place.

While present day Christian homosexuals may justifiably reproach a soft, culturally compromised and self-indulgent

Western church for its too flaccid view of the "cost of discipleship" in other areas of life than the sexual, they may not legitimately use such pervasive laxity to excuse themselves from the requirements of that discipleship. As Russian Orthodox spirituality teaches unequivocally, authentic Christian life requires *podvig*—"striving with all your might" toward the good. For the Christian gay or lesbian, such *podvig* may well include bearing the pain of unfulfilled romantic and sexual attraction, but throughout the church's history faithful Christians have had to relinquish far more than domestic happiness or erotic satisfaction for their faith, up to and including their very lives, and they have done so in the confidence that, as Jesus promised:

> . . . there is no one who has left house or wife or brothers or parents or children, for the sake of the Kingdom of God, who will not get back very much more in this age, and in the age to come eternal life[24] (Luke 18:29–30).

Moreover, proponents of this view would be quick to add, if gay Christians truly understand that they are "not [*their*] own" but "bought with a price," as St. Paul writes of all believers (1 Cor 6:19–20), they will be ready not only to accept the very real suffering their particular path to faithfulness must entail, but also to look beyond that pain to discern the vocation their disability contains. In so doing, they will discover that the way of the cross is also the only royal highway to joy in the eternal presence of God.

Question 11:
What is the pastoral call of Christ to the church on the issue?

As with any other moral question, the church is called to affirm unequivocally and unapologetically the revealed purpose of God for human sexuality, no matter how much this faithful witness may offend the received opinions of the present culture. Christians have no choice but to proclaim clearly, therefore, that homosexual acts are contrary to the will of God.

At the same time, homosexual sin should be treated no differently than any other sin. As St. James makes clear in his Epistle (Jas 2:10), if one has broken any part of God's law, one stands equally condemned with every other sinner. Gays and lesbians, therefore, stand no more (and no less) in need of God's redemptive grace than all other human beings.

Furthermore, in keeping with Christ's example of particularly seeking out those sinners deemed most reprehensible by his own time and culture, the church should acknowledge a special calling to compassion for and ministry to gays and lesbians. Gay people should be able to be open about their struggle within the community of faith without fear of rejection or contempt, since there is no room for moral superiority or homophobia among those who recognize their own brokenness and are bound together by the love of Christ. Homosexuals in the church should be given support through whatever means a particular Christian community employs for ministry to its people—prayer, the sacraments, spiritual direction, small group ministry. Mature individual heterosexual Christians may also serve the particular needs of homosexual believers by providing supportive spiritual friendship or inclusion in a family context for holidays and other occasions when the unpartnered homosexual may feel especially isolated and lonely, and consequently vulnerable to temptation.

Since the homosexual committed to celibacy is basically no different than the unmarried heterosexual pledged to abstinence until marriage, the homosexual condition in and of itself is no barrier to leadership in the church, including ordination.

Question 12:

What is the political call of Christ to society on the issue?

Most holding this viewpoint affirm the obligation of Christians to combat discrimination against or persecution of any minority, including homosexuals. On that basis, laws abridging homosexuals' access to housing or employment, for example, would be viewed as unjust and deserving of Christians' opposition. Similarly, the criminalization of private, consensual homosexual acts would be rejected—on the principle that similar acts between unmarried heterosexuals, while sinful, are not matters with which the law concerns itself. At the same time, there is hesitation regarding the support of legislation which would appear to endorse homosexuality as a morally legitimate alternative way of life—legal recognition of same-sex unions, for example.

The Christian repudiation of legal discrimination against homosexuals is well articulated in the Roman Catholic catechism *Life In Christ:*[25]

> As human persons [*homosexuals*] are to be treated with all human respect and unjust discrimination against them is forbidden by Jesus' law of love.

Much hinges, of course, upon the definition of what constitutes "unjust discrimination."

Many Catholic bishops and their dioceses have been in the forefront of opposition to various legislative proposals which are taken by the church to go beyond protecting homosexuals from injustice to actively promoting or endorsing the licitness of homosexual acts or relationships. Such opposition, which has been a primary flash point for conflict between the Church and gay activists, is in fact based upon explicit Vatican policy. In June 1992, the Congregation for the Doctrine of the Faith issued "Some Considerations Concerning the Catholic Response to Legislative Proposals on the Non-Discrimination [sic] of Homosexual Persons." Addressing all the bishops of the Catholic Church, the letter noted that initiatives seeking to make discrimination on the basis of sexual orientation illegal, "even when they seem more directed to support of basic civil rights than condonement [sic] of homosexual activity or homosexual lifestyle, may in fact have a negative impact on the family and society." Accordingly, it is the obligation of the church to oppose them, since "there are areas in which it is not unjust discrimination to take sexual orientation into account."

Although not all holding to this viewpoint would accept the precise terms of the Vatican's edict on this point, most recognize a certain inherent tension in the attempt, on the one hand, to support gays' civil rights within a pluralistic society and, on the other, to avoid the appearance of sanctioning behavior which they understand to be contrary to the revealed will of God.

Representative Denominations and Para-Church Groups

While the previous perspective and its emphasis on healing for the homosexual is the majority opinion among conservative evangelicals and charismatics, this present viewpoint has been for close to three decades the official position of the mainline Protestant denominations. It is also the current teaching of the Roman Catholic magisterium.

Among Protestants, the 8.5 million member United Methodist Church is typical, both in its official articulation of the position and in the ongoing and increasingly public debate that this stance is occasioning within the denomination. In 1984, the church amended its *Discipline* to include declarations that, while gays and lesbians are "people of sacred worth," homosexual behavior is incompatible with Christian teaching and, therefore, no practicing homosexual can be ordained to the Methodist ministry. A resolution passed in 1992 affirmed that, although active homosexuality is contrary to Christian morality, the civil rights of homosexuals should be supported by Christians. In 1996, the denomination barred its clergy from presiding at services uniting gay or lesbian couples.

In January 1997, fifteen prominent United Methodist ministers went on record as opposing the church's ban on same-sex unions and the denial of ordination to otherwise qualified but non-celibate homosexuals. By January 1998, nearly 1,300 Methodist pastors nationwide had signed a statement of dissent from the denomination's teaching on homosexuality, calling upon the church to provide "appropriate liturgical support" for same-sex covenant partnerships. The document was released to the media at that time, at least in part, as an expression of public support for the Reverend Jimmy Creech, who had been suspended from ministry pending investigation of his having violated church law by officiating at a union service for two women in Omaha, Nebraska.[26]

Creech's eventual acquittal on this charge (based on lack of clarity as to whether the 1996 ban had the force of binding church law) led to an appeal by a number of conservative bishops to the denomination's nine-member Judicial Council, which an official Methodist spokesman likened to the Supreme Court, "the decision [*of which*] is final."[27] In August 1998, the council ruled that "ceremonies that celebrate homosexual unions" are in fact contrary to church law and that Methodist ministers who perform such rites can be tried and defrocked. The council's "final" decision was not the end of the matter, however. On January 16, 1999, ninety-five Methodist pastors put their careers in jeopardy by jointly officiating at the union of two women—longtime Methodist lay leaders Jeanne Barnett (68) and Ellie Charlton (63)[28]—in a Sacramento, California, ceremony attended by an estimated 1,200 people.[29]

Many Methodists fear the increasingly polarized dispute over homosexuality will eventually split their denomination, as did the debate over slavery in the last century.[30] In the Northern California–Nevada Conference, an "Evangelical Renewal Fellowship" of conservative congregations has been formed to resist what its member churches consider the "blatant" disregard of scriptural norms on the part of liberal Methodists on the issue of homosexuality, and some pastors and congregations have already left the denomination.[31]

The situation in the Presbyterian Church USA is similar. In 1978, its General Assembly approved a resolution setting forth a policy regarding homosexuals within the denomination. According to that resolution, homosexuals are children of God, as are all human beings, and therefore should be welcome in the church. Homosexual behavior, on the other hand, is "incompatible with Christian faith and life." Nonetheless, the Presbyterian church should work to abolish legal discrimination against homosexuals. The General Assembly also offered what it termed "definitive guidance" against the ordination of "unrepentant, self-affirming, practicing homosexuals."[32] This official denominational policy did not deter a number of Presbyterian congregations over the next twenty years from declaring themselves "More Light" churches which welcome gays and lesbians into their fellowship and support the ordination of responsible non-celibate homosexuals to all levels of ministry.[33]

The 1988 General Assembly commissioned a report reassessing the church's stand on sexuality. Three years later, that report—"Sexuality, Spirituality and Social Justice"—created a firestorm of controversy within the denomination over its handling of homosexuality. In fact, *two* reports were submitted to the

1991 General Assembly: a majority draft proposing that, in light of current scriptural scholarship and scientific knowledge regarding homosexual orientation, the church should apply the same moral standards to homosexuals and their relationships that it does to heterosexuals, and a minority report which, also citing Scripture and scientific data, unequivocally condemned homosexuality on both moral and psychological grounds. After considering both versions of the report, the General Assembly, by a vote of 501 to 7, accepted the minority draft and sent it to the congregations for five years of study, reflection and response. The denomination also issued a statement affirming that homosexuality is not God's wish for humanity and forbidding the ordination of "openly" homosexual persons.[34] In 1993 and again in 1997, the church reaffirmed its judgment that practicing homosexuals are not eligible for ordination, and the 1994 General Assembly passed a measure forbidding Presbyterian ministers to perform same-sex union rites understood "to be the same as marriage."[35]

In 1996, after the prescribed five year period of study by the congregations of the 1991 report on sexuality, the General Assembly amended the denomination's *Book of Order* to require that pastors, elders and deacons practice abstinence in singleness or fidelity in marriage between a man and a woman—language which clearly excluded non-celibate homosexuals from ordination—and the 1998 General Assembly, after a week of debate, rejected by a vote of 412 to 92 a proposal to reopen the question of ordaining practicing homosexuals. Despite the national church's stand, numerous liberal Presbyterian churches, not all of them self-identified as More Light congregations, continue to ordain gays and lesbians as deacons and elders.

As a final example, the Episcopal Church is also significantly divided on this issue at present, despite the fact that it has historically been more receptive to gay members than almost any other American denomination. In 1979, the church's General Convention codified the denominational consensus and practice by passing a resolution that homosexual acts are incompatible with Christian moral teaching. The resolution also enjoined any Episcopal bishop from ordaining a practicing homosexual.[36] Despite this stated policy, a number of bishops continued doing what they had done for years: ordaining non-celibate homosexuals to the diaconate and the priesthood so long as these candidates evinced the appropriate "discretion" as to their lifestyle. More recently, some bishops have gone public with their acceptance of such candidates and there are now urban Episcopal congregations served by openly gay priests who share their rectories with a life partner who is listed on diocesan registries as a clergy spouse. Services of gay union are also being performed, at least in some instances with the consent of the bishop. In several dioceses, an episcopally sanctioned organization, Oasis, promotes the acceptance of homosexuals in parish life, the ordination of non-celibate gays and lesbians, the blessing of gay unions and church support for homosexual rights. A "traditionalist" group within the church, on the other hand, The Episcopal Synod of America, opposes any change in the church's teaching or policy regarding homosexuality.

Several years ago, heresy charges were brought against now-retired Bishop Walter Righter by a group of conservative Episcopal prelates over his having knowingly ordained to the diaconate a postulant who was in a committed relationship with another man.[37] The charges were dismissed by a church court on grounds of lack of jurisdiction (the issue was not, the court held, "a matter of doctrine"), and the question of ordaining non-celibate gays and lesbians was referred to the church's triennial General Convention (held in Philadelphia in the summer 1997). Many, both in and outside the church, anticipated as heated and potentially divisive a debate over this issue as that occasioned by the matter of the ordination of women in the mid-1970s. This did not in fact take place, however. Instead, the controversy surrounding the increasingly self-confident presence of gays and lesbians in the Episcopal Church found its focus in a resolution that the church approve the blessing of same-sex unions and that the denomination's liturgical commission be instructed to develop "a rite or rites for the blessing of committed relationships between persons of the same sex." This resolution was the subject of sometimes emotional floor debate, with conservatives charging that the proposal, if approved, would violate the Christian consciences of the vast majority of rank and file Episcopalians and cut the church off from virtually every other Christian body—not only from the Roman Catholic and Orthodox churches, but from conservative and even many mainline Protestants, as well as from the mind of the

Anglican communion worldwide. Such a step, it was charged, would also do irreparable harm to the church's teaching on the meaning of Christian marriage and would represent capitulation to a "pressure group which has taken the novel approach of raising experience to normative authority over Scripture."[38] Those supporting the resolution, on the other hand, insisted that "[w]e are not attempting to subvert the sanctity of marriage. Far from it. We are asking to join in the sanctity of marriage through full participation in it."[39] In the end, the measure was by the very narrowest of margins defeated in the convention's "lower" house (the House of Deputies, made up of clergy and lay delegates) and therefore was not sent to the "higher" House of Bishops for consideration.[40] Nonetheless, supporters of gay union rites were pleased by the narrow margin of their defeat. And, as the Reverend Michael W. Hopkins—a member of the Episcopal gay and lesbian organization Integrity—noted, whatever the official position of the church on the matter, certain priests would continue their practice of blessing same-sex unions: "They've been going on for years and they will continue to go on."[41]

Conservative Episcopalians were considerably heartened when the 1998 Lambeth Conference[42] of Anglican bishops issued a resolution on human sexuality which—while it called for sensitive pastoral ministry to all people "irrespective of sexual orientation," committed the church to "listen to the experience of homosexual people," and condemned homophobia—nevertheless unambiguously proclaimed that Scripture mandates a life of sexual abstinence for those not called to heterosexual marriage, that homosexual practice is "incompatible with Scripture," and that the conference could not recommend the "legitimizing or blessing of same-sex unions, nor the ordination of those involved in such unions." While such conference resolutions are advisory in nature and not binding upon the constituent national churches of the Anglican communion, the strong statement—which Archbishop of Canterbury George Carey described as "wholeheartedly with traditional Anglican Orthodoxy and . . . what we've all held . . . Anglican belief and morality [to] stand for"[43]—was clearly a moral victory for conservative Episcopalians concerned over what they see as an erosion of their church's ethical and theological integrity.[44]

Like these and other Protestant denominations, the Roman Catholic Church, as already noted, teaches that gays and lesbians unable to attain heterosexual adjustment must accept the discipline of lifelong celibacy. Since the Roman church has long affirmed celibacy as a high moral good in and of itself, calling homosexuals to permanent sexual abstinence does not tend to carry the same note of moral rigor for Catholics (at least for Catholic moral theologians) that such a demand often conveys to Protestants who have traditionally emphasized the goodness of domestic and sexual satisfaction and viewed celibacy with a certain degree of suspicion. Further, since *all* Roman Catholic priests take a vow of celibacy, homosexual orientation, apart from other factors, is rarely seen as an impediment to ordination—the gay priest is essentially no different than his heterosexual brothers in choosing to channel his emotional and sexual energies into nonerotic forms of love and service.[45]

Despite the church's official teaching on the matter, prior to the 1986 release of the Congregation for the Doctrine of the Faith's "Letter to the Bishops of the Catholic Church on the Pastoral Care of Homosexual Persons,"[46] virtually all chapters of the Catholic gay and lesbian organization Dignity celebrated their masses in parish churches or university Newman Centers, even though Dignity and the priests who served it were fairly open about the fact that they did not accept the church's position on the inherent sinfulness of homosexual acts. The situation changed dramatically, however, after the release of the pastoral letter, which, without specifically naming Dignity, condemned church-related "organizations in which homosexual persons associate with each other without clearly stating that homosexual activity is immoral" and noted that the "practice of scheduling religious services and . . . the use of Church buildings by [*such*] groups, including the facilities of Catholic schools and colleges" is "contradictory to the purpose for which these institutions were founded," as well as being "misleading and often scandalous." On the basis of the Congregation's admonition, the American bishops moved relatively rapidly to deny Dignity access to ecclesiastical property and, by 1992, only two or three chapters nationwide were still meeting in Catholic churches.[47]

Few if any Protestant para-church organizations have arisen basing their ministry to homosexuals on this viewpoint. The Roman Catholic group "Courage," however—founded in 1980 by Father John Harvey, an Oblate of St. Francis de Sales, under the sponsorship of New York's then archbishop, Terence Cardinal Cooke—does provide spiritual support for Roman Catholic gays and lesbians seeking to conform their lives to the church's moral teachings. From relatively modest beginnings, the group has grown to thirty-six chapters in twenty-six dioceses in the United States,[48] six chapters in Canada, and additional chapters in England, Ireland and the Philippines. While a group spokeswoman states that Courage is supportive of any individual member who might desire, as a "personal goal," to "develop into heterosexuality," it applies "no moral pressure to change orientation," but rather seeks to aid members in developing an "interior life of chastity."[49]

Cross-Perspective Critique

To those on the far right of the spectrum, this viewpoint is at best naïve and at worst dishonest, since it refuses to acknowledge the truly depraved nature of all homosexual impulses and accepts at face value homosexuals' rationalizations that the lusts they cultivate are in fact a variety of love. It also violates clear scriptural standards for ministry in its willingness to ordain individuals who have refused to renounce deliberately chosen patterns of sinful response, whether acted upon or not. Finally, it is not even genuinely compassionate, since it is content to leave homosexuals in a spiritual state which means, by definition, their eternal damnation. Indeed, to those affirming viewpoint 1, this present position represents a fatal capitulation to the voices of theological liberalism and moral laxity.

Those convinced that healing is God's promise and challenge to the homosexual see in this viewpoint's willingness to accept the immutability of the homosexual condition nothing less than a tragic denial of the redeeming power of God. In a sense, it is argued, encouraging homosexuals to endure a lifelong struggle for celibacy, when God stands ready to do so much more in their lives, leaves them practicing a "form of godliness but denying its power." (2 Tim 3:5) Even worse, it eliminates the very real *hope* Christians can hold out to those trapped in homosexual lifestyles, giving them, as it were, "the bad news but not the good."

On the left, the critique is equally negative, albeit from an entirely different vantage point. Broadly stated, the argument is that it is hardly realistic to expect that all gays and lesbians who would follow Christ are capable of accepting the discipline of life-long emotional and erotic abstinence and, moreover, that it is any-thing but compassionate to demand of them, as evangelical theologian Helmut Thielicke puts it, "a degree of harshness and rigor which one would never think of demanding"[50] of heterosexual Christians. As Bruce Bawer writes with some feeling:

> What kind of compassion is it . . . that leaves the object of that compassion no means of living honorably with his situation other than that of leading a tortured, empty, loveless life? . . . Gay Christians simply cannot conceive of a God who would bless them with the ability to love and yet demand that they spend their lives alone.[51]

C. S. Lewis's comment that the homosexual is "no worse off than any normal person who is, for whatever reason, prevented from marrying"[52] may sound reasonable on its face but, opponents argue, it fails to take into account the very real difference between "not now" and "never." Despite the fact that the gist of Lewis's remark is repeatedly raised by conservative authors ("we all face the same requirement of self-control, regardless of sexual orientation" another writes),[53] the fact is that, while the ordinary heterosexual Christian may go through some years of struggle between puberty and marriage during which he or she must remain chaste, there is always the hope (and, in the majority of cases, the eventual reality) of finding a mate.[54] For the homosexual Christian, on the other hand, no such hope exists; perpetual singleness (if one accepts the principles of this viewpoint) is the *only* option available apart from heterosexual marriage. Furthermore, it is argued, there is much more at stake in such lifelong celibacy than mere sexual abstinence. Also to be renounced is the entire complex web of intimacy, self-revelation, mutual help, familial connection and emotional union which make up the coupled state. Blithe statements by more often than not married heterosexual conservatives as to the equivalent burden chastity places upon homosexuals and unmarried heterosexuals exhibit, opponents insist, a profound failure of empathic imagination, evincing the fundamental refusal of conservatives to take gay people and their lives seriously.

As for analogies to the Roman tradition of priestly celibacy, critics are quick to point out that such celibacy has always been understood by that church to be a special "gift." It would seem highly unlikely, critics point out, that *every* gay or lesbian person would be the recipient of such a gift—and in fact, many gay Christians give emphatic witness to the fact that they have *not* been granted this particular charism. Given that reality, Bruce Bawer argues:

> It is not only unrealistic but heartless to expect someone who is not called to celibacy to forsake physical intimacy throughout his entire life without becoming bitter and spiritually twisted and succumbing to sexual desire.[55]

Others note as well that much of the traditional Christian promotion of virginity and consecrated celibacy is in fact based in antisexual attitudes far removed from authentic biblical teaching and, for that matter, from sound principles of mental health.[56] Indeed, as Ralph Blair notes, quoting the evangelical *International Standard Bible Encyclopedia*,[57] throughout the Old Testament "celibacy was considered abnormal" and "instances of a lifelong state of celibacy are rare in Scripture." Since the Reformation, Protestants have been quick to deny that celibacy, in and of itself, has any particular moral value over and above marital chastity. Martin Luther, never given to reticence in his polemic, denounced celibacy as a "great hypocrisy and wickedness," writing to his friend Spalatin that "not one in a hundred is suited [*for*] the hell of celibacy, totally unclean and condemned as it is through its burning and pollutions." Reflecting on this rather fevered passage, Ralph Blair comments wryly: "But today . . . [*conservative*] Christians claim that one in ten must be so suited."[58]

Even among Roman Catholics in recent years—given a catastrophic drop in vocations and repeated scandals over priestly pedophilia—increasingly pointed questions have been raised by a number of scholars and theologians as to whether lifelong sexual abstinence is either an asset in ministry or particularly healthy in most cases. Notre Dame theology chair and widely read Catholic apologist Richard McBrien sums up this growing opinion (which is decidedly not shared by the Vatican) in a flat assertion that, as a

general principle, mandatory clerical celibacy is "unrealistic and
. . . counter-productive."[59] Ralph Blair, for one, does not find this
surprising—after all, "[i]t was God who, at the dawn of human history, took note that it was not good for a person to be alone."[60] As
Bruce Bawer, a practicing Episcopalian, notes, reflecting traditional Protestant conviction:

> A loving, committed human relationship isn't a distraction from
> [ministry] but a support to it; it doesn't hinder, but rather enhances,
> one's responsiveness to the problems of others.[61]

If this is true of consecrated celibacy accepted as a condition of
pastoral ministry, critics contend, it is entirely specious to claim
that every gay or lesbian layperson's "vocation" in Christ is in
some manner to be discovered within a lifelong struggle to avoid
sexual and intimate emotional expression.

As for the suggestion that, for at least some gays and lesbians, a
heterosexual marriage may provide a fruitful alternative to the single life, Bawer summarizes critics' take on such proposals succinctly:
"any intelligent, sensitive person who has ever seen such unions in
real life knows that they are [a] mockery of marriage."[62] This is true,
opponents contend, because there is more to authentic marriage
than conservative Christians seem willing to admit when suggesting
heterosexual wedlock as the solution to the dilemma of the gay
Christian. Evangelical Thomas Schmidt, for example, writes
that—in terms of what is essential to a successful heterosexual marriage for the "ex-gay"—"minimally, all that is required is the ability
to function heterosexually and the ability to control homosexual
behavior."[63] To many, this is a grotesque, sterile picture of marriage
and one utterly lacking in that community of spirit, mutual desire
and genuine emotional connection—the rising up of soul to soul—
that are essential to happy, life-giving union. Reflecting upon the
situation of the heterosexual spouse in such a relationship, critics
ask: who in his or her right mind would choose to come to the most
intimate relationship of life knowing that one was always "second
best" in the heart and desire of one's mate?

It has also been pointed out that, for most people, a primary
(though certainly not the only) context in which the individual's
natural tendency to selfishness is whittled away and supplanted by
focus on the needs of others is the day to day reality of marriage
and family life. By denying gays and lesbians the possibility of

such coupled intimacy, it is argued, this viewpoint would cut them off from a key means of God's transforming work in the human heart. Critics also question the ultimate psychological effect of viewing a fundamental element of one's core being[64] as a "disability," and suggest that expending one's energies in a lifelong struggle against emotional and erotic feelings cannot help but limit the psychological resources available for growth, ministry and creative expression.

Attempts to make a moral distinction between the homosexual condition and the specific acts that flow from and express that condition are generally dismissed by critics as well-meaning casuistry. As Bruce Bawer puts it:

> [T]o recognize homosexual orientation as naturally occurring and morally neutral, while insisting that acting upon that orientation is, in every instance and without exception, abnormal, unnatural, and perverse, makes no sense. If homosexual "behavior" comes as naturally to gays as heterosexual "behavior" comes to straight people, then how can heterosexual sex in marriage be seen as a blessing, a virtue, and a force for good, while homosexual sex within a committed, long-term relationship is seen as an evil, deviant urge that must be resisted?[65]

As is the case with the previous two viewpoints, this position is also criticized for its selective enforcement of biblical norms. The few biblical passages which condemn homosexual activity are held by conservatives to be universally and inflexibly binding, whereas other texts which speak with equal force on issues such as remarriage after divorce, the accumulation of wealth, or participation in violence are ignored or explained away.[66] As Bawer writes:

> Certainly one could make a long list of things that are more inconsistent with both the spirit and the letter of Christ's gospel than homosexuality: being rich, for one. Though Christ says nothing in the gospels about homosexuality, he does say unequivocally that it would be "easier for a camel to go through the eye of a needle than for a rich man to enter the kingdom of heaven." But Christians accumulate wealth and are celebrated for it.[67]

As to which biblical standards will be upheld and which abridged, critics contend that the issue generally seems to come down to whose ox is being gored. If the teaching of Scripture is sufficiently onerous on a point at which a sufficient number of believers have become vulnerable, Christians will find a way to accommodate the scriptural witness to the "realities" of their situation. Examples of this process at work range from Augustine's "just war" theories of the fifth century, to the redefinition of usury in the sixteenth, to the gradual acceptance of remarriage after divorce by evangelicals over the past four decades. This being the case, it is argued, it is both intellectually dishonest and spiritually pernicious to insist on strict adherence to a half-dozen proof texts relating to homosexuality at the expense of gay people's need for (and right to) emotional and sexual fulfillment.

The Viewpoint Responds

From the perspective of those holding this viewpoint, their critics on the far right too often confuse invincible ignorance (a determined attachment to prejudice and misinformation) with fidelity to biblical norms. Every age and every Christian tradition and community has its blind spots, to be sure, points where it confuses cultural context or opinion with unchanging revealed truth or bases its theology on textual misunderstanding rather than the actual message of the Scriptures. But the viewpoint of Condemnation is to be particularly faulted for refusing to do the difficult, but far from impossible, work of distinguishing between the clear biblical teaching that sex outside of heterosexual marriage is a violation of the Creator's intent, and any number of extra-biblical notions which it holds with equal passion, notions regarding etiology and the psychosocial consequences of homosexual orientation which are not only *not* questions of faith, but are clearly contrary to fact

As for arguments that the church's answer for the homosexual is spiritual healing and movement toward heterosexual adjustment, the majority of those holding this present viewpoint conclude—often with deep regret—that in most (but possibly not all) cases, such a solution, as appealing as it clearly is on many levels, is simply not a realistic option. Therefore, the church—if it is to be both faithful to the teaching of Scripture and honest about the facts of the matter—is left upholding what has always been a fundamental element in its message, albeit one which finds little favor in today's indulgent, consumption-driven Western world: a call to the arduous work of discipleship, an invitation to follow Christ to the cross.

It is precisely this historic understanding of the nature and purpose of the Christian life that those sharing this viewpoint see as missing in much of the criticism directed at their views from the left as well. Put perhaps too baldly, the fundamental premise of such attacks seems to be a conviction that not only does everyone somehow have a "right" to sexual and emotional fulfillment, but that the absence of such fulfillment must entail, as Bawer puts it, a "tortured, empty, loveless life."[68] Such thinking, proponents of this present perspective respond, simply reflects the obsession with sex which so marks the spirit of this age, as well as our current culture's pervasive insistence upon one's right to gratification of every kind. Despite contemporary assumptions to the contrary, however, there is in fact extensive evidence down through the centuries (not exclusively within the Christian church) of men and women who have lived happy, contented, full and productive lives in which there was a deep experience of love, both divine and human, but who nonetheless never married or experienced coupled erotic intimacy. Indeed, in any age but our own, it is argued, a statement like Bawer's would be received with, at best, polite incredulity.

Furthermore, while the homosexual determined to follow Christ may well be called to a degree of self-denial (in particular areas of affectional and erotic life) not required of most heterosexuals—in other words, to put it colloquially, the gay or lesbian person may have a "harder row to hoe" than the contentedly married "straight"—the question remains whether a complaint that the call of Christ is "too hard" is ever a legitimate issue in Christian moral discernment. When, it is asked, has true discipleship not been "hard?"

Within our present, ubiquitous cultural consensus, so quick to assert "rights" and so leery of acknowledging responsibilities, so certain that the goal of life is fulfillment, satisfaction and relative ease, the plain statements of Jesus that those who would seek God's Kingdom must forsake everything, must leave home and family and social acceptance and follow him, must die to self, are shocking in their dissonance. Yet this has always been the Christian message, along with the promise that, for those who will accept it with grateful hearts, the burden of such discipleship is paradoxically "light."

Therefore, as Christian homosexuals struggle, in contradiction to the spirit of the age, for a sometimes costly faithfulness within the particular requirements of their unique situation, one vocation immediately evident in their disability might well be that of serving as prophetic mentors to their heterosexual brothers and sisters in an enculturated church too quick to assume that the days when Christian commitment was costly are over and that God has now settled himself comfortably into the cozy confines of a bourgeois church that asks little and promises much in this life as well as the next.

- 4 -

PASTORAL ACCOMMODATION

F or all their differences, the previous three viewpoints are in agreement on a fundamental point: homosexual acts are intrinsically evil and therefore never an acceptable moral option. With this present perspective, a very significant step is taken, however cautiously and with however many qualifying disclaimers: homosexual acts are viewed not so much as intrinsically evil as essentially *imperfect*, albeit profoundly so, which raises the consequent possibility that, in certain very specific and narrowly limited contexts, there might be such a thing as morally acceptable *hm.* (though never "idealized" or "sanctioned") homosexual expression.

Although the name most often associated with this viewpoint is that of German evangelical Helmut Thielicke, the fact is that Thielicke in a sense lays all the theological and theoretical groundwork for such a step but then appears unready to take it himself, instead suggesting that, apart from the extraordinarily rare "possible exception" of a morally acceptable committed homosexual partnership, "Christian pastoral care will have to be concerned primarily with helping the [*homosexual*] to sublimate his homosexual urge."[1] It remains for others—among them respected evangelical Lewis B. Smedes, controversial Roman Catholic Charles E. Curran, and United Methodist pastor and counselor H. Kimball Jones—to cross this particular threshold. That so doing opens one to condemnation from both sides of the discussion goes without saying. As Smedes notes, such a viewpoint and its arguments will be "misunderstood by Christian heterosexuals as flabby concession and by homosexuals as unfeeling intolerance."[2] Nonetheless, proponents hold, no other viewpoint does justice both to the biblical witness regarding God's intent for human sexuality and the sometimes painfully ambiguous realities of life in a fallen world.

Question 1:

What is the ultimate authority upon which any moral judgment regarding homosexuals and/or homosexual acts is to be based?

When it comes to moral questions, the preeminence of the scriptural witness must be acknowledged by any ethical formulation worthy of being called Christian. True, this witness is understood by Roman Catholics, Orthodox and Anglicans to be but one aspect of the living tradition of the church, whereas Protestants will, at least in theory, affirm the Reformed doctrine of *sola Scriptura*. True, as well, as Charles Curran notes,[3] Roman Catholics will also look to a natural law methodology for moral guidance. Nonetheless, all holding this viewpoint would agree that, as Helmut Thielicke puts it, "the theological interpretation of homosexuality cannot ignore the relevant statements of the Bible." At the same time, however, Thielicke also writes that "we would not be satisfying this principle of Scripture if we merely cited the Holy Scriptures instead of interpreting the quotations in accord with the kerygmatic purpose" and warns against "a merely legalistic citation of Scripture which [*does*] not inquire into its significance."[4]

In whatever way those relatively few biblical texts which make reference to homosexual activity may be understood to relate to the overriding kerygmatic intent of the sacred Word, Lewis Smedes is confident that the Bible communicates "a clear and certain message: it tells us that homosexual practices are unnatural and Godless. There can be no doubt about this."[5]

At the same time, Smedes recognizes that the only explicit Old Testament condemnations of homosexual behavior (Lev 18:22; 20:13) appear within the Holiness Code alongside numerous other acts which Christians now accept as harmless—marital relations during the wife's menstrual period, for example (Lev 18:19, 20:18).[6] This fact means that "[w]e need some interpreter's rule for selecting one law as a moral norm and the other as cultic fussiness."[7]

Thielicke, in similar fashion, notes that while "there can be no doubt that the Old Testament regarded homosexuality and pederasty[8] as crimes punishable by death," the question of whether this fact connotes a "direct injunction" for Christians must be considered in light of the concerns regarding cultic defilement which underlie the strictures of the Holiness Code:

> [T]he prohibition of divination, the drinking of blood, sexual intercourse with a menstruating woman, and many other things are put on the same level with the capital offense of homosexuality. It would never occur to anyone to wrench these laws of cultic purification from their concrete situation.[9]

Moving on to the New Testament, Lewis Smedes argues that these Scriptures are "just as intolerant of homosexual practices as is the Old Testament. Along with other less reprehensible doings, homosexual acts disqualify a person for the kingdom of God (1 Cor 6:9–10)."[10] Further, commenting on Paul's line of argument in Romans 1, Smedes writes that the scriptural message is that "[w]hen God lets people go, homosexual depravity is one of the intolerable upshots."

Although Thielicke does note that the subject of homosexual acts goes unmentioned in the gospels and that Jesus dealt with "sensual sinners incomparably more leniently than he did with the sinners who committed sins of the spirit," he too affirms that "there can be no doubt" that Paul saw homosexual behavior as sinful and as a "perversion of the order of human existence willed by God."[11]

Despite this unequivocal assertion as to Paul's convictions regarding the spiritual and ethical meaning of homosexual acts, however, Thielicke goes on to give particular attention to the specific *use* Paul makes of those convictions within the biblical texts in which they are mentioned. Put simply, Thielicke's argument runs as follows: Paul's denunciations of homosexuality are never in and of themselves the *point* of the passages in which they appear (Rom 1:26ff.; 1 Cor 6:9–10; 1 Tim 1:9–10); rather, they are in every instance illustrative *examples* (drawn from stock lists of vices available to the apostle from both Jewish and pagan sources) used to buttress his argument on another, more significant issue which is the real focus of discussion. That this is so, Thielicke argues, "cannot be without significance" for our interpretation and application of these condemnations of homosexuality.

Turning to Paul's argument in Romans 1 for an example of the distinction he is arguing, Thielicke notes that the focal thrust (what is "kerygmatically 'binding'") in this text is the fact that disruptions of humankind's vertical relationship with God inevitably result in distortions in the horizontal relationship between people. Indeed . . . "the point of the Pauline statement lies precisely in this correspondence between the two dimensions." Within that overriding context, then, "[t]he individual demonstrative references, including the reference to sexual perversion, are simply illustrations of this point."[12] That being the case, Thielicke reasons, even though there can be "no question that Paul is here rejecting homosexuality," it is nevertheless significant,

> . . . as far as the relative theological emphasis is concerned . . . that [*this rejection of homosexuality*] is not made the subject of separate theological statement, but that it appears only in the context of another, theologically fundamental, statement and as an illustration of it.

Thielicke explains what he understands to be the hermeneutical significance of this "relative theological emphasis" by reference to another Pauline passage he considers less liable to provoke contention: the discussion in 1 Cor 11:3ff. of the male's divinely ordained "headship" over the female.[13] In this text, Thielicke argues, the "essential intention"—which "must be distinguished from the illustration"—is to refute the notion that men and women are to all intents and purposes indistinguishable in the order of creation. The illustration the apostle uses in support of his argument is drawn from the unstated but well understood (to his initial readers) facts of then-contemporary dress conventions.[14] The conclusion Paul draws is that men should pray with heads uncovered, while women should cover their heads in Christian worship—all this as witness to God's hierarchical arrangement of human gender relationships.

Thielicke admits that Paul himself, caught up as any writer tends to be in the customs of his own time and place, was not capable of realizing the difference in ultimate significance—what Thielicke terms "quality"—between the essential point he was making (the divinely mandated difference between male and female) and the illustrative means he used to convey that point (the symbolic meaning of dress in the culture of his day). Nevertheless, Thielicke goes on to point out, Christians today *can* recognize that difference:

[T]he differentiation between the sexes, which is the point that Paul is here stating, is just as important for us today as it was then. It would never occur to us, however, that when we accept these statements of difference between the sexes we must also take over the dress regulations which had symbolical force at that time.[15] We have the freedom to choose other symbols of this difference which come from our own time and situation.[16]

Thielicke is quick to add that "obviously" Paul's "statements concerning dress and those concerning homosexuality are different in importance." Nonetheless, he argues,

[T]he fact that homosexuality . . . appears in the context of the symbolical and illustrative statements and thus is a means of statement [sic] and not the object of the statement of intention itself, gives us a certain freedom to rethink the subject.

Further, such "rethinking" must take into account yet another fundamental issue related to the scriptural data on homosexuality: the biblical authors were, despite their being inspired, still men of their particular time and culture. They did not share, and could not be expected to share, our contemporary understanding of the nature of constitutional homosexual orientation (any more than they shared our knowledge of genetics or atomic fission). What the inspired authors wrote regarding homosexuality was premised upon an anthropology in which all human beings were by "nature" heterosexual with any homosexual act representing, at least to some extent, a willful and conscious "going against the self" in order to practice perversion.

That being the case, Scripture—as Thielicke puts it—"does not provide us with an evident, normative dictum" with regard to the moral options available to a constitutional homosexual (as we today understand that person) since such a question is "alien" to the Scriptures "for purely historical reasons."[17] Those reasons are reducible to the single, simple fact that the scriptural writers had no understanding that some people are constitutionally homosexual. Therefore, while the biblical witness on the question of homosexuality must be given the most serious attention, that to which it speaks and that to which it does not speak must be distinguished, and our application of its witness nuanced accordingly.[18]

Father Charles Curran, reflecting at once a more Catholic and, to a degree, a more liberal perspective, goes beyond even the issues of context and primary intent raised by Thielicke, writing:

> The Scriptures do not have a monopoly on ethical wisdom and thus do not constitute the sole way into the ethical problem for the Christian ethicist . . . [T]he Christian ethicist derives his general orientation from a scriptural base . . . [but] in the case of specific conclusions about specific actions, Christian theologians realize the impossibility of any methodological approach which would develop its argument only in terms of individual biblical texts taken out of their context.[19]

Despite these somewhat varying approaches, the bottom line on the question of authority within this viewpoint can be summarized as follows: Scripture is the ultimate authority for deciding moral issues, but that authority is legitimately employed not through proof texting but rather through serious contextual analysis that takes into consideration the limits of authorial understanding, the literary form and intent of a given passage, and the difference between culturally-conditioned opinion and the underlying eternal verities being expressed through that opinion.[20]

Question 2:
What is the God-given intent or design for human sexuality?

In agreement with the previous three viewpoints, this viewpoint affirms that the divinely ordained heterosexual order for human sexuality is established by both Scripture[21] and empirical fact (sexual differentiation and the biological "imperative" of reproduction).[22]

What is distinctive in this perspective's handling of that heterosexual given is the importance it ascribes to the relational aspects of the one-flesh union.[23] While certainly not excluding the significance of generativity, those articulating this view tend to focus their attention on the psychospiritual mutuality which sexual intercourse is meant to express and deepen within marriage—what Smedes terms a "deeply personal union."[24] For participation in such mature mutuality to be possible, sexuality must be "integrated into the total development of a person's character"[25] and for the Christian this means it must be grounded not only in erotic and romantic love but in that *agape* which is the mark of any Christlike (and, therefore, any fully human) action.

Question 3:

What are the necessary criteria for morally legitimate sexual expression?

As already noted, it is on this point that the present viewpoint makes an extremely significant departure from those which have preceded it. Despite an unequivocal affirmation that the divine intent for human sexuality is heterosexual marriage open to conception and involving a deeply intimate personal union, proponents of this viewpoint understand that intent to be an *ideal*. In light of that ideal, homosexual acts must be seen as—in Thielicke's phrase—"in every case not in accord with the order of creation"[26] because they are not generative.[27] It must also be recognized, however, that *heterosexual* acts rarely if ever measure up to that ideal either, because few if any of them fully achieve the level of self-emptying other-centeredness which is an equally significant element within the Creator's purpose. As H. Kimball Jones argues:

> [I]t is questionable [*whether*] human beings are capable of consummating perfect marriages in which every act of coitus is a perfect, selfless expression of mutual love coupled with a desire to have children. At most, marriage can only approximate this goal. Due to man's sinful nature, lust and selfishness are never completely absent from coitus.[28]

This being the case, it is argued, before any consideration can be given to the specifics of the homosexual's particular moral dilemma, there is an underlying question which must be addressed: on what basis is the morality of *heterosexual* acts to be assessed? The answer, clearly, is that these acts are, in fact, not judged by their *absolute* fidelity to the created intent, since after the Fall no human sexual act can fully escape the effects of sin. Rather, they are judged in terms of how closely they *approach* that intent, taking into consideration the limitations imposed upon the participants by the ubiquitous reality of sin, a reality which will be expressed both through the cultural context in which they must live out their moral lives and through the individual psychological factors which may constrict or deform their ability to fulfill the created intent in all its perfection.

Charles Curran articulates the rationale for such an approach by means of an ethical paradigm he titles "The Theory of Compromise."[29] As Curran explains:

> The presence of sin means that at times one might not be able to do what would be done if there were no sin present. In the theory of compromise, the particular action in one sense is not . . . wrong because in the presence of sin it remains the only viable alternative for the individual. However, in another sense the action is wrong and manifests the power of sin. If possible, man must try to overcome sin, but the Christian knows that the struggle against sin is never totally successful in this world.[30]

In other words, in a fallen world, many (if not most) of the ethical decisions we are called upon to make involve some degree of ambiguity and, more often than we might care to admit, a choice for the lesser of two evils. To recognize that this is so in no way diminishes the importance or authority of revealed moral truth; it merely acknowledges that the inescapable fact of sin not only tempts us to do evil but to some extent limits our ability to do good.

When applied to the issues of sexual morality facing heterosexuals, such an approach means that—to choose an obvious and simple example—if spouses are incapable of conceiving children, this inability to fulfill the "conceptional" aspect of the Creator's purposes for sexuality does not render their conjugal relations morally wrong, even though their sexual expression—though through no fault of their own—falls short of the ideal. Perhaps more significantly for the question at hand, it also means that the polygamous marriages and concubinage of the Old Testament saints—while significantly inferior to the created intent for sexual relationships—were not strictly speaking culpably sinful, since, given the social realities of the time and culture,[31] polygamy was in a sense the closest men and women could come to that created intent.

Proponents of this present viewpoint point out that, as startling as such "accommodationism" may seem (especially when applied to questions of sexual ethics), it is hardly a novelty in Christian moral reflection. Most Christians throughout the church's history, for example, have been willing to recognize (albeit reluctantly in some cases) that war is contrary to the perfect will of God. Nonetheless, the majority after the third century have also been convinced that, in a fallen world, the reality of sin sometimes requires Christians' participation in war. This fact, according to the traditional line of argument, does not make war any less objectively sinful. It does, however, mean that—given the other alternatives available in particular circumstances—certain forms of violence may be less sinful than any other option available. In such a situation, then, the moral imperative becomes one of as far as possible limiting the *subjective* sinfulness of such *objectively* sinful behavior. Indeed, the entire logic of St. Augustine's just war theory lies in an attempt to do precisely that.

To turn to another, more recent example: the majority of conservative evangelicals have, over the past thirty or so years, amended their absolute condemnation of remarriage after divorce. It continues to be acknowledged, to be sure, that the divine ideal, explicitly taught by Jesus himself, is monogamous marriage for life. The failure of any marriage is therefore not only an interpersonal tragedy but to some extent an objective expression of sin, whether the causative issues be willed failures in commitment and love or psychological limitations which are themselves a result of the Fall. Nonetheless, the fact is that some marriages do irrevocably break down.

At one time, conservative Christians insisted that, in such cases, the estranged partners had only two choices: (1) remain in a marriage that was, on every level but the contractual, dead or (2) accept the discipline of celibate singleness for so long as their former spouse remained alive. More recently, however, it has been argued (and widely accepted) that preserving the form of a marriage when the reality of the marital relationship no longer exists is not only a prescription for human misery but an actual affront to what the gift of marriage was created to be. Further, it is held, for any number of reasons—ranging from the need of children for two parents to a longing for the joys of committed partnership–lifelong singleness for the divorced is not always either reasonable or desirable. Therefore, while recognizing that the failure of any marriage is a part of the fallen, sinful situation of humankind, Christians may nevertheless conclude that the "highest good" for all concerned (what Curran would term the moral compromise), and indeed the most *redemptive* alternative, is to allow for a second marriage, even though a lifelong union continues to be affirmed as the God-given ideal.

On these and countless other moral questions, then, Christians—sometimes not without painful struggle with the ethical ambiguities involved—have recognized that the existential realities occasioned by living in and being a part of a broken world must be taken into account in forming any specific moral judgment.

If this is true for heterosexuals, those holding this viewpoint argue, it must also be true for homosexuals, since it would be both unjust and inconsistent to apply one standard of judgment to heterosexuals (*degree of conformity* to the ideal, taking into consideration the fact of the Fall) and another, more stringent standard (*absolute conformity* to the ideal) to homosexuals.[32] Indeed, to do so would be to fail completely in one's moral responsibility to the homosexual, since the only thing the gospel could then do for such a person would be, as Smedes puts it, to "leave the homosexual . . . in his sin."[33] In light of the universal reach of the redemptive love of God, such a bleak option is simply untenable.

Given the inescapable fact of the Fall, therefore, and the consequent brokenness of every human being, gay or straight, the criterion for morally legitimate sexual expression is that both partners come as close to the divinely ordained ideal as is possible given the effects of sin (both personal and contextual) upon the capacities of the individuals involved. Such a standard, it is insisted, in no way compromises the reality of the God-given intent for human sexuality, which continues to be upheld as both a hope and a standard. Rather, it merely applies to sexual questions the same pastoral realism that Christians have long practiced in numerous other less emotionally charged areas of life.

Question 4:

Is there a "homosexual condition" (orientation) and, if so, what is its cause or origin?

The fact that a homosexual orientation exists is no longer a subject for debate among reasonable people: science has established indisputably the existence of the "constitutional" homosexual, the person whose sexual and emotional attractions are to all intents and purposes exclusively same-sex directed.[34] This determination is based in large part upon the testimony of countless gays and lesbians as to their experience of themselves as sexual beings.[35]

Theories of etiology, on the other hand, are numerous and often conflicting, have varied over the years and continue to be a matter of some dispute among therapeutic and clinical professionals.[36] The best that can be said for most of them is that they more often than not seem to fit some cases but not all. Indeed, the specific causative factors of constitutional homosexuality may well differ from individual to individual. This being said, it must be recognized—as noted previously—that etiology is not properly a theological or moral question in the first place, but rather a subject for scientific inquiry. Insofar as science can move beyond hypothesis to demonstrable fact, its judgments should be accepted by Christians as true.

Question 5:

Can a legitimate moral distinction be made between a homosexual condition (orientation) and homosexual acts?

In agreement with viewpoint 3, this perspective holds that the homosexual condition, while a result of the fact of sin in the world, is never culpable, because it is not chosen. As Smedes writes:

> No homosexual, to my knowledge, ever decides to be a homosexual; he only makes the painful discovery at one time or another that he is homosexual . . . He is a product of forces over which he had no control. He merits blame for being homosexual no more than a mentally retarded child does for being retarded.[37]

Thus, even though "it is impossible to think of [*the homosexual condition*] as having no ethical significance, as being a mere vagary or sport of nature,"[38] the homosexual should "simply refuse to accept a burden of guilt for [*it*]," since he or she is "a victim either of biological accident or someone else's folly."[39]

On the matter of homosexual acts, however, gays and lesbians must recognize that they are morally responsible for what they *do* with their unchosen condition, and these acts—like their heterosexual counterparts—may or may not be culpable depending upon their context and meaning.

Question 6:

What is the psychological significance of homosexuality?

In that homosexuality is "abnormal"—both in a purely statistical sense and in its divergence from the implicit "imperative" of human biology and reproduction—homosexual orientation is to be understood as a species of psychosexual disability.

This does not mean that homosexuals are necessarily mentally ill, or less psychologically whole than heterosexuals, despite Thielicke's equation of homosexuality with "abnormal personality structure,"[40] or H. Kimball Jones's insistence that the homosexual is "a sexually-handicapped person . . . there is no getting around this."[41] As Curran notes:

> a review of the [*scientific*] literature plus personal experience would seem to indicate that homosexuality does not necessarily make every individual a neurotic or emotionally disturbed person . . .

But, Curran adds, affirming the potential mental health of homosexual people does not mean that homosexual orientation is "normal" or that homosexual acts are the moral equivalent of heterosexual acts, since "even the well-adjusted person can have proclivities and perform acts which are 'abnormal' and/or morally wrong."[42]

Therefore, as Jones points out, while homosexual love can often "reach a height of fulfillment equal to that of many heterosexual relationships," such love is always:

> . . . doomed, by its very nature, [*never to*] pass beyond a certain point. Two homosexuals can never complement one another in the same sense that male and female can, and they can never know the joy of having children, a joy that brings a heterosexual relationship into a whole new dimension.[43]

Question 7:

What is the spiritual significance of homosexuality?

As already noted, homosexual orientation is one of the many results of the Fall, an evidence and a consequence of sin in the world. To acknowledge that this is true is not to deny the fact that "[t]housands of homosexual people live highly moral and often deeply religious existences."[44] Nor is it to ignore the reality that every human person, not just the homosexual, has "sinned and fall[s] short of the glory of God." (Rom 3:23) As Thielicke writes:

> The [homosexual] predisposition itself . . . dare not be any more strongly deprecated than the status of existence which we all share . . . in the disordered creation that exists since the Fall . . . Consequently, there is not the slightest excuse for maligning the constitutional homosexual morally or theologically. We are all under the same condemnation and each of us has received his "share" of it.[45]

Yet the gay person's struggle for moral integrity is to some extent exceptional, even within the community of sinners. In the first place, homosexuals "must grope their way painfully into a creative and useful life amid a community of [heterosexual] people who—try as they will—cannot fully sympathize with [their] struggle."[46] Furthermore, the moral options open to the homosexual involve either a degree of self-denial or a level of moral "imperfection" (as against the ideal) which, in either case, far exceeds that faced by most heterosexuals. Thus, the homosexual seeking to live a morally responsible life must in a perhaps unique fashion grapple with the ambiguity which lies at the heart of all human experience after the Fall.

Question 8:

Can a homosexual become heterosexual (the question of "cure")?

Most holding this viewpoint contend that the gay person has a responsibility to attempt to change the direction of his or her emotional and sexual attractions, whether through conventional  psychotherapeutic methods, various Christian spiritual techniques or a combination of the two. Smedes is exceedingly straightforward on this point:

> [The homosexual] ought to believe that change is possible . . . He ought to seek change. The Christian homosexual ought to open himself to the possibility of divine healing . . . Further, he should seek psychiatric help to modify his behavior.[47]

Curran, too, states that "[a]ttempts should be made to overcome this condition if possible."[48] and Thielicke writes that "[t]he homosexual must therefore be willing to be treated or healed so far as this is possible; he must, as it were, be willing to be brought back into the [*created*] "order."[49]

Despite these unequivocal affirmations of the homosexual's moral obligation to pursue the possibility of "cure," however, these same authors are less than optimistic as to the likelihood that such methods will prove effective. Thielicke writes:

> But now experience shows that constitutional homosexuality at any rate is largely unsusceptible to medical or psychotherapeutic treatment, at least so far as achieving the desired goal of a fundamental conversion to normality is concerned.

Furthermore, Thielicke admits, the great majority of homosexuals belong in this classification [*those for whom change is not possible*] and their number is considerable." Curran seems even less inclined to hold out the prospect of change in orientation, noting simply in passing that "[t]herapy, as an attempt to make the homosexual into a heterosexual, does not offer great promise for most homosexuals."[50]

Even Smedes, despite his insistence that the homosexual is obliged to hope for change, admits that "[s]tatistics on homosexual conversion are certainly not promising." Nevertheless, he argues, "no homosexual person can be absolutely sure of what is possible for him." As for divine healing (as opposed to traditional therapy), Smedes notes that there are simply "too many testimonies to God's help in changing a person's sexual orientation . . . to be ignored," but then, within the same paragraph, again acknowledges that, here too, "the statistics are not encouraging."[51]

In short, while upholding the duty of the homosexual to seek both therapeutic and pastoral assistance in attempting to alter his or her orientation, those holding this viewpoint in the end recognize that, for constitutional homosexuals (who comprise the majority of adult gays and lesbians), such efforts at change are most likely doomed to be unsuccessful.

Question 9:

What is the moral opinion arrived at, given the responses to Questions 1 through 8?

Homosexual acts, whatever their context or the subjective dispositions of the individuals involved, always "fall outside the bounds

of the order of creation"[52] and, "by their very nature, negate the
male-female complement and [the] vocation of parenthood, both
of which are essential"[53] to morally acceptable sexual expression.
They are never, therefore, an objective good. Such acts always
express, to a greater or lesser degree, the effects of sin in the world.
Nonetheless, for the constitutional homosexual, they may be sub-
jectively the optimal moral alternative possible. In such a case,
they are to be judged by exactly the same ethical standards applicable to heterosexuals: monogamous fidelity to one partner in a
relationship in which love, "respect and regard for the other as a
person dominates [the] sexual relationship."[54]

This is not, as Smedes writes,

> . . . to accept homosexual practices as morally commendable. It is,
> however, to recognize that the optimum moral life within a deplor-
> able situation is preferable to a life of sexual chaos.

Jones concurs:

> [T]he homosexual who cannot change must be accepted for what he is
> and encouraged to live responsibly within his own given sexuality; at
> the same time, we should surely see his position as being unenviable
> and his way of life as one not to be recommended as being desirable.[55]

Or, as Curran puts it, underscoring clearly the limits of this viewpoint's cautious pastoral acceptance of homosexual expression in
certain narrowly defined circumstances:

> There are many somewhat stable homosexual unions which afford
> their partners some human fulfillment and contentment. Obviously
> such unions are better than homosexual promiscuity.
>
> . . . The individual homosexual may morally come to the conclusion
> that a . . . permanent homosexual union is the best, and sometimes
> the only, way for him to achieve some humanity.

This being the case, "at times one may reluctantly accept homosexual unions as the only way in which some people can find a satisfying degree of humanity in their lives."[56]

[handwritten marginal notes]

effets of Fall

best given circumstances

* does this viewpt. responsibly
deal w/ question of FALL or
irresponsibly deal w/ fact of
Redemption ???

Question 10:

What is the personal call of Christ for the gay man or lesbian?

Of the representative authors under discussion, none addresses this particular question more exhaustively than Smedes. Although not all those identifying with this viewpoint would agree with every one of Smedes's contentions, the very scope of his treatment on this point merits first consideration.

According to Smedes, the preliminary step for every homosexual is relentless honesty:

> He should courageously face the abnormality of his condition. There can be no "okay, stay gay" attitude in his own assessment of his homosexuality. He must resist the temptation to say: "This is my nature, so it is normal for me."[57]

As a part of this honesty, the gay person should also acknowledge personal responsibility for what he or she does with homosexual feelings and drives. "I can't help myself" is never a legitimate basis for moral choice, no matter how overwhelming one's urges or emotions in a particular situation.

Secondly, the homosexual has an obligation to hope for change. He or she "has no right to be fatalistic." While acknowledging, as already noted, that statistics regarding change of orientation are "not promising," Smedes argues that the gay person must aspire to such a change nonetheless and take concrete practical steps to achieve it, through both psychotherapeutic and spiritual methods. In this effort, the homosexual should not only seek "conversion" to functional heterosexuality but, if that attempt proves futile, "consider whether it might be better to convert *from* homosexuality even if he cannot convert *to* heterosexuality."[58] Despite the fact that such hope might seem inordinately costly, both emotionally and financially, particularly in light of considerable evidence that real and lasting change in sexual orientation is unlikely at best, Smedes insists that "given the abnormality of the homosexual condition, a person whose tragic misfortune it is to suffer it is morally responsible to gear his choices in the direction of changing the condition that victimizes his life."

But what of the gay or lesbian who has hoped and prayed and sought both pastoral care and therapeutic treatment and has still been unsuccessful in achieving change in orientation (as Smedes admits is apt to be the case, particularly with mature people)? Smedes's response is that, in such situations, it should at least be considered whether the homosexual condition constitutes, in itself, a call to celibacy. While celibacy can prove "extremely diffi-cult" to achieve, achieved it can be, at least with help, at least in some people.[59] Given that a homosexual life is always ethically problematical and most likely personally unsatisfying as well, the option of celibacy "should be very seriously weighed."

However, Smedes goes on to write, it must be acknowledged that for some gays and lesbians, neither change, asexuality or celibacy are viable alternatives. In those cases, "we must follow the homosexual person to the edge of his options." What this means in practical terms is that the homosexual "in this tragic situation" must:

> . . . develop the best ethical conditions in which to live out his sexual life . . . Within his sexual experience, he ought to develop permanent associations with another person . . . in which respect and regard for the other as a person dominates their sexual relationship.

Clearly, for Smedes, this solution—what he terms "optimum homosexual morality"—is a concession made most unwillingly and only in the face of a lack of other options within a situation he does not hesitate to label "deplorable." Such accommodation should never be confused with even the most marginal approba-tion of homosexual acts in and of themselves.

Unlike Smedes, Curran does not detail all that might be involved in a serious effort to put into practice his rather perfunc-tory admonition that "attempts should be made to overcome [*the homosexual*] condition if possible." He turns instead to the truly constitutional gay or lesbian for whom change is clearly not a pos-sibility, proposing for such persons a cautious and qualified accep-tance of stable same-sex relationships. At the same time, however, like Smedes, he is quick to stress that "[h]omosexuality can never become an ideal." The necessary moral compromise in the case of the constitutional homosexual

> . . . never does away with the distinction between heterosexuality and homosexuality, even though not all heterosexual relationships [*themselves*] are moral and good . . . The basic meaning or "structure" of human sexuality remains, even though some individuals may not be able to live in accord with [*that structure*] because of the infecting power of sin.[60]

Jones, like Curran, does not dwell on the responsibilities of gays or lesbians prior to an individual recognition that their condition is immutable and that they have not been given the specific charism of celibacy. He does, however, note that his proposals are directed only to the situation of the "absolute invert," the "homosexual who cannot change." For such a person, Jones argues, mere sublimation "is not a practical answer," since—as D. J. West writes—forced abstinence based on guilt "often leads to neurotic disorder."[61]

That being the case, for the truly constitutional homosexual a genuinely loving gay or lesbian relationship is not only a valid moral option, it may well be the *only* option available since it is the sole context in which full "humanization" for the gay person can begin to become a "concrete and achievable reality . . . however short [*such a relationship*] may fall of perfect humanity."[62] This is true despite the fact that societal attitudes, a lack of legal and culturally sanctioned support structures and the "absence of a natural mutuality" will no doubt "make it difficult for a homosexual relationship to reach the heights of mutual satisfaction and fulfillment that are possible within a heterosexual marriage."

Like Smedes and Curran, however, Jones insists that acceptance of such a viewpoint is "by no means . . . an endorsement of homosexuality," nor an "idealization of the homosexual way of life." Rather, it is simply "a realistic, and thus responsible, solution to an otherwise insoluble problem."

As already noted, Thielicke's arguments take him to what Smedes has termed "the edge of [*the homosexual's*] options." Having arrived at this precipice, however, and after giving every evidence of readying himself to take the leap across it, the stalwart German evangelical at the very last moment pulls back, insisting that Christian pastoral care must focus primarily on assisting the homosexual in efforts at sublimation.[63] Nonetheless, until this final word, Thielicke's line of reasoning would appear to lead with persuasive inevitability to the same conclusion reached by Smedes, Curran, Jones and others of this viewpoint.

Thielicke begins his argument with both a negative and a positive moral imperative for the homosexual. On the negative side, since "homosexuality cannot simply be put on the same level with the normal created order of the sexes," the gay person "is called upon not to affirm his status *a priori* or to idealize it . . . but rather

[*to*] regard and recognize his condition as something that is questionable." In terms of positive action, he or she must "be willing to be treated or healed so far as this is possible . . . willing to be brought back into the [*created*] 'order,'" willing both to consult a psychotherapist or psychiatrist and to receive pastoral care. But what of those who make up what Thielicke admits is the "great majority" of homosexuals—those for whom such efforts will prove unavailing? Thielicke responds:

> Our attitude toward an ailment that is recognized as incurable changes . . . [W]e must accept it . . . [*but*] what . . . does "acceptance" mean here? It can mean to accept the burden of this predisposition to homosexuality . . . as a divine dispensation and see it as a task to be wrestled with, indeed—paradoxical as it may sound—to think of it as a talent that is to be invested.

Even though the homosexual condition is always "something questionable," then, it can also be "the vehicle of a blessing and a creative challenge." As to how the gay person is to approach engagement with this task, investment of this talent or the living out of such a challenging blessing, Thielicke writes:

> Perhaps the best way to formulate the ethical problem of the constitutional homosexual, who because of his vitality is not able to practice abstinence, is to ask whether within the co-ordinating system of his constitution he is willing to structure the man-man relationship in an ethically responsible way. [64]

Such an approach would clearly comport with the arguments of Smedes, Curran and Jones, as would Thielicke's further observation that:

> The homosexual has to realize his optimal ethical potentialities on the basis of his irreversible situation. Here one must seriously ask whether in this situation . . . the same norms must not apply as in the normal relationship between the sexes.

In other words, if the homosexual cannot change and has not been given the special charism of celibacy,[65] is it reasonable to suggest that his or her moral responsibility might be to live out an actively homosexual life within a committed, mutually self-giving, monogamous relationship?

Still appearing to squirm before the prospect of providing the answer which his entire line of discussion would seem to suggest, Thielicke instead restates the question: "It is the question of how the homosexual in his actual situation can achieve the optimal ethical potential of sexual self-realization."

Having said this, and while recognizing that the divinely intended heterosexual order itself is "fraught with hazards and temptations," Thielicke goes on to note that "the homosexual is exposed to even greater dangers," among them a lack of supporting institutions for monogamous homosexual coupling (i.e., marriage and social approbation), the gay subculture's embrace of promiscuity, the social ostracism and criminalization which drive the homosexual into the demimonde, and a need to hide the truth of one's orientation from others so as to function in daily life. Given all these negative factors, Thielicke finally recoils from the logical end of his argument—a qualified acceptance of committed gay and lesbian relationships. Instead, admitting his own share in the "despair" Christian theologians often feel over the homosexual's "minimal chances of being able to live ethically with homosexuality and achieve an acceptable partnership," he concludes that "we ourselves do not venture to credit these chances with anything more than being a possible exception."

Thielicke's ultimate reversal aside, the view of this position as to the call of Christ to the gay person could be summarized as follows. You must recognize that your condition is contrary to God's created intent. You must sincerely and tenaciously struggle to change your sexual orientation through both therapeutic and spiritual means. You must—if such change is not possible and celibacy and singleness prove untenable—reject promiscuity and seek a loving, monogamous relationship with a same-sex partner. Even if you achieve such a mature homosexual relationship, you must always acknowledge that however deep the caring, love and commitment you share with your partner, your union is by its very nature imperfect and incomplete, an accommodation to the fallen state of the world, and never to be granted any sort of moral parity with heterosexual marriage.

Question 11:

What is the pastoral call of Christ to the church on the issue?

The church must not only staunchly defend the authority of God's created order for sexuality, but also positively affirm the goodness and the moral beauty of that order. Unapologetic fidelity to the divine purpose is of particular importance in an age when the common wisdom trivializes sexuality and focuses ethical concern on individual "rights" to self-determination, moral autonomy and the pursuit of emotional and sensual gratification on one's own terms. Indeed, paradoxical as it may seem, such fidelity is the first vital form of pastoral care to the homosexual, in that it makes clear the moral significance of his or her particular struggle for wholeness and authenticity. Neither concern for popular opinion nor a well-intentioned desire to ease the admittedly difficult situation of persons wrestling with homosexual feelings can justify a compromise of the church's witness to God's normative design for sexuality.

Alongside this public, proclamational responsibility, however, the church also has an obligation to minister individually to gay and lesbian people in the immediacy and intimacy of their unique personal journeys. This means that, while upholding the unchanging intent of God for human sexuality, the church must be ready to walk with homosexuals through the progressive stages of self-discovery and openness to healing which Christian faithfulness requires, providing support at each step (and misstep) of this painful, exacting process.

But what if it finally becomes clear that, in a particular case, the homosexual condition is immutable and the special charism of celibacy has not been given? In such instances the church must—privately and discreetly—encourage the gay or lesbian to strive for the optimally ethical way of life possible by establishing a monogamous and loving same-sex partnership in which faithfulness, commitment, stability, mutual support and genuine self-giving transcend and, as far as is possible, transform the sexual components of the relationship.

While such a relationship may be—within the necessary moral compromise—licit and even the source of considerable psychological and spiritual good, it is never to be confused with the heterosexual ideal. Therefore, there can be no question of the church's publicly blessing a same-sex union, much less creating some form of "gay marriage." As Thielicke notes, even the most ethical and loving "homoerotic self-realization" can never be "an open and public thing," for the simple reason that "it falls outside the bounds of the order of creation."[66]

As for ministry in the church, the fitness of the gay man or lesbian who has chosen sublimation and lives as a celibate should be judged no differently than that of an unmarried, chaste heterosexual. The ordination of a homosexual committed to a same-sex union, however, poses a significant problem for at least two reasons. In the first place, the public nature of ordained ministry makes nearly impossible that discretion upon which the church's conditional sanction of a same-sex union is premised. Secondly, even in the most non-sacerdotal ecclesiologies, the ordained minister is seen not only as a servant of God's people but also as a role model for them—albeit always a more or less imperfect one. A homosexual union, however, no matter how loving and mature, can never be held up by the church as a model because, as Thielicke notes, it violates the fundamental order for human sexuality. Given these realities, most holding this view would oppose the ordination of homosexuals living in a same-sex relationship.[67]

Question 12:

What is the political call of Christ to society on the issue?

As was the case with the previous viewpoint, this perspective affirms that neither personal prejudice nor legal discrimination is ever justified against any minority, whether that minority be one of race, creed, conviction or sexual orientation. Christians are called to expunge such prejudice from their own hearts, to work actively to eliminate discrimination in their societies and to demonstrate by the inclusive welcome offered within the community of faith the universal reach of the love of God.

Consequently, those holding this viewpoint are sympathetic to legal initiatives aimed at eliminating discrimination based on sexual orientation. They also encourage Christian participation in organized opposition to hate crimes aimed at gay people or other forms of extra-legal intolerance. At the same time, their commitment to upholding what they understand to be the divinely mandated standard for human sexual expression requires that they draw the line at support for any legislation or social convention which would imply any moral correspondence between homosexual partnerships and heterosexual marriage.

Representative Denominations and Para-Church Groups

As is evidenced by the authors quoted above, this viewpoint has found champions within a wide spectrum of Christian conviction—from liberal Methodist, to mainstream evangelical, to Roman Catholic. Twenty-five years ago it would certainly have been seen as the cutting-edge, "progressive" opinion within the church. Time and an escalating gay Christian presence and confidence (some might say "assertiveness") have served to render it to all intents and purposes obsolete on the institutional level, however. Conservative denominations remain steadfast in their rejection of any even conditional sanction for homosexual acts, no matter what the context. Those churches seeking to be more open and responsive to gays, on the other hand, are likely to reject this viewpoint as offensive to the sensitivities of the very people they seek to reach, dismissing its arguments as homophobia-riddled double-talk.

Individual, as opposed to institutional, exceptions to this widespread rejection of the viewpoint do exist, to be sure, particularly among some of the more liberal Roman Catholic clergy who utilize the "internal forum" of the confessional or spiritual direction to counsel gays and lesbians along lines such as those proposed by Curran, while continuing to uphold—at least tacitly—the church's teaching on sexuality in public. Some evangelical therapists and pastors, again of a more liberal persuasion, follow Smedes in similar fashion. In both cases, however, such pastoral practice represents the conviction of an individual priest, counselor or minister, not the publicly affirmed approach of the denomination or communion itself.

Cross-Perspective Critique

To those holding one of the more conservative perspectives on the spectrum, the fundamental defect of this viewpoint is self-evident: it sanctions behavior which Scripture states unequivocally will result in eternal exclusion from the Kingdom of God. As a consequence, those who advance its arguments make themselves accomplices in the damnation of all those gay men and lesbians encouraged by their reasoning to act upon homosexual feelings.

Furthermore, critics on the right contend, the cornerstone of the viewpoint's thinking, the point upon which all else stands or falls, is an assumption that Christian faithfulness is simply "too hard" for homosexuals, so some sort of exception must be made for them. Yet real commitment to the call of Christ is *always* "hard," these critics insist—not just for homosexuals but for anyone who takes the gospel seriously. When has authentic Christianity ever suggested otherwise? Jesus made it inescapably clear that those who wish to be counted among his disciples must take up their crosses and follow him. (Matt 10:38; Mark 8:34; Luke 9:23; 14:27) Over the centuries this has meant loss of family, property, social position and respectability, even life itself. In the light of such sacrifices, it is argued, homosexuals' complaints at being asked to forsake certain forms of sensual and emotional gratification cannot help but take on a certain moral puniness. Only in an age when self-indulgence of every variety is both practically possible and socially validated, an age in which sexual fulfillment has been elevated to the status of a fundamental human "right," would an argument from the difficulty of obedience even be granted a hearing in Christian moral deliberation.

Also disputed from the conservative side is this viewpoint's contention that an immutable homosexual orientation does, in fact, exist. Whether asserting with Payne that "there is no such thing as a homosexual"[68] or with Moberly that change of orientation is "entirely possible,"[69] Christians advocating healing for homosexuals see this acceptance of the notion of "constitutional" homosexuality as nothing more than capitulation to the self-serving rationalizations of gays and lesbians unwilling to practice self-restraint or bear the personal cost of entering into the struggle for wholeness.

Many non-Catholic conservatives reject as well the idea of celibacy as a special calling—which is the premise underlying claims that sexual abstinence cannot be expected of most homosexuals. The notion of a "gift" of celibacy, it is argued, is an invention of the patristic and medieval church aimed at justifying its demands for such celibacy from its clergy. The fact is, however, that all people who for whatever reason are not married are called to sexual abstinence. Such a situation may be temporary or it may last a lifetime, but in either case, chastity—while sometimes difficult—does not require any special charism beyond the grace of God available to all Christians in their efforts to be faithful to God's will.

Critics from the right also take issue with the analogies this viewpoint would draw between the moral compromise proposed for homosexuals and the church's previous accommodations on matters such as remarriage after divorce and Christian participation in war. In the first place, it is pointed out, not all believers acknowledge the legitimacy of a second marriage while the first spouse still lives, just as some still hold to the primitive church's pacifism. For these Christians, one mistaken compromise of gospel principles can hardly be used to legitimize yet another such compromise.

Even those defending remarriage after divorce, however, insist that—despite whatever "compromise" this ethical judgment may involve—the heterosexual partners in a second marriage still remain fully within the structural parameters of God's male/female order for sexuality. The compromise proposed on the issue of homosexual relationships, on the other hand, would move entirely outside the created order; in fact, it would establish a new model for sexual expression directly contrary to that order.

As for the church's endorsement of Christian participation in war, it is noted that there is extensive scriptural support for the non-pacifistic position, not only in the many Old Testament passages in which God is portrayed as specifically directing the chosen people to wage war—in fact, as being the "God of Battles" who fights with and through them—but also in the New Testament's positive use of military imagery[70] and its approving portrayals of various members of the occupying Roman army.[71] No such support for a homosexual "alternative" appears in the biblical witness, critics contend—not one single verse. While the relative paucity of biblical texts specifically condemning homosexual acts may be striking to some on the liberal side of the debate, the complete lack of any even indirectly positive statements on the subject is far more significant to conservatives.

Proponents of this present viewpoint are also charged with what might charitably be termed a willful naiveté in their assumptions regarding the ethical options open to Christian homosexuals within the larger gay community. Precisely how, it is asked, is the gay or lesbian Christian to go about finding his or her monogamous partner within a subculture in which casual sex is a given? Is the church supposed to provide some sort of discreet, underground dating service for gay Christians who intend to remain chaste until a formal commitment has been made?

Not only naiveté but outright hypocrisy is alleged in the fact that well-meaning heterosexual supporters of this viewpoint, for all their talk of lifelong monogamous partnerships, tend to turn a blind eye to the realities of gay experience: relatively short-term, serial relationships among many gay Christians (even those who publicly pledge their commitment in some sort of union ceremony); the acceptance by many long-term gay male couples of an "arrangement" in which sexual activity outside the relationship is permitted under at least certain circumstances; and, in general, a tendency among gay Christians toward too easy a slide into the permissive mores and attitudes of the gay and lesbian subculture.

Finally, many from the conservative side of the spectrum question the whole stance from which this viewpoint approaches the issue to begin with. What Christians should be concerned with, they insist, is ever greater and deeper faithfulness to their high calling in Christ. They should not be expending their energies attempting to find (or create) "loopholes" in the scriptural witness to that calling.

For those to the left of it, this perspective's qualified acceptance of certain homosexual relationships is an improvement over the absolute rejection afforded such relationships by all the previous viewpoints, but it is not enough. As Curran himself admits, "one can object that such a view still relegates the homosexual to second class citizenship."[72] And in fact, liberal critics argue, that is precisely what it does.

Indeed, many would contend, what is most notable about this viewpoint is the fact that—despite its apparently genuine compassion and concern for gays and lesbians—its proponents seem unable to escape the grip of their own deep-seated homophobia. Thielicke may insist that "there is not the slightest excuse for maligning the constitutional homosexual."[73] Smedes may admit that heterosexual Christians should exercise humility when presuming to make pronouncements about homosexuals "because we are very ignorant."[74] Nonetheless, what those on the left perceive to be at work at the heart of this viewpoint is a thinly veiled contempt for the desires and affections of gay people, a condescending certainty that their love, commitment and caring are always by definition somehow "less" than those of their heterosexual counterparts simply by virtue of being homosexual.

This patronizing "heterosexism"[75] is evidenced by the fact that proponents of this viewpoint feel the need to give repeated assurances that a limited acceptance of certain homosexual relationships is not to be confused with sanction or idealization of homosexual love or acts. Heterosexism is also clear, critics argue, in Thielicke's equation of homosexuality with psychopathy[76] and Kimball's insistence that the homosexual is a "sexually-handicapped person" whose love is "doomed, by its very nature, to never pass beyond a certain point."[77] Smedes's suggestion that homosexuals may have some sort of "built in obstacle to meaningful sexual relations" so that, for them, the integration of sexual development within the wholeness of personhood is "perhaps impossible"[78] is seen to arise from a similar bias.

How are gays and lesbians ever to achieve integration and psychological health, critics ask, when they must label their most intimate, loving relationships as inherently defective, inferior by definition to heterosexual pairings far less objectively healthy? What sort of pressure does it place upon even the strongest, most caring Christian homosexual union to insist that it must never be an "open and public thing,"[79] must always be treated as something unholy and broken? The requirement that gays and lesbians keep themselves and their relationships permanently in the closet in order to gain even limited toleration from Christians flies in the face of everything that gay people have gained over the past twenty-five years in self-esteem and pride, liberal critics contend, and the psychological cost in terms of the self-loathing that such a retreat would engender is simply unacceptable.

Particularly criticized is the notion that the church should encourage gay men and women to hope for "healing" (and expend tremendous time and money in attempting to attain it) when the evidence is clear that chances for such "healing" taking place are slim to nonexistent—which proponents of this viewpoint themselves admit to be the case. While Smedes's insistence that "no homosexual person can be absolutely sure of what is possible for him[, *h*]e has no right to be fatalistic,"[80] may sound appropriately pious at first hearing, critics charge that it is not only fallacious but spiritually harmful to encourage what even Smedes himself concedes is in nearly all cases a false hope. Gays and lesbians would be better served by spending their time, efforts and money working toward mature self-acceptance and a healthy partnership within the context of their immutable orientation than they would by struggling fruitlessly to achieve a change which even proponents of this viewpoint acknowledge is unlikely to occur.

The Viewpoint Responds

Critics from the right, those holding this viewpoint argue, are simply unwilling or unable to recognize the fact that there is an inevitable element of ambiguity in many of our moral choices as Christians. Throughout its history, the church has seen perfectionist sects split away from the body of the faithful, determined to reject the worldly compromises of the larger Christian community and live by biblical norms in all their purported simplicity and clarity. Many of these sects have eventually moved on to outright heresy and, more often than not, have disappeared. Those which have survived have always found themselves before long facing the same dilemma that has confronted the church since its infancy: how to live out scriptural principles in the midst of a fallen world which not only defines the context in which Christians must conduct their lives, but which is busily at work—both by its assumptions and its fundamental rebellion—in Christians' own redeemed but still unperfected hearts as well.

The practical solution to this tension, more often than not, has been that some relaxation, some compromise, of absolute fidelity to scriptural principle is made. The church took this step in terms of economic and political issues fairly early on, so that now only a few "radical Christian" groups and denominations even question the Christian's obligation to the state and its power to make war, or the right of believers to their comfortable share (and more) of this world's goods. Similarly, at the end of the Middle Ages, the church changed its longstanding, biblically-based prohibition on usury and now few Christians even consider the possibility that there might be some problematic moral dimension to one of the undergirding principles of the capitalist system, the lending of money at interest.

But even in those areas where the church has not officially endorsed the compromise of biblical principle, in actual daily living, Christians—whether they recognize it or not—often find it difficult to practice a consistent biblical ethic. Middle class Western believers often protect themselves from this disconcerting truth by narrowly limiting and, as it were, domesticating the scope of legitimate moral concern, in particular shielding themselves from the realities of their incidental participation in larger structures of evil.[8] But the hard reality remains: simply by virtue of our inescapable participation in the world as it is, we are all deeply involved in sin, both directly and indirectly.

Thus, the accommodationism proposed by this viewpoint must be recognized as, to a greater or lesser extent, the *modus vivendi* of all practical Christian ethics and all Christian living in the real world. Once that reality is admitted, there then follows at least the possibility of a cautious, nuanced reconsideration of the moral options available to the constitutional homosexual who is not graced with the gift of celibacy, since to deny the homosexual person the sort of pastoral concessions that Christians have accepted on a host of other moral issues over the centuries is manifestly unjust. Christian discipleship may indeed be a hard and challenging calling, but there is no scriptural evidence that it was ever intended to be made completely impossible (or psychologically ruinous) for certain people.

As for those on the left who object to this viewpoint's insistence on a continuing public affirmation by the church of the created male/female sexual order, with a consequent requirement of life-long "discretion" on the part of those homosexual Christian couples who share in its fellowship, proponents of this viewpoint insist that fidelity and commitment to God's revealed purpose for his creation permit no other stance. It is one thing to recognize that, in a fallen world, certain individuals through no fault of their own may be unable to conform to God's full intention for human sexuality, and thus to work pastorally so as to provide such men and women with optimal opportunities for fulfillment and humanization. It is quite another to suggest that the church turn its back on the consistent witness of the Scriptures and its own unbroken tradition and propose a new model in which heterosexuality is only one of several equally acceptable options for human sexual realization. If this be labeled "heterocentrism" by some, so be it. To the faithful Christian, it is something much simpler: a humble submission to reality.

- 5 -

AFFIRMATION

This viewpoint takes a significant step beyond even the qualified moral acceptance of monogamous same-sex partnerships offered by the previous viewpoint to those constitutional homosexuals unable to change and lacking the gift of celibacy. It does not merely tolerate gay and lesbian relationships, it *affirms* them as positively good. Committed homosexual relationships are seen as holding all the same potential for a self-transcending exchange of love as heterosexual relationships. They too can be a means of growth into fuller humanity through mutual self-giving. In fact, for those who are by "nature" homosexual, same-sex love is the ontological equivalent of opposite-sex love for heterosexuals.

Homosexual acts, therefore, are not to be evaluated in isolation, or viewed simply as categories of behavior to be approved or condemned. Rather, they must be considered contextually, in terms of the *quality* of relationship they express. They must be judged, in other words, by precisely the same criteria that are applied to their heterosexual counterparts: whether (or to what extent) they are "genuinely consensual and nonexploitative. . . characterized by mutual commitment, faithfulness and intended permanence."[1]

In response to charges by conservative critics that such a viewpoint represents a complete abandonment of scriptural authority and, with it, the historic Christian understanding of sin, proponents insist that they do not reject the legitimate role of the scriptural witness in Christian moral deliberation, nor are they "soft on sin." Rather, they simply perceive the Scriptures' true authority differently than do conservatives and, as a result, come to a different understanding as to what constitutes faithfulness to God's call to us.

Question 1:

What is the ultimate authority upon which any moral judgment regarding homosexuals and/or homosexual acts is to be based?

Christian moral inquiry must begin by giving serious attention to the Scriptures, to be sure, since they are a record both of God's gracious self-revelation through human history and of humankind's struggle to understand and respond to that revelation.

Recognizing the significance of the Scriptures to Christian moral reflection does not mean, however, that one can simply assert—as do some fundamentalists—that "the Bible says what it means and means what it says" and then proceed to approach any given text with the sort of prosaic literalism one might bring to the owner's manual of an automobile. Rather, as Anglican theologian Norman Pittenger writes, we must take the Scriptures, as we take all the rich Christian heritage, "with utmost seriousness," yet not necessarily always literally.[2] This is because, as even conservative Gordon-Conwell Seminary biblical scholar Moises Silva acknowledges:

> The Bible is divine, yet it has come to us in human form. The commands of God are absolute, yet the historic context of the writings appears to relativize certain elements. The divine message must be clear, yet many passages seem ambiguous.[3]

To admit to this paradoxical quality of the biblical writings is not, as conservatives so often charge, to "deny the inspiration of scripture." Peter J. Gomes, the African-American Preacher to Harvard University, clearly understands himself to take the Bible "with utmost seriousness" when he writes that it is:

> ... dynamic, living, alive, lively ... This means that behind the letter of the text is the spirit that animates it, the force that gave it and gives it life ... The fixed text has a life of its own ...[4]

Nonetheless, as Gomes recognizes, the Bible is "a result or consequence of a complex process that is both human and divine." It is a library of encounter with God, its constituent volumes composed, edited and selected over more than a millennium, written in languages not our own, from within cultures and circumstances drastically different from ours, in a variety of genres and for a variety of purposes. This means that the Living Word which addresses us in Scripture can never be adequately served by proof texting; interpretation of any biblical text is always necessary. In fact, as Gomes notes, interpretation "is impossible to avoid," because "to read is to interpret." That being the case, it follows that human reason and experience must be brought into dialogue with the literal words of any scriptural text if we are to avoid unwittingly distorting the true scriptural message by our own subjective biases and ignorance.[6] Contrary to what conservatives sometimes charge, such a reasoned dialogue does not mean we are presumptuously setting ourselves "above" Scripture—passing judgment in our human frailty and sinfulness upon that Word of God which should now and ultimately will judge us. It means, rather, that we are willing to recognize (and give ourselves over to) the sometimes elusive, always *interactive* process by which God reveals God's self and will to us.

And what is the nature of that process? How does God, according to this view, work in and communicate with God's world? The answer goes to the very heart of Christian faith. God engages the world *incarnationally*—that is to say, by revelation within and through the particularity of specific human history. This fact is most profoundly evidenced in the person of Jesus himself: God does not come to us in the form of some sort of some abstracted "ideal" of a human being existing outside time, place and culture. The eternal Word becomes flesh in a particular man, Yeshua ben Yusef (as he would have been known to his contemporaries), with a particular face, a particular personality, a particular personal history and a particular "worldview" created by and mediated through his family, his community and his society.

If this is true of God's ultimate revelation, the Son of Man, it is even more true—so the argument goes—of God's revelation through those who spoke, wrote, edited and selected those particular words which now make up the Scriptures. What this means, in practical terms, is that God graciously accommodates the divine Word to the grid through which it must pass to reach us: our human capacities, assumptions and understandings. As a consequence, those holding this viewpoint contend, the either/or often posed by conservative Christians—either the Scriptures are the Word of God and therefore absolutely, literally true in every detail, or they are not literally true in every respect and therefore cannot be the Word of the God who is Truth—grossly misapprehends the nature of the biblical witness.

In order to read Scripture aright, those of this viewpoint argue, we must recognize, first of all, that the biblical authors and editors were not working in a vacuum. They brought to their encounter with the living Word of God the culture, worldview, values and moral consciousness of their time and place, of the community to which revelation was first addressed and by which it was passed on in oral or written form. Secondly, the content of revelation is not a static thing, it is *progressive*. Finally, the divine gift of revelation is not a matter of the *words* of any biblical text read in stark isolation, powerful as those words can often be. Revelation is not merely propositional. Rather, in its most profound sense, revelation is an experience, a life-changing encounter with the Living God, as God's Word is mediated by the Spirit *through* the scriptural text[8] and through our interaction with that text within the community of faith, both past and present.

Given, then, what the Bible is and how it came to be, if we are to use Scripture as God intends it to be used, we must consider any particular biblical text in light of four fundamental questions:

+ What do the words of that text really say (a question of translation)?

+ What is the intended message of that text in context (a question of exegesis)?

+ What effect do the limits of authorial intention and understanding have on our contemporary application of the text?

+ What is the relationship of the particular text to the larger message of the Bible?

Issues of Translation

Scriptural translation, in particular the interpretation of idiomatic words and phrases, is not always the exact science many devout Christians might assume (or wish) it to be.

Several Old Testament verses once assumed by most Christians to speak to the issue of homosexuality, for example, are now recognized by virtually all biblical scholars as having nothing to do with homosexuality as that word is understood today. These are the various Old Testament allusions to the *qadesh* (plural, *qadeshim*), which the Authorized Version[9] translates as "sodomite."[10] In fact, the term *qadesh* is entirely unrelated to Sodom or any particular theory as to that city's sin. The *qadeshim* (literally, "holy ones") were male cult prostitutes whose dormitory-brothels were attached to the temples of certain Canaanite deities and who were at least tangentially connected with periodic corruptions of Israel's worship as well.[11]

The matter of accurate translation also figures significantly (and far more contentiously) in discussion of two of the New Testament texts still widely understood to condemn all homosexual acts between men: 1 Cor 6:9–10, which catalogues those who will not inherit the Kingdom of God, and 1 Tim 1:10, a list of the reprobate for whom the Law "is made." At issue in these verses are two Greek words: μαλακοί (*malakoi*), which literally means "the soft" and appears only in the Corinthian passage, and ἀρσενοκοῖται (*arsenokóitai*), a compound idiom of disputed derivation and meaning which literally translates into English as the awkward "man-beds" (ἀρσεν—man; κοίτη—bed) and is used in both texts:

> Do you not know that wrongdoers will not inherit the kingdom of God? Do not be deceived! Fornicators, idolaters, adulterers, μαλακοί, ἀρσενοκοῖται . . . none of these will inherit the kingdom of God.
> 1 Cor 6:9–10

> . . . the law is laid down not for the innocent, but for the lawless and disobedient, for the godless and sinful, for . . . fornicators, ἀρσενοκοῖταις . . .
> 1 Tim 1:9–10

Before beginning a discussion of these words, it should be noted that gay Christians, along with many others sympathetic to their viewpoint, take considerable exception to the fact that, in what appears to be little more than an excess of delicacy, the 1946 Revised Standard Version New Testament lumps together what in the Greek text of 1 Corinthians are two clearly discrete terms (μαλακοί and ἀρσενοκῖται) under the single English word "homo-sexuals."[12] In the first place, it is argued, this conflation ignores whatever distinction the apostle intended to indicate by his use of two separate words in his list of vices. Secondly, and more impor-tantly, it distorts the clear intention of the passage, which is to condemn those who *do* certain things, by employing an English word which refers not only to those who do certain things but those who *are* a certain thing. Taken at face value, the RSV transla-tion (or, more properly, paraphrase) of Paul's statement would exclude from the Kingdom of God not only those who "commit" certain presumably homosexual acts but everyone whose erotic and affectional attractions are to their own sex—even those who have remained heroically chaste for their entire lives.[13]

The rendering of the Authorized Version resolves this particu-lar problem, since it translates each word individually, rendering μαλακοί as "the effeminate" and ἀρσενοκῖται as "abusers of themselves with mankind."[14] But were the Authorized Version's seventeenth-century translators accurate in their understanding of what Paul intended to condemn? To begin with their choice of "the effeminate" (which in the usage of the time denoted overly sensual, enervated, voluptuous males—see note 14) for μαλακοί, this translation is supported by the fact that, among Greek patris-tic writers, variants on μαλακός were used to refer to nonspecific dissolute behavior, immorality in general or, upon rare occasions, to masturbation, but, as John McNeill notes, "never to homosexu-ality as such."[15] Roman Catholic exegetes for a number of centu-ries were more specific in their interpretation of the term, but they did not see in μαλακοί any reference to same-sex erotic activity; rather, they took it as a proof text for the proposition that men who masturbate are barred from the Kingdom of God.[16]

Given the linguistic evidence, McNeill concludes that "there is no justification for applying *malakós* specifically to homosexual-ity."[17] Yet Derrick Sherwin Bailey, himself so often cited by those urging a more liberal interpretation of biblical strictures against homosexual behavior, states with an assurance fully equal to

McNeill's that μαλακοί "denote[s] . . . those males who engage passively . . . in homosexual acts . . ."[18] Robin Scroggs, however, focusing his inquiry on the social structures of classical pederasty, proposes yet another meaning for the term, arguing that the μαλακοί were "effeminate call boys" who—after the age at which one usually ceased being a "beloved" in conventional pederastic practice—maintained a girlish appearance through affect, dress, facial and body hair removal, and, upon occasion, even castration.[19] Scroggs's point is that (as with the *qadeshim* of the Old Testament) such a meaning would clearly limit the application of this particular biblical condemnation to male prostitution, not to all homosexual behavior irrespective of context.

When it comes to ἀρσενοκοῖται (or the variant plural ἀρσενοκοῖταις used in 1 Timothy),[20] translation becomes even more treacherous, in part because Paul's vigorous idiom does not appear in any prior Greek literature available to us—presumably he either coined it himself (John Boswell's contention)[21] or borrowed it from a vernacular usage for which we have no extant documentation. In "Lexicography and Saint Paul," a twenty-page appendix to his *Christianity, Social Tolerance and Homosexuality*, Boswell cites a wide-ranging variety of evidence to support his conclusion as to the meaning of this term.

When used as a prefix in compound koine Greek words, Boswell contends, the form ἀρσενο- (as used in ἀρσενοκοῖται) is generally employed to indicate an adjectival relationship to the second part of the compound (which would point to the reading "men who bed"), whereas a variant form, ἀρρενο-, is most often used when "male" is the object of the second half of the word ("those [men] who bed men").

In what Boswell terms the "vast amount of writing extant on the subject of homoerotic activity in Greek," not one author reasonably contemporaneous with Paul uses the term ἀρσενοκοῖται in a way which clearly indicates any connection with specifically homosexual activity (indeed, no extant document predating Paul's letters uses the word at all).

According to Boswell, none of the many patristic writers who were unequivocal in their condemnation of homosexual activity uses the term ἀρσενοκοῖται in his discussion of homosexual acts. Further, various Latin fathers cataloging scriptural proof texts that condemn homosexual activity consistently fail to cite the references to ἀρσενοκοῖται in 1 Corinthians and 1 Timothy, leading one to conclude that they understood this term to refer to something other than homosexual activity per se.

In the Vulgate (late fourth century), St. Jerome follows earlier Latin translations by rendering ἀρσενοκοῖται as *masculorum concubitores* ("male concubines"), which Boswell describes as a "vague phrase suggestive of multiple interpretations," but leaning most specifically toward that of active ("inserter") male whores.

Given these and numerous other lexicographical factors which he cites in extensive detail, Boswell comes to the conclusion that the most reasonable understanding of ἀρσενοκοῖται is men whose distinguishing feature is the fact that they "bed"—i.e., male prostitutes. McNeill concurs with Boswell's judgment,[22] pointing out as well that had Paul intended to indicate general homosexual activity as such, he had a number of other, more specific Greek words at his disposal, and "it is probable that he would have selected one of these terms" instead of ἀρσενοκοῖται.

An alternative etymology is proposed by Robin Scroggs, however. Scroggs's treatment of ἀρσενοκοῖται in *The New Testament and Homosexuality*[23] looks not to the antecedent pagan Greek literature considered by Boswell but rather to intertestamental Judaism, the Hellenized Jewish culture of the Diaspora and the Septuagint. As he notes, using his own translation for the Levitical phrases:

> . . . there was no Hebrew . . . word for homosexuality. When the [*Old Testament*] raises the issue . . . it points to it by the awkward phrase "With a male you shall not lie the lyings of a woman" (Lev 18:22), or, "A man who lies with a male the lyings of a woman" (Lev 18:22). Rabbinic scholars picked up part of that phrase "lies with a male," made it virtually into a noun, and gave it nearly the status of a technical term. The term that thus emerged and that is used frequently in [*the rabbinic*] literature is *mishkav zakur* (lying of a male) . . .

The Pauline ἀρσενοκοῖται, Scroggs goes on to argue, "is an almost exact Greek parallel to the Hebrew" technical term. Moreover, the Septuagint translation of Lev 18:22 closely juxtaposes the two parts of the Greek compound used by Paul ("with ἄρσενος you shall not lie the κοίτην of a woman"), as does Lev 20:13 even more notably (. . . "whoever lies with ἄρσενος [*the*] κοίτην of a woman"), which could have influenced either Paul or the

Hellenized rabbis of the Diaspora before him to choose ἀρσενοκοῖται as a near-literal rendering of the rabbinic term *mishkav zakur* into "understandable Greek."[24]

Since, according to Scroggs, the *mishkav zakur* in rabbinic discussion is always the active, not the passive, partner in homosexual intercourse; and since, furthermore, in Greek thinking regarding pederastic relationships the active partner was presumed to be the "older" sponsoring male; and since, finally, in this usage ἀρσενοκοῖται appears to be paired with the preceding word, μαλακοί (which Scroggs has understood as "effeminate call boys" who always took the passive role), Scroggs concludes that what Paul is specifically denouncing in 1 Corinthians (and, by partial extension, in 1 Timothy) are these girlish male prostitutes and their customers. Therefore, as opposed to being a condemnation even of classical pederasty in general, much less all modern day forms of homosexual partnership per se, only a "very specific dimension of pederasty is being denounced with these two terms," a dimension, Scroggs goes on to note, that even the pagan defenders of pederasty universally censured.

Yet Bailey[25] argues differently, pronouncing without elaboration that just as μαλακοί are the "passive" partners in homosexual intercourse, ἀρσενοκοῖται are the "active" partners (an interpretation reflected in the 1913 Moffat translation's "catamites and sodomites").[26] Boswell denounces Bailey's contention forcefully, however, insisting that "[t]he argument that in 1 Cor 6:9 the two words "μαλακοί" and "ἀρσενοκοῖται" represent the active and passive parties in homosexual intercourse is fanciful and unsubstantiated by lexicographical evidence . . ."[27]

Whatever interpretation of these two troublesome Pauline terms is favored, most holding this viewpoint would agree with McNeill's final verdict:

> The variation in translations points to the fact that there is very little understanding of the precise meaning of Paul's terms . . . Translations appear at times to be based on preconceptions rather than serious scholarship.[28]

That being the case, it is argued, any attempt to assert a scriptural basis for condemnations of contemporary committed homosexual relationships on the basis of either 1 Corinthians or 1 Timothy is simply untenable.

Issues of Context

For those of this viewpoint, the preeminent example of misinterpretation (and therefore misapplication) of a scriptural citation due to a failure to understand its context is the notorious story of Sodom in Genesis 18 and 19.[29] Branded on the Western mind as the epitome of male same-sex degeneracy, the name of this ancient "city of the plain" became in most European languages the commonly accepted designation both for homosexual acts (in English, "sodomy") and those who commit them ("sodomite"). The story also fed a number of popular notions regarding homosexuals: their sin is sufficiently outrageous to provoke a particular "outcry" to God, they are by nature predatory (crowding around a peaceable man's house to sexually assault two strangers in the middle of the night), and their very presence in a community constitutes an evil of such enormity as to call down divine retribution of the most spectacular sort.

Some conservative Christians still defend this inflammatory reading of the Sodom account, to be sure,[30] concurring with evangelical author Thomas Schmidt's quip in a college student newspaper that Sodom was "the first gay community."[31] The mainstream scholarly consensus, however, has shifted dramatically over the past forty years in its understanding of the nature of the sin at issue in this story.

Derrick Sherwin Bailey was not the first scholar to propose rethinking what is actually being condemned in the Sodom narrative, but his *Homosexuality and the Western Christian Tradition*[32] was the initial work of its kind to gain attention beyond certain narrow academic circles. Not surprisingly, Bailey's book has been cited by virtually every revisionist exegete since it first appeared in 1955. Although a part of Bailey's argument involves a detailed word-study of a particular, pivotal Hebrew verb used in the Genesis text,[33] the conclusions he draws from that word-study are dependent upon the *cultural context* of the tale, a context which—he contends—traditional readings have entirely ignored.

That context is: Lot himself is, as the text makes clear, a resident alien in Sodom (a *gēr*). As such, in the violent, tribal society of his time and place, he is to some extent a suspect personage by definition—not one of "us." Add to that reality the fact of his bringing two strangers into his house at night (behind the security of the city's walls and locked gate) and a situation is created in which Lot's neighbors might well feel there was legitimate reason for concern (the two visitors could be spies, the advance party of one of the many hostile nomadic groups that perpetually swept the Fertile Crescent, pillaging and enslaving the more settled communities in their path. In such a situation, the demand that the strangers be brought out, interrogated (no doubt roughly), even, perhaps, publicly debased,[34] could be seen as to some extent reasonable from the Sodomites' perspective and would entail no real "homosexual" motivation on their part)

If one takes into account this contextual understanding, a significant shift is seen to occur in the moral focus of the story; that focus is no longer sexual at all (or, at most, only incidentally so). Rather, it is now clearly social. The evil being denounced is not homosexuality but rather the vicious treatment the Sodomites sought to inflict upon two strangers in their midst. By the same token, Lot's "righteousness" resides not in his averting sexual misconduct but in his willingness to put himself and his family at risk in order to honor the solemn obligations of hospitality as his society understood them.

While such an interpretation of the Sodomites' sin may seem more than a little far-fetched to those accustomed to reading this account through the grid of traditional assumptions, Bailey and many other exegetes following him have pointed out that such a reassessment of the story's meaning is solidly supported by subsequent scriptural references. Indeed, the biblical witness after Genesis consistently fails to characterize Sodom's sin as homosexual. Rather, Sodom is held up as a symbol of apostate worship (Deut 29:18–25), false prophecy (Jer 23:14), pride (Jer 49:16–18; 50:31–40) and, in particular, economic injustice (Isa 1:9–17; Amos 4:1–11). Ezek 16:49–50, it is often noted, forthrightly summarizes the Old Testament understanding of Sodom and its notorious evil:

> This was the guilt of . . . Sodom . . . pride, excess of food, and prosperous ease, but [the Sodomites] did not aid the poor and needy. They were haughty and did abominable things before me . . ."[35]

Similarly, it is pointed out, as recorded in Matt 10:15 and its parallel in Luke 10:12, Jesus linked Sodom's destruction to the fate of those towns which would fail to offer hospitality to his disciples, not to that of the sexually reprobate.

Finally, many commentators after Bailey have noted that even if the intention of the men of Sodom *was* to sexually violate the angelic visitors (from whatever motive), a story of an attempted gang rape can hardly be used to condemn all homosexual activity per se, nor can it adequately exemplify the character or desires of all homosexual people today. Therefore, they argue, despite its venerable association with male homosexual acts, the Sodom story in fact has nothing whatsoever to say about the moral legitimacy of loving, consensual relationships between people who are by orientation gay or lesbian.

Context is equally important to our understanding of the two Levitical references to homosexuality (Lev 18:22 and 20:13), it is held. Indeed, context is *everything* in our reading of these texts which, if taken at face value and out of their context, would assert unequivocally that homosexual acts between men are not only prohibited by the law of God, but that they are to be punished by death (that they are, in other words, as Bahnsen argues,[36] not just a sin but a crime).

The first thing to be considered in terms of context is the nature of the "Holiness Code" (Leviticus 17–26) in which these two edicts appear. This code is a complex compendium of public and private regulations related to the distinctiveness of God's chosen people as opposed to the religious and cultural life of those Canaanite peoples whom they are to supplant[37] in Palestine (". . . you shall not do as they do in the land of Canaan, to which I am bringing you. You shall not follow their statutes. My ordinances you shall observe and my statutes you shall keep . . ." [Lev 18:3, 4]).[38]

As well as recognizing the nature and purpose of the Holiness Code, an adequate consideration of context must also take into account the ancient Hebrew understanding of and attitudes toward human sexuality, in particular its reproductive function. As McNeill writes:

> One must keep in mind the pro-fertility bent of the Old Testament authors due to underpopulation . . . [*and*] the strong Hebrew stress on preserving the family name through progeny.[39]

Given these two contextual realities, those of this viewpoint contend, the vital question which must be asked in addressing the two Levitical proscriptions of male homosexual acts is not *what* they prohibit but *why* they prohibit it. The answer to this question is that, first and foremost, in the ancient Hebrew mind, male homosexual acts were associated with those very idolatrous Canaanite religious practices from which the Code is designed to protect God's chosen people. Therefore, such acts are prohibited not because they are necessarily intrinsically wrong in and of themselves (a moral evil) but because they represent a compromise— through their association with Canaanite religion—of the Hebrew's call to monotheistic worship (a cultic violation).[40] Secondarily, since the ancients believed that new life is transmitted whole in male semen, with the female serving as little more than an incubator or the "soil" for the male "seed," the "waste" of semen in non-generative acts was seen as tantamount to murder. Since homosexuality as we know it today has nothing whatever to do with Canaanite or any other idolatrous religious practice, since Christians have always considered themselves freed from the requirements of Old Testament cultic law (circumcision, dietary restrictions, and so on) and, finally, since our understanding of both the biology and the larger meanings of human sexuality is no longer that of the ancient Fertile Crescent, these prohibitions—it is argued—are no longer applicable.

In contrast to arguments by some conservatives that the description of homosexual acts as an "abomination" indicates that they are in fact a grave *moral* evil as opposed to a mere violation of cultic purity or religious distinctiveness, those holding this present viewpoint counter that, far from signifying that something is, by its very nature, a uniquely pernicious form of evil, "abomination"—*to'ebah* in the Hebrew—is a quasi-technical term specifically denoting acts or things *associated with idolatry*.[41] The use of "abomination" in the Levitical ban on homosexual acts therefore makes it inescapably clear, defenders of this viewpoint argue, that such acts are being condemned as a species of cultic defilement related to idolatrous practice, not as inherently immoral in their own right irrespective of context.

L. William Countryman, Professor of New Testament at the (Episcopal) Church Divinity School of the Pacific (Berkeley,

California), takes a somewhat different approach to the Levitical prohibitions. For Countryman, all the significant biblical materials dealing with sexuality are expressive of either a purity ethic (purity being understood as a matter of social and cultic distinction between Jew and non-Jew) or a property ethic.[42] Proscriptions of adultery, for example, would fall under the latter, since another man's wife is seen as his "sexual property." The two Levitical laws banning homosexual acts, on the other hand, exemplify the former; they are part of the Hebrew "purity system." Countryman does not argue this assertion simply on the basis of the connection between homosexual acts and pagan cults.[43] Instead, he bases it in the ancient Israelites' understanding of holiness being not so much moral or ethical perfection per se but rather wholeness or completeness (hence, for example, the exclusion of any man with a "blemish" from the priesthood [Lev 21:18–20]). This "attention to wholeness," Countryman writes, "demands two things: first, that every individual should be a complete and self-contained specimen of its kind . . . and, second, that there should be no mixing of kinds." Similarly, Countryman continues, "no one person must seek to combine mutually exclusive perfections. This is the reason for the condemnation of homosexual acts, as the phrasing of the rules makes clear; the offense is described, literally, as a man lying with a male 'the lyings of a woman' . . . The male who fulfills the 'female' role is a combination of kinds and therefore unclean, like a cloth composed of both linen and wool; and the act that renders him unclean is the joint responsibility of both partners."

Having determined, then, that prohibition of male homosexual acts is a purity "issue," Countryman goes on to point out that the first Christians, being essentially Jewish in their theological perspective on the Hebrew scriptures, would have shared the ancient Israelite understanding of the purity system as "more or less of a single piece." Therefore, when the early church, not without controversy and struggle, determined that the purity system would not be applied to Gentile converts, it abandoned that system *in its entirety.*[44]

This does not mean that certain standards of sexual morality did not continue to be operative in the Christian community. Those standards which remained in effect, however (e.g., the condemnation of adultery), were grounded in the *property ethic* as interpreted through gospel principles of justice and concern for community solidarity, not in the now-abandoned purity ethic. Consequently, Countryman determines, the Levitical proscriptions of sexual acts between males are inapplicable to Christians who are no longer bound by any aspect of Jewish purity regulations.

Issues of Authorial Limitation

In reading the Scriptures, it is argued, there are two distinct authorial "limits" that must be considered if one is to interpret and apply any given text with integrity. The first is a limit set by the author more or less consciously; it is what he (and subsequent editors) *intended* to communicate through that particular text.[45] The second is a limit imposed upon the biblical authors and editors by the fact that they were of necessity men of their particular time and culture; it has to do with the question of whether (and, if so, to what degree) that fact affected their understanding of the truth revealed to them or the conclusions they drew from it.

The first of these limits is the less controversial. Put simply, it means that we cannot generally take a biblical text to mean more than its own author understood it to mean, nor can we apply it to circumstances which are not within the scope of that author's original purpose. The principle is, as it were, one of textual self-regulation—which is why it is acceptable to at least some Christians of a more conservative leaning, since the full authority of the text is preserved once its legitimate parameters have been determined.[46]

Such an approach has figured largely in much of the revisionist exegesis of Rom 1:18–28, which—from the perspective of the Christian homosexual—is the most vexing of what Ralph Blair has dubbed the "clobber passages."[47] While for most conservatives this text is the ultimate and irrefutable authority for their negative judgment upon both male and female[48] homosexuality, exegetical revisionists have raised a number of issues relating to precisely what Paul intended to say in it.

It is often argued, for example, that Paul's explicit linking of homosexuality to idolatry means he cannot be addressing the situation of present-day homosexuals, in particular Christian homosexuals, who are *not* idolaters. Furthermore, Paul's emphasis on the lustful nature of the passions he describes, while clearly speaking to promiscuous, abusive and dehumanizing homosexual expression in both his age and our own,[49] is held to be entirely inapplicable to loving, committed, consensual relationships between gays or lesbians, the nature of whose partnerships clearly has nothing in common with in the forms of sexual expression being condemned.

As for Paul's argument from what is "natural" (φυσικὴν [phusikēn], from φύσις [phúsis], "nature"), which conservatives interpret to mean "that which is in accord with the order of creation," i.e., heterosexuality, liberal exegetes contend that this term does not necessarily signify what it has traditionally been assumed to mean. Paul also uses φύσις in 1 Cor 11:14, it is pointed out, to argue that it is contrary to nature for men to have long hair.[50] Thus, some suggest, Paul's polemical use of "nature" in Romans 1 (as in 2 Corinthians 11) may not necessarily speak to any overriding order of creation, but rather to something considerably more relative and malleable—cultural gender role expectations.[51]

Others contend—on the principle that limits of intention are sometimes due to lack of information—that Paul's argument from nature in this passage reflects his lack of awareness that some people's "natures," that is to say, their internal, spontaneous affectional and sexual responses, are same-sex directed. Since the apostle assumed, along with the rest of his Jewish subculture, that everybody is "by nature" heterosexual,[52] and that homosexual acts and desires therefore always represent a deliberate choice to act "against" the integrity of one's internal selfhood (for purposes of experiment, religious practice or unbridled sensuality), what Paul is really condemning here is deliberate, conscious perversity. As a result, Romans 1 has nothing at all to say about men and women whose "natures" are truly homosexual.[53] Indeed, it has been suggested that—since what is at issue here is a deliberate violation of the structures of one's personality and innate sexual orientation—this passage could even support an argument that it would be wrong for a true homosexual to attempt to function as, or change into, a heterosexual.

Nearly all exegesis reinterpreting this particular passage in terms which would allow for the moral legitimacy of loving, committed homosexual partnerships has invoked one or more of the above arguments.[54] While more conservative Christians might well remain unconvinced by such revisionism, many would not reject in principle the concept underlying it—that the biblical text cannot legitimately be pushed beyond the bounds of its author's intent.

Assertions as to the second aspect of authorial limitation, however—claims that cultural limits to the scriptural authors' understanding sometimes led them to draw erroneous conclusions—occasion considerably more opposition. The reason such thinking is a point of contention for conservatives is obvious: their understanding of scriptural inspiration precludes the possibility that the human limitations of a biblical author's knowledge could have any effect whatever upon the text itself. Since that text is "God-breathed," it must by definition be protected from all error.[55] Despite conservative objections on the point, however, many of those identifying with this viewpoint are willing to say without equivocation that the limitations of the scriptural writers' understanding upon occasion led them into error.

On the matter of homosexuality, it is argued, while honesty requires that we recognize that the man Paul, bound by his time and his Jewish culture, would no doubt have condemned all homosexual acts and all homosexual love, we cannot let his "ignorance be an excuse for our own."[56] Since Paul had no awareness of the existence of a homosexual orientation which is both unchosen and immutable, nor any models for responsible, loving, committed homosexual relationships, we must conclude that he was simply mistaken in his blanket condemnation of all homosexual acts (just as, for different reasons, he was mistaken in his tacit acceptance of slavery[57] and his exclusion of women from leadership in the church).[58]

If such a bald-faced assertion seems heretical to more conservative sensibilities, Bawer and others would remind their fellow Christians of Peter's rooftop vision relating to the conversion of the centurion Cornelius and his family (Acts 10). The "conservative" view among faithful Jews of the time, buttressed by strong biblical evidence and consistent tradition, was that Jews could have no intimate dealings with Gentiles. But God's purpose was greater even than Scripture or the traditions of the household of faith. In imagery that can only have seemed extraordinarily shocking to Peter (just as shocking as it would be to many conservative Christians today to consider, for example, affirming the moral legitimacy of a loving, committed, monogamous gay union), God showed Peter a sheet writhing with nonkosher animals and instructed him to "kill and eat." When Peter protested that he had never in his entire life eaten anything unclean (as, it is important to note, the Scriptures themselves had defined "unclean"), God's shattering answer was: "What God has made clean, you must not call profane. Every Gentile Christian today is welcomed into the fellowship of the church only because Peter's response was to reach beyond biblical literalism to a new and wider inclusivity. In so doing, he was implicitly judging the divinely mandated traditions of his people, expressed through their sacred Scriptures, as insufficient for the all-embracing purpose of God's love. We can do no less, it is argued, for God's beloved gay and lesbian people.

Issues Relating to Larger Biblical Themes

For those holding this present view, moral questions relating to homosexuality cannot properly be decided solely on the basis of the handful of isolated, often ambiguous scriptural statements conventionally thought to refer to homosexuality, nor can those texts be imposed with absolutist literalism upon the lives and moral choices of contemporary gay and lesbian people. Rather, these few, scattered texts must be evaluated in light of larger themes which are ultimately what the biblical communication is all about. This is true in part because, as Gomes notes:

> Given the appeal to the Bible in the case against homosexuality, one would assume that the Bible has much to say on the subject. It has not. The subject of homosexuality is not mentioned in the Ten Commandments,[59] nor in the Summary of the Law. No prophet discourses on the subject. Jesus himself makes no mention of it . . .[60]

More importantly, it is argued, turning from proof texting to consideration of the major biblical themes is also necessary because those themes, properly understood, undermine any attempt to pronounce an unequivocal and universal condemnation upon either the homosexual condition or homosexual acts in every context.

What are these themes? The answer varies somewhat from author to author.[61] The common thread running through them all is a conviction that the overriding truth of the biblical message is a

two-fold affirmation: God is love and God is just. As a consequence, human beings, made in the image of God, are called to live
lives which embody and give practical expression to divine justice
and love. This call is the fundamental starting point for all moral
discernment.

That being the case, it is asked, what sort of justice is it that
would condemn all God's gay and lesbian children because of an
orientation they did not consciously choose and cannot change?
How could it be just to require them (on account of that orientation) to renounce permanently one of the most fulfilling and
humanizing of life's experiences, coupled intimacy, including the
sexual aspects of such intimacy? Where is justice to be found, it is
further questioned, much less love, in supporting—tacitly or
directly—discrimination, persecution, prosecution and prejudice
against an entire group of people on account of their immutable sexual and affectional natures? What sort of love, divine or human,
would categorically reject the abundant evidence of genuine,
self-transcending, partnered love between gay and lesbian couples,
love which many testify has even opened them more fully to the love
of God? For those of this viewpoint, the answers to such questions
become obvious when we submit our exegesis of particular condemnatory texts to the larger authority of the scriptural witness.

In summary, then, when the limited scriptural material on
homosexuality is considered in terms of accurate translation, context, the human limits of its authors' intention and understanding,
and the larger biblical themes of justice and love, those holding to
this viewpoint would agree with Bawer when he writes:

> The point that emerges . . . from a careful study of the biblical pas-
> sages that are invoked in attacks on homosexuality is that one can-
> not divorce them from their historical and textual settings.
>
> . . . To be sure, biblical scholars differ on the specific interpretations
> of [those] passages . . . Whatever their differences, however, the
> indisputable fact remains that this is an issue about which intelli-
> gent, serious, and responsible scholars can disagree. . . The lesson of
> Jesus is one of love, not of denunciation of love.[62]

Or, as Gomes puts the matter, considerably less dispassionately:

> . . . no credible case against homosexuality or homosexuals can be
> made from the Bible unless one chooses to read Scripture in a way

that simply sustains the existing prejudice against homosexuality and homosexuals.[63]

Question 2:

What is the God-given intent or design for human sexuality?

Those holding the current viewpoint are generally of the opinion that this question is not the appropriate place to begin Christian moral reflection on sexual issues. As Michael Keeling puts it, "the fundamental problem should be formulated first in the question: 'How should human beings relate to one another?' rather than in the question: 'What should human beings do about sex?'"[64] By starting with specifically sexual questions, it is argued, traditional Christian moral reflection inevitably mires itself inextricably in law, or what Keeling terms a "morality of rules." But for the Christian, law will always be seen to fall short of the humanizing purposes of God's grace, a grace which is constantly drawing us to perceive our lives not in terms of rules, but in terms of *relationships*, relationships both with God and with each other.

Pittenger expresses this conviction in terms of the theological "end" of human life:

> [T]he objective or goal or end or aim of each human existence is to become more fully human . . . to realize and establish [*one's*] possibility of living in love . . .[65]

To be truly human, Pittenger insists, is to be in authentic, self-giving connection with others. For most people, he continues, "[*this*] means being with another [*particular*] person with whom we can be in intimate and fulfilling relationship."[66] As we grow and deepen in our capacity to love, a capacity which is not to be limited to its romantic or erotic forms but which certainly cannot exclude those aspects either, we more and more come to actualize the image of God within us and, in so doing, "we . . . realiz[e] and express . . . our basic humanity."

That being the case, if we are to begin to comprehend and rightly act upon God's loving purposes for us as sexual beings, we can neither spurn our sexuality as the "lower" element of our natures (or, should that prove impossible, restrict its legitimate expression to biological functionality, i.e., reproduction), nor can we simply "do what comes naturally"—do, as the '60s adage had it, "whatever turns you on." We must, as Keeling, Pittenger and others argue, look to the fuller meaning of our lives as human persons and images of God, and seek to articulate our understanding of sexuality in terms of that greater significance. When we consider human sexuality from this perspective, Pittenger argues, we come to understand that it "ought to be interpreted as essentially unitive or conjunctive in nature, rather than seen as nothing more than reproductive."

That being said, how are we to answer our question: what is the God-given intent for human sexuality? Those holding this viewpoint argue that we must answer that question by affirming that the sexual component of our personhood is given to us, as is everything else that we are, as a means for our growth in love, which is to say, for our salvation. In many, perhaps most, human beings, it will be linked to the creation of new human life, which in itself profoundly expands (or at least should expand) one's capacity for self-giving love. But whether or not this biologically generative aspect is fulfilled in a particular relationship, sexuality properly used will fulfill its fundamental unitive purpose—no less for homosexuals than for heterosexuals, albeit always imperfectly for both. It will provide a primary means for our growth from selfishness to that self-transcendence which is the essential quality of mature love, creating thereby a sacred place where—as the German poet Rilke puts it—"two solitudes protect and border and salute each other."[67] Thus, like all God's good gifts, sexuality is given not only for our salvation, but for our delight.

Question 3:

What are the necessary criteria for morally legitimate sexual expression?

Those holding this present viewpoint are agreed that, as Norman Pittenger writes, moral evaluation of any sexual act, heterosexual or homosexual, must begin with "the centrality and primacy of love—love which is mutuality, sharing, giving and receiving, life together in the most radical sense of the phrase."[68]

As Brother Stephen Edward, Spiritual Director of the (Episcopal) Mercy of God Community, writes in *Footsteps*, his community's newsletter:

Jesus taught a love ethic: non-exploitative, non-dominating, respon-sible, mutual, caring and loving . . . Our task is to apply the love ethic of Jesus in [*all areas of*] our own lives. This does not mean "anything goes," but it does mean that all our actions [*are*] measured by Jesus' commandment to love one another. For same-sex oriented persons as well as for heterosexuals, [*this*] means rejecting sexual practices that violate their own integrity and that of others . . . valu[ing] their sexual-ity, us[ing] it responsibly and lovingly, and never harm[ing] others.[69]

In *A Time for Consent,* Pittenger develops the positive aspect of this position more fully. In a morally appropriate sexual relationship, he writes:

The two persons must be committed one to the other, in such a fash-ion that neither is "using" the other. They must give and receive in tenderness, so that there is no element of coercion, undue pressure or imposed constraint which denies the freedom of either partner. They must intend some loyalty to each other, accepting what we might style a mutual belonging. They must purpose to entertain in respect to each other an expectation of fresh and new manifestations of personality, which they will not only "put up with" but which they will welcome and appreciate.[70]

Ralph Blair, setting the tone on this question for Evangelicals Con-cerned, sees this "bond that can keep [*the homosexual couple*] together" as essential. In numerous addresses, interviews, booklets and EC's quarterly *Review,* Blair repeatedly stresses that responsi-bly loving sexual expression requires a context of committed monogamy for its full actualization.[71] Peggy Campolo, wife of well-known evangelical leader Tony Campolo, strikes a similar note when she calls for the preaching to homosexuals of a "true biblical lifestyle that values persons and their loving relation-ships." Such "monogamous, loving relationships between people of the same sex," Campolo adds, are something she "enthusiasti-cally affirm[s] for Christians" and is confident "God wants to bless."[72] The Episcopal Diocese of Michigan's Commission on Homosexuality makes much the same point when it comments that the "accent" of Christian sexual teaching should be "lifetime personal commitment, a couple's taking responsibility for one another, mutual love and faithfulness." This is the case, the com-mission continues, because "[c]aring for one another is a reflection of the essence of God's care for mankind."[73]

In short, the necessary criteria for morally legitimate sexual expression remain the same whether the partners are of opposite sexes or the same sex: love, commitment, faithfulness, mutuality, openness to each other as persons (not just as sexual objects) and the aim of unitive self-transcendence. Given the realities of human experience, Pittenger adds, this does not require of heterosexuals or homosexuals that they achieve the perfect maturity of a life "lived [*fully*] under the mastery of supreme love" before they form sexually intimate relationships. It does mean, however, that sexual partners should be "on the way, moving towards the goal and open to possibilities which conspire to promote such actualization." When that is the case, insofar as particular sexual acts contribute to the movement of the persons involved "towards mutual fulfillment and fulfillment in mutuality, with all the accompanying characteristics of love, they are good acts. Insofar as they do not contribute towards mutual fulfillment in love, they are bad acts."[74]

Question 4:

Is there a "homosexual condition" (orientation) and, if so, what is its cause or origin?

Given both the overwhelming scientific evidence and extensive personal testimony from gays and lesbians themselves, any attempt to argue that an innate, immutable homosexual orientation does not exist must represent an indefensible rejection of established fact.

As for questions of etiology, proponents of this viewpoint tend to dismiss them on principle, since "etiology" is a medical paradigm presuming pathology. No one asks how certain people become heterosexual. The fact is that—whatever the reason—a consistent minority of people discover themselves to be gay or lesbian.[75] That they do so does not mean that something "went wrong" either in their prenatal or early childhood development. Homosexuality is simply a natural variant occurring consistently throughout history and cultures, much like left-handedness.[76] Therefore, a homosexual orientation can be understood by the Christian who discovers himself or herself to be gay as yet another gift of God, with the confidence that God only gives good gifts.

Question 5:

Can a legitimate moral distinction be made between a homosexual condition (orientation) and homosexual acts?

A *practical* distinction can be made in the sense that a person who is homosexual may choose to be celibate or to live as a heterosexual.[77] One can be homosexual, in other words, without ever engaging in an explicitly homosexual act.

This distinction is ultimately meaningless on the moral level, however, since sexual orientation is a morally neutral fact about a person (it would make as much sense to question the "morality" of having green eyes or a genetic predisposition to baldness) and the morality of any given sexual act, homosexual or heterosexual, is entirely dependent upon its context.

Question 6:

What is the psychological significance of homosexuality?

In and of itself, homosexual orientation does not signify anything at all regarding psychological health or lack thereof. As Bruce Bawer notes:

> [I]f homosexuality were a psychological disorder, it would have to be considered a unique one: for the "sufferers" who experience the greatest emotional health are those who confidently reject the idea that it is a psychological disorder, while the greatest psychological damage is suffered by those homosexuals who have allowed themselves to be persuaded that they're suffering from a sickness.[78]

Just as heterosexuals' affectional and erotic urges can be blunted, bent and muddled by various forms of neurosis, so can those of homosexuals. Indeed, given the realities of life in a still profoundly homophobic society, homosexuals may even be somewhat more susceptible to psychological difficulties related to their sexuality than heterosexuals. Where this proves to be true, however, it is not attributable to homosexual orientation per se, but rather to the difficulties of achieving sexual maturation within a hostile environment lacking most of the supportive structures—familial, cultural and ecclesial—available to heterosexuals.

Question 7:

What is the spiritual significance of homosexuality?   *None*

Either as an orientation or a form of sexual behavior, homosexuality has no specific spiritual significance beyond the significance all human sexuality has as a vehicle not only for pleasure, but for self-transcendence and the deepening and sharing of intimate partnered love.

Homosexual desire can of course be lustful (as can heterosexual desire)—lust being understood as an attitude which "treats persons whether in reality or in fantasy as means, not as ends in themselves, as objects to gratify desire, not as persons existing in their own right."[79] But for the homosexual as for the heterosexual, the sexual act, when entered into with other-focused love, honesty and vulnerability, and in the context of a committed, exclusive relationship, becomes in the deepest sense an act of knowledge, both of oneself and of one's partner. The longing for this knowing and being known—which is perhaps most exquisitely, though certainly not exclusively, fulfilled in sexual intercourse—is a fundamental element of the human condition as created by God.

Question 8:

Can a homosexual become heterosexual (the question of "cure")?   *No*

No; nor is there any reason for the homosexual to attempt to do so.

Bawer puts the matter bluntly when he writes that the idea that homosexuality can be reversed is "nonsense":

> It's no more possible to turn a homosexual straight through therapy than it is to turn a heterosexual gay. Sexual orientation is an essential element of a person's identity . . . What has happened [*to those claiming to be "ex-gay"*], quite simply, is that these people—who wouldn't be trying to "change," of course, if they had ever fully accepted their sexual identity—have returned to a state of denial.[80]

The Christian message to the homosexual, therefore, should not consist of false promises of "change" or "cure." To attempt to change what is in fact immutable—sexual orientation—simply diverts a person from the real task set for us by our sexuality, be it gay or straight: bringing *eros* under submission to *agape*, thereby integrating desire and its fulfillment into a life of commitment, caring and self-abandoning love.

Question 9:

What is the moral opinion arrived at, given the responses to Questions 1 through 8?

Homosexual acts are to be evaluated exactly as are heterosexual acts. In a context of a committed, monogamous, loving relationship, they are a positive moral good insofar as they are open to mutuality, growth and deepening knowledge of the self and the other. They can serve the unitive intention of human sexuality every bit as fully as can heterosexual relations. They can "signify good and . . . be a means of redemption."[81] Therefore, as Pittenger writes, "[h]omosexual acts between persons who intend a genuine union in love are not sinful nor should the church consider them as such."[82] Indeed, such acts are *blessed*. "God is present in them," Pittenger continues, "He is present in the loving relationship and present also in the acts which express and cement that love." Pittenger is certain this is true, he says, because "I have seen it to be true."

Question 10:

What is the personal call of Christ for the gay man or lesbian?

For many homosexuals, the vital first step in responding to the call of Christ—and often a far from easy one—is trusting that they are, in fact, included in that loving call *as gay or lesbian persons,* that they truly have a place in the new community created by the incarnation, death and resurrection of Jesus no matter what their personal history or the public stance of certain Christian groups may have led them to believe to the contrary. Despite conservatives' use of the Bible to "clobber" them and their longings for intimacy and partnership, gay people must claim their right to a share in the biblical message of God's all-embracing love. As Peter Gomes puts it, that message is inclusive "not . . . simply in the abstract and in principle. It is inclusive in particular." Like every other person, the gay or lesbian can be sure that "[y]our story is written here, your sins and fears addressed, your hopes confirmed, your experiences validated, and your name known to God."[83]

Once the gay or lesbian embraces his or her orientation, Christ's call in terms of specific sexual morality is no different than his call to the heterosexual. Homosexuals who would follow Christ are to discipline their sexual and affectional urges so as to avoid promiscuity, exploitative sexual contacts or contentless relationships in which either they or their partner is treated as less than an independent image of God, with all the significance and respect that dignity entails. In terms of life goals, gays and lesbians not specifically called to singleness should seek a same-sex partner with whom they can build a loving, monogamous union. Such a relationship, if it is to be an authentically Christian partnership, will be marked preeminently by that quality which Dominican Richard Woods terms "reciprocal care": "the capacity and desire to respond to another person as a uniquely valuable and therefore infinitely loveable self in terms of bodily intimacy, psychological mutuality, and spiritual growth."[84] A Christian gay or lesbian union, in other words, will involve a conscious commitment by both spouses to the challenging, ongoing task of psychospiritual integration. Such integration, as it is achieved, is the very definition of Christian maturity, a maturity in which sexuality—like every other element of the personality—is subordinated to the unifying principle of *agape*, self-emptying love.

Woods also challenges Christian gays and lesbians to recognize that they are particularly called by Christ to serve as agents of "the redemption of the gay world itself, by authentic witness and by creating alternatives to the morally destructive forces and structures in that world." Such prophetic ministry to their own community could include resistance to or criticism "from within" of the objectifying, sexualized aspects of the gay subculture, in particular the prevailing "pornographic conception of sex" which accepts and in fact celebrates anonymous, promiscuous, exploitative and/or commercialized sex, justifying such dehumanization by the notion that "sex (or, rather, orgasm) is a constant and undeniable need and therefore a right which must be satisfied as frequently and easily as possible."[85]

Question 11:

What is the pastoral call of Christ to the church on the issue?

As an essential first step to correcting its long history of censure, exclusion and theological justification for persecution of gay and lesbian people, the church is called prayerfully to examine and repent of its own homophobia. It must undertake the hard work of changing attitudes and expunging vestigial prejudices, including public confession of past wrongs against gay people when appropriate. Individual Christians are under a similar obligation if they are to live out the gospel mandate to their gay and lesbian neighbors. Christians should also be vigilant in exposing and countering misinformation regarding homosexuals, particularly when such slander has its origin in ostensibly Christian sources.[86]

In faithfulness to the biblical call to justice for all people, the church should "speak publicly for repeal of all laws which make criminal offenses of private, voluntary sex acts between mature persons . . . oppose police harassment of homosexuals. . . and speak publicly on behalf of homosexuals in the area of civil rights legislation."[87]

Given the biblical witness to God's particular compassion for the outcast and despised, the church should also be leading the way in affirming, welcoming and serving gay and lesbian people. It should enthusiastically invite them to full participation in the Body of Christ. Christians, by the genuineness and warmth of their welcome of gays and lesbians into their own circles of friendship, association, work, family, worship and neighborhood, should provide a model to the rest of society for that true inclusivity which is a cardinal mark of the coming reign of God. In terms of its own leadership, the church should apply the same standards to homosexual candidates for ordination that it does to heterosexuals. As the Episcopal Church's Commission on Human Affairs recommended in 1991:

> [T]he Church [should] be open to ordaining gay men and lesbians otherwise qualified who display the same integrity in their sexual relationships which we ask of our heterosexual ordinands.[88]

Understanding as it does the true unitive meaning of human sexuality, the church should also be setting the example for a world too quick to accept functional or hedonistic views of sex by creating Christian structures for supporting committed gay partnerships.

This means offering gays and lesbians public blessing for their unions in rites which unapologetically celebrate the Christian significance and moral goodness of these relationships. Indeed, for many gay and lesbian Christians, the question of same-sex union is *the* crucial issue for the church, a point which Bawer makes in personal terms:

> . . . to be gay and sit in . . . church week after week beside your partner of five or ten or thirty years and hear announcements of weddings and . . . know that the two of you can't be married in the church is to be reminded that you're *not* really full, equal members.[89]

If gays and lesbians are recognized as "full, equal members" of the Body of Christ, however—as they must be if the church is to be true to itself—then, Bawer concludes, "the only Christian way for the church to respond to the fact of homosexuality and the identicality of homosexual love and commitment to heterosexual love and commitment is [*for it*] to bless gay unions and allow the ordination of openly gay clergy."[90] Anything less than such active inclusivity, it is argued, constitutes a refusal to heed the call of Christ and a rejection of the church's role as the preeminent sign of divinely-constituted community in a divided world.

Question 12:
What is the political call of Christ to society on the issue?

The entire Judeo-Christian tradition makes clear God's call to communities and nations to establish and practice justice. On the basis of that clear biblical principle, "[t]here should be no discrimination against any person in housing, employment, business services, or public accommodations on the ground of sexual orientation."[91] Furthermore, not only should all statutory penalties for consensual homosexual acts between adults be revoked, the state should grant legal status to committed same-sex relationships.

Bawer writes extensively on this last matter in *A Place at the Table*, contending that—as radical a notion as it may seem to conservatives—it is an "essentially conservative" issue. This is so, he writes, because:

> [A] tolerant society, by agreeing not to interfere with the operation of such institutions as gay bars and bathhouses, makes it vastly easier and less stressful for homosexuals to lead promiscuous sex lives,

but, by refusing to grant committed gay couples legal rights comparable to those granted married heterosexual couples, doesn't effect a
similar improvement for gays who want to live in monogamous relationships.[92]

As a result, he continues:

> . . . laws and social conventions regarding homosexuality have long
> had the effect of discouraging monogamous relationships and of
> encouraging covert one-night stands.

Nevertheless, Bawer argues, while the "subculturally oriented" gay
may embrace the "narrow, sex-obsessed [model] of gay life" which
is most often perceived by the rest of society due to the image presented by self-appointed gay spokespersons and the gay media,
most gays and lesbians are far more mainstream in their aspira-
tions. They hope to find a partner with whom they can build a
loyal, loving, committed relationship which will allow them to create a home, a place of refuge and mutual support, a sense of family.
Therefore, if the state is to fulfill its God-given purpose of establishing justice and promoting the optimal humanization of all its
citizens, there must be full civil recognition for same-sex unions
through the legalization of gay marriage.[93]

Representative Denominations and
Para-Church Groups

The only major denomination officially espousing this viewpoint
at present is the United Church of Christ (UCC) which, in 1972,
became the first church to ordain an openly gay person to its ministry. In 1983, UCC national delegates issued a statement that sexual orientation should not be grounds for barring anyone from
ordination; the church also performs same-sex union ceremonies.

While the other mainstream denominations continue to bar
non-celibate gays and lesbians from ordination (at least in theory)
and to prohibit their clergy from presiding at the blessing of
same-sex relationships, it is widely recognized that among mainline national leadership, liberal clergy and seminary faculties, the

majority opinion leans heavily toward a viewpoint similar in most respects to this one.

Most of the "gay caucus" groups within or loosely related to the major denominations—Dignity (Roman Catholic), Integrity (Episcopal), Presbyterians Concerned, Affirmation (United Methodist), GLAD (Disciples of Christ), Lutherans Concerned—would also identify with at least the major points of this perspective, as would growing numbers of individual Protestant, Catholic and evangelical clergy and laity who are becoming increasingly bold in pressing their respective communions to move toward full inclusion of gays and lesbians in the life of the church.[94]

The national nondenominational organization Evangelicals Concerned ("EC"), founded and still directed by New York psychotherapist Ralph Blair, has for more than two decades been the standard-bearer for this perspective among evangelicals, amassing an impressive roster of evangelically identified guest keynote speakers for its annual "Connections" conferences.[95] Through local chapters throughout the United States, EC provides Bible studies, prayer groups and social activities for evangelical gays and lesbians, and the national organization's quarterly newsletters, *The Record* and *Review*, both the work of Dr. Blair, reach all chapter members, as well as a considerably wider audience of interested supporters.

Cross-Perspective Critique

Not surprisingly, critics on the right are unimpressed by this viewpoint's conviction that love and love alone is the definitive principle for all moral inquiry. St. Paul certainly understood the primacy of love (1 Corinthians 13), these critics note, but that did not keep him from urging the fledgling Christian communities under his charge to conform their new lives in Christ to any number of other ethical precepts as well, including the principles of sexual morality common to Jews at the time, principles understood to have been ordained by God.[96]

The apostle's Epistle to the Galatians, for example, is a sustained and passionately argued polemic against those who would replace salvation through faith in Jesus with a reimposition of the law. Nonetheless, within a few sentences of writing that "the whole law is summed up in a single commandment, 'You shall love your neighbor as yourself'" (Gal 5:14), Paul goes on to list a series of "works of the flesh" which, if Christians do not avoid them, will result in their exclusion from the Kingdom of God (Gal 5:19–21).[97] This does not represent inconsistency on Paul's part, conservatives insist. Rather, it evidences the fact that there is more at issue in sexual morality than the subjective intentions and feelings of those involved, no matter how lofty these might be. Mutuality, commitment and other-focused love are certainly among the divinely intended criteria for sexual intimacy, but these things, good though they are, must still find their expression within the bounds of the will of God as made clear in creation and revelation.[98]

Indeed, conservatives contend, if one truly loves God, a primary way that love will be expressed is through honoring God's wisdom as manifested in the natural order God made and called good. The negative proscriptions of law, subordinate as they may be to positive admonitions to love of God and neighbor, exist in part to make clear which acts run contrary to the practical consequences of that love and the integrity of that order. Love of God and obedience to God's law are not to be set against one another; rather, our love for God is to be expressed *through* our willing submission to God's revealed will. If appeal is to be made to larger biblical "themes," critics argue, it should be recognized that it is contrary to the entire thrust of Scripture to claim that love for God can coexist with rebellion against God's sovereign intent for creation.

In reality, it is charged, those defending this viewpoint are guilty of an intellectually indefensible monism. God is, as St. John writes, love (1 John 4:8[b], 16[b]), it is true; and self-transcending love—in sexual as in all other relationships—is certainly the ultimate human calling. This does not mean, however, that nothing else remains to be said about either the nature and will of God or the moral limits to human action. To affirm that "God is love" does not mean—as proponents of this viewpoint are felt too often to assume—that God makes no demands upon us, asks nothing of us that might be painful or difficult, desires only that we find fulfillment on our own terms. Yes, God loves us unconditionally "just as we are," but that love, by its very nature, seeks true good for us; it is not content to leave us in our brokenness and sin, simply overlooking our fallen state. God respects us as creatures so much that God will not be satisfied until we become whole, become holy, become all that we are created to be. Liberal arguments from the "love of God," conservatives complain, slide too easily into that notion of divine love which C. S. Lewis once scorned as a "senile benevolence" unconcerned with particulars just so long as "the young people are enjoying themselves" and "a good time was had by all." Such thinking is appealing, to be sure, as Lewis admits:

> I should very much like to live in a universe which was governed on such lines. But since it is abundantly clear that I don't, and since I have reason to believe, nevertheless, that God is Love, I conclude that my conception of love needs correction.[99]

This, critics suggest, is precisely where liberal Christian conviction finds itself on the matter of the love of God: its understanding of that love "needs correction" because it is at once too sentimental and too shallow, falling far short of the passionate, self-emptying, active and holy desire for our true and eternal good that is fundamental to the character of the God of the Bible and Christian tradition.

Conservatives allege that this viewpoint's grasp of sin is limited as well, nearly as limited as its conception of divine love, in that it has adopted from contemporary non-Christian culture the notion that, before an act can be considered wrong, some unwilling party must be hurt by it.[100] Liberal Christianity, in other words, has baptized as a spiritual postulate the secular principle that there is no such thing as a "victimless crime." If all those involved in and affected by a particular act are "consenting adults" and there is no observable harm done, then, the reasoning goes, that act cannot be said to be sinful. The difficulty with such thinking, critics contend, lies in the fact that the divine moral law is premised on something greater than our subjective sense of injury—the purposes of God in creating us in the first place.

This viewpoint's narrow view of sin has a parallel, it is charged, in an unjustifiably restricted understanding of the effects of the Fall upon human judgment and self-awareness. Christianity traditionally taught that one of the consequences of that Fall was concupiscence—which means considerably more, theologically, than the commonly accepted definition of "strong sexual desire." Theologically speaking, concupiscence is a disordered relationship between God-given—and therefore good—human appetites of any kind and their intended "ends."

According to traditional argumentation, before the Fall, there was in the human psyche an innate balance by which, under the governance of reason, all human desire moved naturally to the end for which it had been created. Hunger for food, for example, did not express itself in gluttony or in craving for that which was unwholesome; rather, it led—by automatic self-regulation—to eating only that which was healthy, and in an amount sufficient to nourish and no more. After the Fall, however, this balance between desire and its end was shattered. The appetites burst beyond the limits of their intended ends to seek gratification for its own sake, often at the expense even of these appetites' legitimate, created ends. Reason was no longer the spontaneous governing principle of the human personality; rather, its authority would have to be imposed by conscious self-discipline and moral effort. What had come naturally to humankind before the Fall, in other words, was now a matter of often arduous struggle. Given its unique power, the sexual appetite has been particularly affected by concupiscence, it was held—a situation clearly evidenced by the fact that, once roused, erotic passion can neutralize nearly any restraint of reason or conviction. Therefore, when it comes to sex, particular vigilance and a fair amount of external control were felt to be required to ensure that desire did not overwhelm its divinely intended boundaries.

The direction of liberal theological thinking over the past fifty years has had little patience with such venerable theological constructs as concupiscence. The liberal anthropology is considerably more optimistic than that of traditional theologians; its evaluation of the erotic drive a great deal more benign. Indeed, the entire concept of a primal Fall from perfection is often called into question, if not flatly rejected. In light of current theological attitudes, any attempt to introduce the concept of concupiscence into discussions of sexual morality is likely to invite dismissal as a sexual neurotic.

Despite the tide of the times, however, conservative critics argue that the liberal view of the human person is simply unrealistic. This is nowhere more apparent, it is held, than in that view's focus on subjective states like "mutuality"[101] or the desire for "genuine union in love"[102] as the measure of morally appropriate sexual expression. Appeal to such criteria, it is claimed, grossly overestimates our ability to appraise accurately our own intentions and feelings when under the powerful pressure of *eros*. How, it is asked, are those in the throes of cathexis (gay or straight), or even those simply roused by desire, supposed to know when they have reached the necessary level of "mutuality" for sexual expression to become appropriate?[103] Subjective states are, by their very nature, highly unreliable indicators of objective reality. Therefore, this viewpoint's attempt to ground sexual morality in subjective concerns related to intention and feeling not only misapprehends the normative significance of the created order and the biblical witness, it reveals an extraordinary naiveté as to the fundamental realities of human nature.

As for this viewpoint's reinterpretation of those scriptural statements traditionally held to condemn homosexual acts, conservative scholars charge that those advocating such revisionist exegesis have entirely failed to make their case. Furthermore, the fact that liberal Christians have been so uncritical in their embrace of the arguments of Boswell, Scroggs, Countryman and others of similar opinion is seen as a clear indication that these liberals are ultimately indifferent to scrupulous biblical scholarship—at least when such scholarship runs afoul of what they think the Bible *should* say, as opposed to what it actually says.

The work of the late John Boswell has come in for particularly vigorous criticism. Despite the fact that his *Christianity, Social Tolerance and Homosexuality*[104] was awarded the 1981 "American Book Awards for History," several subsequent scholarly articles have "call[ed] into question Boswell's scholarly ability, if not his scholarly integrity."[105] In what Guenther Haas (Associate Professor of Religion and Theology, Redeemer College, Ontario, Canada) describes as a "devastating critique"[106] of Boswell's celebrated lexicographical study of ἀρσενοκοῖται,[107] for example, David F. Wright flatly contradicts Boswell's claim that, when used as a prefix in koine Greek compounds, ἀρσενο- most often indicates an adjectival relationship to the second part of the word (pointing to Boswell's reading of ἀρσενοκοῖται as "males who bed," i.e., male prostitutes). In fact, Wright argues, the structural determinant in ἀρσενοκοῖται is actually its second part, κοῖται (κοῖταις), and in all similar compounds it has a verbal force, with the first part of the word (in this case ἀρσενο-) functioning as the object of the "bedding" (which would make a more accurate rendering "those [*males*] who bed men," i.e., male homosexuals).[108] Furthermore, Wright charges, Boswell is simply wrong in asserting that, in most other compounds employing the prefix ἀρσενο-, that prefix functions adjectivally. In the great majority of instances, Wright counters, where the second part has a verbal force (as is the case here), ἀρσενο- denotes the object, which lends further credence to the contention that—as Wright puts it in a subsequent article— ἀρσενοκοῖται denotes "'male homosexual activity' without qualification."[109] In addition, contrary to Boswell's categorical statements that ἀρσενοκοῖται or its variants were never used by patristic writers in reference to homosexual acts and that neither 1 Cor 6:9 nor 1 Tim 1:10 (the two Pauline passages in which the word appears) was cited by early church fathers in their condemnations of these acts, Wright documents numerous instances in early Christian writings in which some form of ἀρσενοκοῖται is used to describe homosexual acts or appeal is made to one or both of the Pauline texts to condemn them.[110]

Robin Scroggs has also been the object of conservative challenge on scholarly grounds. While his tracing of ἀρσενοκοῖται to the Septuagint's translation of Lev 18:22 and 20:13[111] is seconded by Wright (indeed, Wright terms the parallelism "inescapable"),[112] Scroggs's larger exegetical framework for both μαλακοῖ and ἀρσενοκοῖται (commercialized pederasty, with the terms denoting, respectively, the effeminate call boy and his older male customer) has been faulted for being premised upon an error in fact. As Haas notes, a primary "pillar"[113] of Scroggs's interpretation of these two words is the claim that there is no textual evidence from Plato through the first century of the Common Era for any generally recognized form of homosexual relationship other than pederasty, with all its inherent inequalities and potential for exploitation, both sexual (on the part of the older male) and financial (on the part of the younger "beloved"). Therefore, Scroggs concludes, since the only form of homosexuality known to Paul would have been pederasty, the apostle's condemnation of the μαλακοῖ and ἀρσενοκοῖται can only relate to some form of pederastic practice. In a 1996 article in the *Journal of the American Academy of Religion*,[114] however, Mark D. Smith contends that this presuppositional "pillar" of Scroggs's interpretive theory is demonstrably untrue, citing materials from the fourth century BCE through the first century CE—both written texts and art works—as evidence of the prevalence of non-pederastic homosexual practices in Greco-Roman society among both men and women. That being the case, Smith argues, there is no factual basis for assuming that the behavior Paul condemns on the part of the μαλακοί and ἀρσενοκοῖται must be limited to pederasty. Indeed, D. F. Wright asks rhetorically, if Paul had intended to limit his condemnation to a particular form of pederasty, "why did he not use one of the several Greek words or phrases for it current in Hellenistic Jewish writings? . . . Why did he (create or) adopt a (relatively) new, certainly unusual term inspired by a Levitical prohibition and therefore one which prima facie has a broader meaning than pederasty?"[115]

Apart from the two disputed Pauline terms employed in 1 Corinthians and 1 Timothy, conservative assessment of revisionist perspectives on the remaining commonly cited biblical texts runs along the following lines.

As for the story of Sodom (Genesis 19), early attempts (in particular by Bailey)[116] to explain the Sodomites determination to "know" Lot's angelic visitors as merely a desire to examine their credentials[117] cannot be sustained when the Hebrew word in question (yādhă) is interpreted in context—in particular the offer to the mob of Lot's daughters, whose virginity is indicated by a phrase which includes the same term. Nonetheless, most conservatives—though not all—would agree with Haas when he writes that, while the Sodomites' intention was homosexual rape, "there is validity in connecting this sin to the violation of the norm of hospitality. The desire to rape the visitors is less the expression of homosexual desire . . . per se, and more the use of forcible homosexual rape to express domination over the strangers, thereby humiliating them."[118]

Turning to the Levitical prohibitions of male homosexual acts (Lev 18:22 and 20:13), conservatives absolutely reject revisionist claims that, as part of the Holiness Code, these laws are no longer binding on Christians, either because they are part of a now abrogated Jewish system of "purity law" (as Countryman contends), or because their true moral concern is avoidance of Canaanite practices related to idolatry, not homosexual behavior in and of itself (per Boswell, McNeill and Nelson). As for Countryman's argument, critics note, the fact that certain practices may be part of Israel's purity code "does not preclude [*their having*] a moral force apart from their connection with ritual purity. We are not always forced to choose between ritual and moral import, but can find the two concerns coinciding in injunctions in the Holiness Code."[119] Indeed, conservatives note, most liberals themselves acknowledge this to be the case in that they consider other of the Code's sexual prohibitions—of adultery and bestiality, for example—still morally binding.[120] Arguments by Boswell, McNeill and others that the rationale for the Levitical condemnations of male homosexual acts lies in the association of these acts with idolatrous Canaanite worship are also unconvincing to conservative scholars. The fact that such behavior was characteristic of the Canaanites (even that it may have had some connection with idolatry) "does not warrant the conclusion that homosexual acts were condemned purely because of their cultic association."[121] As for the use of "abomination" (*to'ebah*) in these two texts, the word's recognized connection with idolatry does not require an *exclusively* cultic interpretation of the ban on homosexual acts, it is argued. As Haas writes, summarizing Bailey on this point, while "abomination" does have idolatrous connotations for the Levitical authors, its meaning is "extended to whatever reverses the proper natural order. Because homosexual acts reverse the natural order of sexuality, they manifest the subversive spirit of idolatry."

Conservatives particularly fault revisionists' handling of Paul's passionate excoriation of Greco-Roman iniquity in Romans 1. They find indefensible on either contextual or linguistic grounds, for example, Countryman's (to them) tortuous attempts[122] to explain away the plain meaning of Paul's words in that passage as nothing more than a rhetorical device designed to win over Jewish readers used to such cataloguing of Gentile vice.[123] Conservative commentators are equally unimpressed with Countryman's argument that, because Paul never specifically uses the word "sin" (ἁμαρτία, *hamartia*) in reference to the homosexual desires and acts he describes in Romans 1 (despite the fact that he terms them "degrading passions" [1:26], "lusts" [1:24], "shameless" [1:27] and "unnatural" [1:26]), this means that Paul merely views these things as "dirty" according to the Jewish purity code which is no longer binding on Gentile believers, a "recompense" for sin, but not sin in and of themselves.[124]

Also disputed are claims that Paul's condemnations cannot be applicable to contemporary Christian homosexuals, since Romans 1 describes a process which begins in conscious turning away from God to idolatry and continues in a consequent turning away from heterosexuality. While it is true, as Haas acknowledges, that not all contemporary homosexuals are "consciously rebelling against God and engaging in idolatry," this misses the point Paul is making:

> Paul's argument in Romans 1 does not hinge on individual homosexuals' engaging in conscious and deliberate acts of rebellion and idolatry. His argument paints a general portrait of humanity with broad and sweeping brushstrokes. He describes humanity's corporate rebellion against God . . . which leads to the worship of idols . . . which results in the corporate corruption of humanity.[125]

Debates as to whether or not contemporary homosexuals "choose" to turn away from some personally inherent heterosexual orientation misread Paul in similar fashion, it is held. As Schmidt argues, "Paul's . . . concern is not with motivation—whether described in modern terms or ancient terms—but practice . . ."[126]

As for claims by Gomes, Boswell and others that, since Paul was unaware of there being a constitutional homosexual orientation, his denunciation of same-sex acts and desires can only be applied to heterosexuals who choose to act "against" their actual orientation and engage in homosexual behavior, conservative critics point out that even Bailey, noted for his revisionist reading of the Sodom account, rejects this argument. In fact, Bailey explicitly reverses its conclusion, insisting that since Paul's cultural assumptions made him unable to differentiate between the true "invert" and the heterosexual "pervert," one cannot apply such a distinction—which Paul himself would have been unable to comprehend—to his statements. So far as he knew, Paul was condemning *all* people who engaged in homosexual acts. Therefore, Bailey contends, we must apply the Pauline judgment to all such acts, whether committed by those with a genuine homosexual orientation or by heterosexuals choosing to go against their "natural" inclinations.[127]

Finally, regarding the much-debated matter of Paul's argument that homosexual acts are "against nature" (παρα φύσιν, *para phúsin*) and the question of what "nature" should be taken to mean in the context of that argument, numerous conservative scholars[128] maintain that Paul is not merely referring to "the *personal* nature of the pagans in question" (as Boswell[129] asserts) or to some biologically-based paradigm related to reproduction (as Countryman[130] construes the intertestamental Hellenistic Jewish sources which use similar language). Rather, conservatives contend, Paul's understanding of "nature" is grounded in the creation order itself as set out in Genesis 1 and 2, nature as it was intended by God to be, not as we find it in a fallen world. Read in this light, the argument "from nature" perfectly fits the flow of Paul's thought in this passage: just as in idolatry humankind turns away from the one true God, in homosexual behavior men and women turn away from God's created order for sexuality. In that sense, as Haas puts it, "Homosexual practice is always implicitly idolatrous, for it involves a rejection of the sovereignty of the Creator."[131]

Summing up conservative criticisms of revisionist exegesis, Haas writes:

> [T]hese revisionist arguments fail. They do not deal properly with biblical texts. [*Their*] arguments do not let the context and the natural sense of the key biblical terms determine their meanings . . . They attempt to read into the biblical texts . . . distinctions, qualifications and misunderstandings that are not there. [*They*] distort the historical evidence on same-sex relations in the ancient world . . . and on the early church's view of same-sex relations.[132]

Given such gross mishandling of the sacred text by liberal exegetes, Haas finds it "difficult to avoid the conclusion that the various revisionist authors come to the biblical texts with preconceived notions of what the texts should say, and that they exegete these texts to fit their preconceived notions."

Responding to the often-noted fact that biblical references to homosexuality are scanty at best and that Jesus himself is never recorded as mentioning it, conservatives counter that even a single biblical proscription would be sufficient to condemn homosexual acts morally. Moreover, homosexual behavior is so self-evidently a violation of the created order that the point does not require extensive scriptural explication. As for the lack of recorded comment by Jesus on the subject, conservative critics point out that an argument from silence is the weakest form of proof. Furthermore, some add, if πορνεῖα (*pornēa*) is in fact a generic term for any violation of Jewish sexual codes, as a number of conservative exegetes suggest is the case, then Jesus on at least two occasions refers to homosexuality (Matt 15:19; Mark 7:21), and in both instances the reference is negative.

Opponents of this viewpoint also note that its argumentation assumes as fact certain points which are not only unproven but vigorously contested—the conviction that some people are simply "born gay," for example. While the data is certainly complex, and even in certain instances appears contradictory, critics contend that sufficient evidence exists as to there being some sort of relationship between adult homosexuality and damaging childhood experience[133] to call into serious question any claim that the source of homosexual orientation is entirely "nature" as opposed to "nurture." If proponents of this viewpoint are honest, it is argued, they will admit that assertions of being born gay are in the end statements of *faith*, not of fact—just as are claims by some conservatives that there is "no such thing as a homosexual."

It is also observed by many, in particular those grounded in more traditional Christian spiritual practice, that the focus of this perspective, as evidenced even in the very language it chooses to communicate its convictions, is almost entirely limited to this life, with little or no indication of interest in the life to come. The center of attention is always the human person as that person seeks fulfillment on his or her own terms; it is rarely if ever a God who might in fact have a prior claim upon that life, a God to whom that person could in some way be answerable. On the issue of homosexuality, as on a number of other issues, it is charged, liberals talk a good deal about humanization, but they never say anything about sanctification; they attach great importance to wholeness, but rarely seem concerned with holiness. Yet Christianity has historically taken a remarkably casual view of earthly happiness—not a bad thing if held loosely and received gratefully, but nothing we are guaranteed (indeed, quite the opposite, if one is to believe Jesus—"in the world you will have trouble" [John 16:33]). Both Christ's teaching and example make it clear that temporal satisfaction or fulfillment are far less important than the joy that comes through faithfulness to the will of God, and it is only when Bonhoeffer's "costly discipleship" is upheld as the model for authentic Christian living that the hungers of the human heart will truly be met.

All that being said, the bottom line for most conservatives, in particular those speaking out of the evangelical tradition, is the matter of scriptural authority. As Stanton L. Jones wrote in 1993 in *Christianity Today*:

> There are only two ways one can neutralize the biblical witness against homosexual behavior: by gross misinterpretation or by moving away from a high view of Scripture.[134]

But absent the historic Christian conviction that Scripture is reliable in its moral and theological teaching (if not in every historical, geographical or cultural detail), that it can be trusted when it speaks definitively, that its authors were speaking for more than themselves and expressing more than their own culture-bound opinions— absent all this and much more that makes up the traditional "high view" of scriptural authority, conservatives insist, we are left with no divinely-grounded basis for belief or action. If Scripture is not to be trusted in its explicit teaching regarding sexual morality, it is asked, what reason do we have for trusting its message on the primacy of love, the imperative of justice, the call to peacemaking or any other principle dear to contemporary liberal Christian hearts? Once we place ourselves in the position of judging that Word which is in fact the standard by which we are to be judged, we make *ourselves* the ultimate moral authority. As Jones concludes:

> The church's historically high view of Scripture is threatened by efforts at revising the church's position on homosexuality . . . We can only change our position on homosexuality by changing our fundamental stance on biblical authority.

From the left, it is often charged that gay proponents of this viewpoint are nothing more than "assimilationists"—standing with hat in hand at the door of the straight church and humbly asking that it judge them worthy of inclusion in the Body of Christ on the grounds that (except for the minor matter of who it is they love) they are really not all that different from nice, middle-class heterosexuals. The fact is, gay liberation theologian Richard Cleaver argues, to expect the bourgeois church "to validate us . . . does not work. We waste our time trying to become respectable enough to be accepted by the majority."[135] This assimilationism is also faulted by some for remaining far too constrained by what are perceived to be "heterosexist" models for sexual relationships—particularly in the emphasis proponents like Blair and Bawer place upon monogamy. Moreover, it is claimed by these same critics, the viewpoint continues to think and speak about sexuality as though it required some moral justification beyond itself,[136] rather than simply celebrating *eros* in its own right as a liberating means of self-discovery and personal fulfillment.

For the new generation of gay Christian theoreticians such as Cleaver, however, the fundamental failure of this viewpoint lies in its method:

> The path of apologetics has led us to a dead end. So has the other path we have been following . . . the scholastic path . . . pulling a word from scripture here and a phrase from scripture there, then arguing about what the words meant in Greece . . . versus what they meant to Jews in the diaspora . . . This is history, it is not theology.[137]

In order to claim their rightful place in the ongoing work of God in history, Cleaver and others argue, lesbians, gays, bisexuals, transgender people and other sexual minorities must reframe the methodological context of the debate according to paradigms developed by feminist and Latin and African-American liberation theologians. Anything less, even the well-intentioned "liberalism" of this present viewpoint, will "always lead [*lesbians and gays*] to a dead end because . . . it relies on experts to define who we are and where we stand in relation to scripture." Such an approach lacks both the radical analysis and the existential liberty (a liberty born of living outside the limits of conventional approbation) necessary to accomplish the real work which must be done by queer Christians: freeing themselves from "the falsehood that gayness is the root of our sins" and learning the hard but liberating truth that being queer is, in fact, "the source of our virtues."

The Viewpoint Responds

The "high view of Scripture" conservatives so often cite as an insurmountable obstacle to their making any significant movement toward moral acceptance of homosexuality can no longer be intelligibly defended whether on scholarly, historical or theological grounds. We simply know too much at this point—too much about how the Bible was written, edited and compiled, too much about its use by the church over the centuries, too much about its function in God's ongoing work in history—to find credible old concepts of scriptural authority which define the Bible's significance in terms of infallible statements of propositional truth (a notion which is "hostage to the eighteenth-century illusion that truth and meaning are the same thing").[138] In attempting to make the Bible something it was never intended to be, the conservative "high view" actually strips the Scriptures of their genuinely transformative power, substituting literalistic fidelity to the purportedly unambiguous message of the text for that life-changing encounter with the Living Word to which the written words are meant to draw us.

The conservative argument from a supposedly inviolable commitment to scriptural inerrancy is something of a red herring, as well, since—as has been noted in response to viewpoints 1 through 3—conservative Christians have made and continue to make any number of compromises as regards the "clear teaching of Scripture" when it suits them. As Gomes writes somewhat acerbically, "the authority of scripture seems not to have been challenged by the revision of the church's position on women . . . [or] slavery." Thus, the underlying explanation for conservative Christian inflexibility on the matter of homosexuality must, in fact, lie elsewhere.

As for conservative cavils regarding this viewpoint's allegedly naive trust in our human ability to know our own hearts and motives, and therefore to determine when our subjective experience of "love" is sufficient to justify sexual expression, the viewpoint's defenders counter that a refusal to take responsibility for our own moral life by retreating into the sort of proof texting legalism that makes all our decisions for us stands in diametric opposition to the scriptural call to spiritual maturity—to growing into our "full stature in Christ." The authors and editors of the biblical witness, no less than we, discerned revelatory truth through the grid of their own human perceptions, and mechanistic theories of inspiration that would make the Scriptures the one artifact of history somehow "outside" the realities of all other human experience are simply untenable. This being the case, we must recognize that the biblical writers' theological "process" on moral issues was not that dissimilar from our own when we submit our minds and hearts to the work of the Spirit, and there is therefore no basis for assuming that their ethical discernment is uniformly and universally applicable while our own insights and judgments are inherently unreliable.

Responding to claims that this viewpoint is guilty of theological monism in its focus on self-emptying love as the defining descriptive of the character of God, advocates of the viewpoint note that conservatives have for years faulted more liberal Christians for what they perceive to be an over-emphasis on the love of God to the exclusion of other equally important divine attributes. This debate is certainly not limited to the question of homosexuality, and has to do more with fundamental theological assumptions than it does with differences on any particular moral question. As for themselves, liberal Christians find ample and compelling support for their understanding of the centrality of divine love not only in the example and teaching of Jesus, but in the larger message of the Scriptures, as well as the insights of countless mystics and saints over nearly two millennia of Christian history.

Finally, while criticism of the purportedly "temporal" (as opposed to eternal) focus of this viewpoint's concerns may resonate with those accustomed to the comfort of a traditional theological vocabulary, it should be recognized that conservative complaints in this regard are essentially a semantic quibble. Call it "wholeness" or "holiness," "integration" or "sanctification," the challenge of Christian faithfulness in every age, whatever the descriptive categories used, is ultimately a matter of moving toward an ever more authentic human life, which is to say, a life which in all its aspects (including the erotic and affectional) is grounded in and expressive of that self-emptying love which is the essential character of God. One immediate practical result of such growth in love, as Scripture makes clear, will be a passionate commitment to justice for all God's children. This is the message liberal Christians perceive at the heart of the gospel, and that message leaves no place for theological arguments which would set gay and lesbian people outside the all-inclusive grace of God unless they are willing to renounce a fundamental element of their essential personhood.

- 6 -

LIBERATION

Those holding this final viewpoint maintain that it is not for the heterosexual majority in the church to dictate to gays and lesbians what they can and cannot do with their sexuality. The relevant moral issue for Christians lies elsewhere: in a biblically-based call to struggle against all forms of oppression and domination, including homophobia, in the name of God's Eternal Reign of justice grounded in love.

By giving themselves over to that struggle, "queer Christians" become the vanguard of a new gospel faithfulness which cuts through the stultifying incrustations of centuries to rediscover the radical heart of Jesus' message: the scandalous good news that no one is outside the universal embrace of the Creator's love. Indeed, those whom conventional bourgeois society most readily condemns and stigmatizes are the very people being invited to the head of the line at the feast of Jesus' reign. For Christians holding this view, the moral challenge of their faith is the call of Christ the Liberator to throw off all repressive structures of sexism, misogyny, patriarchy, heterosexism, racism and political and economic injustice and begin to experience—and make it possible for others to experience—the freedom of that "more abundant" life which Jesus himself lived and promised to those who would follow him.[1]

Question 1:

What is the ultimate authority upon which any moral judgment regarding homosexuals and/or homosexual acts is to be based?

For the Christian, the ultimate authority for any moral judgment, sexual or otherwise, is Jesus of Nazareth himself, the one man among all human beings so filled with the love that is God that he can serve as a model to all who come after him for the potentialities of human life lived in the freedom of the Spirit.

This Jesus, it is proclaimed, was never the champion of the sex-phobic, self-righteous, individualistic morality that has marked the church for centuries.[2] This Jesus never cast himself as defender of the status quo of gender, orientational and class privilege, of power politics and marginalization of the unconventional—despite what the pietistic Christology of traditional Christianity has too often attempted to make him out to be. This Jesus launched his public ministry by claiming for himself the prophetic words of Isaiah:

> The Spirit of the Lord is upon me
> because he has anointed me
> to preach good news to the poor.
>
> He has sent me to proclaim release to the captives
> and recovery of sight to the blind,
> to let the oppressed go free,
> to proclaim the year of the Lord's favor.
>
> (Luke 4:18, 19)

By applying this passage to himself, Richard Cleaver insists, Jesus made it clear that he understood his mission to be fundamentally bound up with freedom for the oppressed and outcast and, in so doing, "Jesus is pointing us toward a social resurrection . . . [n]ew communities, new ways of organizing our collective life . . . ."[3] Indeed, the most striking thing about Jesus' ministry was his determined breaking through all those barriers of race, caste, gender and class which were the linchpins of the religious-political "system" of his day, a system which eventually found the freedom he taught and lived so threatening that it felt it had no choice but to kill him.

Once we strip away the pious imagery that has distorted the Jesus of the gospels for so long, proponents of this viewpoint insist, we discover a man who spent the majority of his time with the most disreputable elements of his society: prostitutes, tax collectors (whose closest modern parallel might be the Mafia "bag man") and "sinners" (those Jews who failed to keep even the minimal standards of the Law).[4] Not only did Jesus reach out to such people, he relaxed with them, he went to their parties. And contrary to what too many Sunday School lessons and movies of the *King of Kings* ilk have led us to believe, there is no suggestion in the gospels that all, or even most, of these people had sudden conversions to conventional norms of socially respectable behavior the moment Jesus crossed their paths. There are those exceptional narratives in which a remarkable *metanoia* occurs, of course—the story of the tax collector Zaccheus, for example (Luke 19)—but in most cases, nothing of the sort is indicated. What is noted a number of times, however, is that Jesus was constantly criticized by both religious fundamentalists (the Pharisees) and mainstream clergy (the Sadducees) for the company he kept. What those social outcasts who flocked to Jesus experienced was not, in fact, a call to embrace the mainstream, conservative values promoted by the rabbis and the synagogue. What they found in Jesus was an unconditional love that drew them into the mystery of their own preciousness to God and, with it, an empowering respect which assured them in no uncertain terms that the Eternal Reign of God was *theirs*, that they had a place—indeed, a place of honor—at the table of God's grace.

It is in this sense, many holding this view would argue, that it is entirely legitimate to say that "Jesus was queer."[5] Such a—to some—startling affirmation is not primarily a statement about what Jesus' sexual orientation might have been,[6] although there is no particular reason to insist he might not have been homosexual or bisexual. It is, rather, an assertion of the stance Jesus took toward the self-serving moralisms and conventions of his own society—placing himself squarely on the side of the marginalized, the dismissed, the despised, the outsider and the outcast. As Goss writes, "Jesus the queer Christ symbolizes God's solidarity with the sexually oppressed . . . in the midst of their resistance, conflict, and the struggle for justice."[7]

Along with the example of Jesus himself, those elements of the Old Testament tradition which speak particularly to the great themes of liberation and justice—the saga of the Exodus, the story of Esther, the prophets' fiery denunciations of social inequity—can also provide a rich source of moral reflection and encouragement for contemporary Christians struggling against the death-dealing power structures and bigotries of their own day. As the Central American liberation theology of the '70s made clear, as African-American "liberation preachers" of the last hundred years have consistently proclaimed, God is always on the side of the oppressed, the rejected and the persecuted. God is always the ultimate advocate for the victims of discrimination and social opprobrium. Since homophobia is the last socially acceptable prejudice, since discrimination and violence against gay people are the last such abuses to find at least implicit sanction from many Christian churches, it therefore follows inescapably that God is on the side of gay, lesbian, bisexual and transgender people in their struggle for justice, self-acceptance and full equality in the both the church and society at large.

Only when we take to heart the overriding scriptural themes of liberation, justice, and inclusive love—in particular as those themes are exemplified in Jesus—can we begin to grasp what the moral call to the Christian truly entails. We will not find the gracious breadth of that call in dated, culture-bound sexual regulations from the Old Testament, which also makes God the author of genocide (Deut 7:1[a] & 2[b]),[8] mandates trial by ordeal for wives with jealous husbands (Num 5:11–31), and permits obtaining a wife by rape (Deut 22:28) or a concubine by capture in war (Num 31:18; Deut 20:14, 21:10–12). Nor can that call be circumscribed by a few isolated statements from the writings of St. Paul, statements which reflect not the eternal mind of God but simply Paul's own patriarchal attitudes toward women, his unthinking acceptance of the political status quo or his limited understanding (even neurotic negativity) when it came to matters of sex.

Rather, as Roman Catholic Michael Valente writes, in relating the sexual proscriptions of Scripture to their own processes of moral reflection, contemporary Christians must understand that:

> . . . the moral pronouncements found in Scripture are simply the expressions of the author's convictions as to how everyday problems of living must be resolved in accordance with the thrust of the Judaic-Christian ethical message. They cannot be assigned in

themselves—as isolated pronouncements—the absolute value of inerrancy.[9]

In fact, any attempt to "codify an intrinsic objective morality of sexual acts is another example of the self-righteousness which stands as the very antithesis of true Christian morality." In contrast to such self-serving moralism, "Christ's standard of ethical righteousness and love teaches what men—especially when they are in the majority—find most difficult: tolerance. Indeed, where sexuality is concerned—as in other areas of human life—tolerance and vision are perhaps at once the most uniquely Christian, the most self-fulfilling, and the most important aids to authentic spiritual discovery."

If Valente's radical revisionism is disconcerting to more conservative Christian sensibilities, others of this viewpoint are prepared to go even further. Marvin Ellison, Professor of Christian Ethics at Bangor Seminary, contends in a recent work that feminist theologians are right when they argue that biblical texts related to sexuality and gender relationships are flawed not only in specific application but in fundamental motive, since they were written to "serve patriarchal functions."[10] Therefore, "gay people should acknowledge the . . . errors of biblical traditions" and "call [the Bible] to account for its homophobia," recognizing that the legacy of a racist, elitist, patriarchal society (and church) has been spiritually deadly: "control, coercion and rigidity."[11]

This does not mean, however, that gays and lesbians have no alternative but to abandon the Scriptures to the homophobic exegesis of the churches.[12] Rather, they must claim the Bible as their own, deconstructing its power as a tool of oppression by exercise of their own queer hermeneutic. Such a hermeneutic begins, as does feminist liberative exegesis, with a recognition that "[t]o truly understand the Bible is to read it through the eyes of the oppressed, since the God who speaks in the Bible is the God of the oppressed."[13] This means queer Christians must approach the Bible:

> . . . intertextually with their own resistance to homophobic oppression . . . and the truth of their own queer lives. The lives of queer Christians become another text from which they interpret the biblical text. Queer Christians refigure the meaning of the text by interpreting and applying it to their lives . . . Their commitments to their

queer identities, practices, and the struggle for justice become a framework for interpreting a particular biblical text.[14]

When queer Christians do so, Goss concludes, "they transform any particular story into a narrative amplification of their own struggles. They imaginatively release the elements of struggle and resistance within the text into their lives."

When this imaginative release occurs, queer Christians discover that—despite the homophobic, self-protective, exclusionary, negative morality taught by too many of the churches for far too long—the good news proclaimed by Jesus in both word and deed remains. That radical news is: we are each one an image of God, whatever our sexual orientation; the eternal reign of God is truly inclusive, and that inclusivity does not stop short of the non-heterosexual; love and a justice grounded in love are the essence of any authentic moral vision; and we can each risk the freedom of unhampered self-discovery, confident that the God who creates our diversity delights in the uniqueness (including the sexual uniqueness) of each one of her beloved children.

Question 2:

What is the God-given intent or design for human sexuality?

Attempts to determine appropriate expressions of human sexuality on the basis of some normative "design" in creation are mistaken in principle.

If arguments for such a design are based upon theories of "natural law," it must be recognized that this conventional theological construct presumes a "divinely given natural order that is static and unchanging."[15] Yet the natural order is far from static; it is an ongoing process of evolution, adaptation, change. Moreover, as Valente notes, a part of humankind's appointed place within creation is the ability, and indeed the duty under certain circumstances, to subject nature to reason—"Reason therefore liberates man from a so-called 'natural law,' when that law is unreasonable."[16]

While it is true that—for reproductive purposes—the male body "fits" the female and the female the male, this can not be taken as defining the boundaries of all human sexual relationships, since reproduction is only *one* of the "'primary characteristic[s]' of sex." Human sexual expression has capacities far richer than those of the other animals, in which sex is to all intents and purposes limited to reproduction; in human beings, sex can be "sensitive, subtle, and varied, with many ways of one human body touching another human body and so creating love."[17]

If the argument turns from natural law to revelation—in particular to the two creation accounts in Genesis—for its justification of a controlling, God-given "design" for all legitimate human sexual expression, it must be recognized that these poetic stories were composed within the context of a very real social agenda created by the "cultural needs of the monogamous agrarian family unit . . . fear of Canaanite and other apostate idolatrous sexual-religious practices, the primitive reverence for semen, and . . . biological misunderstandings regarding the conception and birth processes."[18]

Traditional arguments from a purportedly divine intent, proponents of this viewpoint charge, are actually little more than self-serving attempts by the heterosexual male majority to justify its continuing dominance over those it marginalizes and oppresses: women and sexual minorities. Given that reality, gay and lesbian people must "claim their authority as moral agents [and] . . . theological subjects . . . on their own terms," just as women and people of color have done before them, recognizing that authentic theological reflection starts "not with revelation" but with "liv[ing] from within ourselves . . . [being] responsible to ourselves in the deepest sense . . . experiencing our experience."[19] As Goss insists:

> [N]o one "not involved" in and committed to the struggle for gay/lesbian liberation can write a gay/lesbian liberation theology. Nor can anyone who is not out as gay/lesbian write a liberation theology. There is no apologizing in an authentic gay/lesbian liberation theology . . . Institutional Christianity has failed to listen to the truth of gay and lesbian lives, the truth of their sexuality, and the truth of their Christian witness.[20]

Since a postulate of a queer liberation theology will be the refusal "to accept a God who is not identified with the liberation goals of its community," the questions such a theology will pose to frame moral discourse must differ radically from those of "homophobic/heterosexist ecclesial power." In its reflection on the meaning of sexuality, a queer liberation theology will look not to teleological paradigms claiming universal, objective applicability. Rather, it will listen to the Spirit speaking through the evolving, expressive truth that wells up out of the queer experience of oppression, out of queer "love-making and justice-doing," a truth which will empower gay and lesbian Christians in their struggle for liberation.

Question 3:

What are the necessary criteria for morally legitimate sexual expression?

Although he is in a committed relationship himself and appears to endorse the importance of monogamy to such unions, Will Leckie summarizes this present viewpoint's understanding of the moral parameters for sexuality succinctly:

> [O]ur morality as sexual creatures, whether we are gay, straight, bi, active, or inactive, is about finding genuine, nonabusive ways of relating to one another, not about what we do with our genitals.[21]

Valente makes much the same point, albeit in considerably less colloquial language:

> The guidelines for . . . sexual activity are . . . very definite, and they are concerned with the preservation of the integrity of the human personality. To engage in sexual activity that would be destructive of one's own or another's personality is ethically wrong and dangerous.[22]

It is important to note that the sort of standard proposed by Leckie and Valente does more than simply affirm that genitalized sexual activity—be it same sex or opposite sex—is morally neutral apart from consideration of its larger context. It also raises the possibility that a sexual act between partners in a heterosexual marriage could be morally objectionable (as in the patriarchal notion of the husband "exercising his conjugal rights" irrespective of his wife's feelings or inclination, for example) while a one-night stand between two men could be morally acceptable if their connection was aimed at mutual satisfaction and there was full acknowledgment of each other as persons.

Anglican priest James E. Cotter, seeking to ground a gay-affirming sexual ethic in some sort of larger moral paradigm, notes that conventional Christian moral reflection regarding sexual acts tends to use a model similar to its treatment of questions about the taking of human life: wrong in general but permitted under a few special circumstances. The moral task for the Christian in such a model, then, becomes determining precisely what those "special circumstances" might be. Rejecting this approach, Cotter suggests:

> We might get a lot further if we compared sex, instead, to eating. Eating is simply a fact of life that in itself is neither right nor wrong . . . Something is out of balance if your behavior is excessive or greedy or compulsive—and also, at the other extreme, [*if*] there is a constant denial, *anorexia nervosa*, and even starvation. But there is a healthy rhythm of fasting and feasting, of abandonment and restraint.[23]

Although Cotter does not take his argument further, it could be noted that eating is susceptible to a wide variety of equally legitimate meanings. A meal can be a banquet, a solemn event of family or community solidarity, drawing together those who share it in connection and celebration. In such instances it can be, in a very real sense, unitive. For the Christian, in the Eucharist, a meal can even be sacred—a medium of divine-human encounter and communion. Yet at other times eating can be a simple matter of satisfying physical hunger. The fact that the act of eating can have, in some circumstances, profound significance does not mean that anything less—a quick snack on the run, a simple meal eaten alone—is somehow "wrong." It is merely a matter of a different but equally legitimate exercise of the same basic biological function.

So it is, Cotter would seem to argue, with sex: there are times when, within the commitment of a deeply shared intimacy, sex can be unitive in the deepest sense; there are times when it can lead to the creation of new life; there are times when it can even be the means of a truly spiritual transcendence. But there are other occasions when a sexual act can simply satisfy a legitimate bodily hunger, providing release for accumulated erotic energy. The "higher" levels of meaning—with sex, just as with eating—in no way invalidate the "lower" levels or make them "sin."

There are, of course, certain moral constraints upon eating just as there are upon sexual activity: one should not steal food, one should not feast lavishly while one's neighbor suffers famine, one should not allow food to become a matter of compulsion or consume so much that eating becomes physically harmful. In other words, the moral constraints upon eating have to do with matters of justice and health. The parallels in sexual ethics are obvious: rape and seduction are prohibited, sexual compulsion should be dealt with, though not so much as a moral issue as a matter of psychological health. In the age of AIDS, "safe sex" would be a necessary moral requirement both in terms of loving respect for one's sexual partner and care for the gift of one's own body.

Furthermore, Christians' call to, as Leckie puts it, "find . . . genuine, nonabusive ways of relating to one another,"[24] would preclude sexual expression based on inequities of power such as those which prevail in most prostitution, in pedophilia, in deliberately objectifying sex which discounts the humanity of the partner—and also in traditional patriarchal marriage.

As for the stress placed by the previous viewpoint on lifelong monogamous commitment, those arguing this present perspective hesitate to dictate any single model as applicable to all people or to all points in any individual's journey. For some, such a commitment may be both possible and desirable. But for others, the reality may be different—just as it has proven to be for more and more heterosexuals, as evidenced by soaring divorce rates.[25] The challenge, Cotter writes, "is to emphasize the quality of a relationship rather than its quantitative length," since there may come a point in any relationship "beyond which the two people can no longer grow together."[26] Indeed, even within the lifespan of a committed relationship, demands for absolute monogamy may be little more than "a cover for feelings of jealousy and possessiveness" and may even represent a spiritually destructive form of idolatry which runs contrary to the Christian warning against "see[ing] another human being as the source of all one's needs." What is more important than objective monogamy, Cotter argues, is "faithfulness"— and, at a level deeper than simple monogamy, "to be 'faithful' is to be 'full of faith,' full of trust, to be willing to let love be vulnerable. Only so can . . . the commitment be creative."

Even Michael Keeling, whose conviction that "long-term—even if not lifelong—relationships are the moral aim" would seem to place him in viewpoint 5 (Affirmation), questions whether sexual acts that take place outside of any particular unitive aim or commitment are "morally wicked." It would seem, on the contrary, that "having no relationships to express, they may not be very much of anything at all."[27]

Marvin Ellison goes further, deriding a "compulsory monogamy" that would "restrict the range and significance of other friendships . . . [and] . . . weaken ties with the larger human community." Christian moral reflection, Ellison argues, should be accepting of unions (gay or straight) which "make room for additional sexual partners," since "the precise requirements of . . . fidelity cannot be determined in advance."[28]

There is, then, considerable difference of opinion within this viewpoint on the matter of monogamy. Whether long-term, exclusive, committed relationships are seen as the ideal, as merely one acceptable option among many, or as a "heterosexist" model inapplicable to the wider potentialities of gay sexuality, however, all holding to this viewpoint would likely agree with Valente when he writes:

> [Homosexuals] should be encouraged to seek relationships that are meaningful and constructive, and that can contribute to the development of their personality as loving.[29]

Question 4:

Is there a "homosexual condition" (orientation) and, if so, what is its cause or origin?

Human beings are richly diverse in their capacity for sexual expression—as is true of every other aspect of their personhood. Many holding this viewpoint, in fact, would assert that everyone is actually bisexual in potential. Indeed, Valente argues, were society not so consumed with establishing boundaries and creating abstract psychosexual definitions in order to suppress the unnerving consciousness of humankind's inherent sexual versatility, our entire notion of sexual orientation might be transformed:

> If society were truly tolerant . . . the effect might be a realization that the division of persons into heterosexuals, homosexuals, and bisexuals is artificial and arbitrary. The division, in fact, is the result of a former worldview that saw the preferences of the apparent majority as the norm for what it means to be human . . . It could thus see deviations as illnesses, perversions, and evils. A new worldview, however, makes it clear that each individual is uniquely capable of turning every interpersonal encounter into something new, something creative.[30]

Others of this viewpoint, however, are more ready to accept as fact what most people perceive to be true about themselves: that, whatever their unconscious, unexpressed erotic potentiality might be, they experience themselves as clearly belonging at one end or the other of the heterosexual-homosexual continuum. When this is the case, one's orientation—gay or straight—should be understood and gratefully received as a positive gift of God. Beyond that, speculation as to "how" one came to be homosexual or heterosexual is pointless.[31]

Question 5:

Can a legitimate moral distinction be made between a homosexual condition (orientation) and homosexual acts?

Given the premises of this viewpoint, such a question is meaningless.[32] Morality is not a matter of, as Leckie puts it, "what we do with our genitals,[33] but of the compassion, caring and practical justice we bring to our dealings with one another. That being the case, a person's sexual orientation—straight, lesbian, gay, bisexual, transgender or "questioning"[34]—is not a moral issue; neither, apart from matters of justice or health, are homosexual acts.

Question 6:

What is the psychological significance of homosexuality?

For the majority of those holding this viewpoint, a gay or lesbian orientation is simply one of the many naturally occurring variations in human psychosexual expression, carrying with it no inherent psychological advantages or disadvantages. For a few on the far left of the viewpoint, a "queer" orientation is felt to be superior to a conventional straight orientation in that the "outsider" perspective it provides opens one more widely to the divergent, multifaceted possibilities of human life, sexual and otherwise.

At least one lesbian theologian, Sally Gearhart, whom Cleaver quotes with approval, argues that homosexual orientation is more psychologically healthy than heterosexual orientation precisely because it is not the result of heterocentrist social conditioning:

> Exclusive heterosexuality has to be understood as a perversion of [*humanity's*] natural state. We very quickly rob infants of their health and wholesomeness. We require them from birth to fall into one of two widely differing and oppositely valued categories: girls and boys. We further require them to obliterate half their loving nature so as to become lovers *only* of a member of the opposite sex

... In this light, it is not the Lesbian or the Gay man who is "unnatural" but rather the heterosexual person ... The motivating energy of the Gay relationship flows ... from inside the persons themselves, from sources that are far more authentic than are responses to external programming.[35]

While not everyone identifying with this present viewpoint would concur with Gearhart's analysis, all would agree that what *is* inherently and universally pathological is homophobia, not only because it leads one to hate other human beings made in the image of God simply on the basis of their being different, but because it requires hatred of that element of one's own being which is, to a greater or lesser extent, consciously or unconsciously, same-sex responsive. Homophobia is also psychologically poisonous in that it is inevitably based in misogyny. As James Cotter puts it:

> The gay woman challenges the notion that women need men to be sexually satisfied ... the "passive" partner in homosexual activity ... simulates the woman physically, for he is the one being penetrated—[*and*] so is called into question the whole image of male superiority.[36]

The gay or lesbian person, confronting both external prejudice and his or her own internalized homophobia, may well have particular psychological work to do in order to achieve full integration and self-acceptance, but that task is not the result of any intrinsic defect in the homosexual orientation itself. Rather, it reflects the destructive impact upon the human spirit of socially sanctioned ignorance and hate.

Question 7:

What is the spiritual significance of homosexuality?

All human sexuality, including homosexuality, is spiritually significant. It provides, by way of powerful physical sensation and sometimes deep emotion, a means of self-discovery, self-revelation and intimate connection. *Eros*, moreover, in many instances, becomes the door not only for *philia* but for *agape*. All that being true, sexuality is also—and here is where it runs into trouble with much traditional Christian thinking—a uniquely potent means of embodiment through which we are brought into particular awareness of ourselves as physical beings.

Conventional Christian attitudes toward sex, advocates for this viewpoint note, have consistently been marked by fear and a pathological rejection of that very thing sexuality reminds us of so forcefully: our physicality. On this point, Cotter writes:

> Behind the traditional Christian fear of homosexuality are other fears, often implied if not directly expressed . . . fears of the flesh (the attitude that only the "soul" matters), of the earthly . . . of the feminine . . . The sexual is held to be so powerful that it must be channeled very narrowly or there will be chaos.[37]

Given these fears, a major element in the church's historic demonization of the homosexual has been the fact that, lacking the procreative justification of heterosexual expression, sex for the homosexual is unabashedly enjoyed for its own sake. In the life of the gay man or lesbian, the physical component of the human person openly stakes a claim for moral parity with the rational and the spiritual.[38]

In the early years of the current reevaluation and debate regarding homosexuality, gay Christian advocates often emphasized the fact that gay and lesbian sexual expression is every bit as open to commitment and unitive meaning, to *philia* and *agape*, as is heterosexual expression. In a sense, this represented an attempt to assure the straight church that for homosexuals—at least for "good homosexuals"—the erotic is just as firmly subordinated to "higher" principles as it is in Christian heterosexuals, even if it conspicuously lacks procreative potential.

More recently, however, gay and lesbian Christian spokespeople have been less reticent about affirming the inherent value of the erotic in its own right, especially as it is expressed in the lives of gay men and women whose discontinuity with straight culture turns specifically upon their divergent erotic focus. Indeed, the Reverend Canon Elizabeth M. C. Kaeton, executive director of Oasis[39] for the Episcopal Diocese of Newark, New Jersey, sees gay and lesbian Christians as having a particular calling in this area. As she proclaimed to members of Integrity, the Episcopalian gay and lesbian caucus, in a July 16, 1997, sermon at an Integrity Eucharist held in conjunction with the church's triennial General Convention in Philadelphia:

> Our special task [*as lesbians and gays*], our specific charism, is to help ourselves and the church reclaim the erotic as a central part of our lives . . . Understanding the erotic is the nursemaid of all our deepest

understanding . . . We know in the deepest places of our knowing that the pathways to our spiritual selves are through our erotic selves. We must chart those paths and make those maps available to the larger church.[40]

Seen in this light, the spiritual significance of homosexuality lies in the fact that it provides the gay or lesbian person the potential of readier and deeper access to the erotic wellsprings of personhood too long ignored and repressed by a sex-phobic church and culture. Whether or not that potentiality is realized in every case, the queer reality of their lives is the very place where gays' and lesbians' particular calling from God is to be found, a calling which is—above all else—a summons to know, receive, give and become that which God is: love. Understood aright, queers' gayness, as Cleaver writes, is truly "the source of our virtues."[41]

Question 8:

Can a homosexual become heterosexual (the question of "cure")?

To propose that a person's fundamental sexual orientation (as opposed to his or her sexual behavior) could be susceptible to change or "adjustment" is absurd on its face, since "sexual orientation pervades and is central to our . . . experience and . . . our sexual identity is at the core of our personhood."[42]

Even if such a change in basic orientation were possible, there would be absolutely no reason for the homosexual to seek it. Our calling as Christians is to receive joyfully all the good gifts God has given (including our sexual orientation) and forge from them a responsible, joyful, life-affirming existence.

Question 9:

What is the moral opinion arrived at, given the responses to Questions 1 through 8?

Sexuality is a natural part of human life and, as such, is subject to precisely the same moral principles as every other part of life: compassion, justice and a liberating confidence in the unlimited love of God. Sexual expression in and of itself is good; therefore one should not approach moral judgment regarding sexual acts from the premise that only particular limiting circumstances can make these acts licit. Rather, one should begin with a positive affirmation of the goodness of sexual expression and then recognize that failures in justice or love can result in misuse of this positive gift in particular instances.

Insofar as a homosexual act between adults is compassionate, responsible, life-affirming and a matter of mutual consent, it is a moral good.

Question 10:

What is the personal call of Christ for the gay man or lesbian?

For those holding this viewpoint, the call of Christ to the gay or lesbian is no different than it is to any human person. Queers must recognize that who they are is precisely who God created them to be. They must claim the gospel mandate of radical opposition to all structures of oppression (including religious structures) and answer the call of Christ the Liberator to new lives built around the embodiment of divine *eros* and the practice of justice. They must reject the homophobia of both culture and church, coming out into their full dignity as children of God and experiencing themselves and their queer sexuality as "graced."[43]

They must be courageous in naming their oppression—heterocentrism and homophobia—and resist that oppression unflinchingly, rejecting the bourgeois church's judgments upon and interpretation of their own life experience.[44] By the way they live and by what they say, queer Christians must proclaim to the homophobic institutional church that God's unlimited love includes gays, lesbians, bisexuals, transgender people and those uncertain of their sexual direction and that God's jubilee justice requires the dismantling of all oppressive and unjust social structures and attitudes.

At the same time, gay and lesbian Christians are called to witness to their own lesbian/gay/bisexual/transgender/questioning community that true Christian faith is not its enemy. Reclaiming the Scriptures, they must affirm that the biblical God "chooses those who have been made to feel powerless or like outcasts" and is "passionately partial" to them in their pain and struggle.[45] Believing that the "risen Jesus stands in solidarity with oppressed gay men and lesbians," they must tell their queer brothers and sisters that "the cross now belongs to us . . . as a symbol of struggle for queer liberation," and that the "promise of Easter" is that "the queer struggle for sexual liberation will triumph." Proclaiming the good news that Jesus the Christ is queer, just as—by the radical solidarity of the incarnation—he is "black . . . female, Asian, African, a South American peasant, Jewish, a transsexual," gay Christians must testify that the "Spirit of the risen Lord is at work within the struggles for gay/lesbian liberation . . . The Spirit is present in gay/lesbian holy anger, their coming out and [*their*] political opposition to institutional and homophobic churches."

Queer Christians are called to stand in solidarity with all other oppressed minorities—women, people of color, immigrants, the poor—and work with them for justice and positive social change, recognizing that all are part of what is ultimately a single struggle to bring into being within history the justice, love and peace of the Eternal Reign of God, a Reign which "is identifiable with the human practice of social justice, the struggle for liberation and freedom." The most immediate and effective path toward actualizing such solidarity, according to Goss, is becoming part of or creating a "queer Christian base community"[46] that will "break the grip that homophobia/heterosexism exercises upon the discourse and practice of the churches," create a nonhierarchical "discipleship of equals" (including the full inclusion of women), pool its economic resources for service to the poor (in particular "those who have been made poor by the ravages of HIV infection"), and engage in "direct actions that transgress the network of homophobic power relations" in church and society (just as Jesus "acted up" by overturning the money changers' tables and shutting down the business of the Temple). Such a queer base community will be "a place where Christians can celebrate the joy of being lesbians and gay men." It will be a "foretaste of liberation, where the diversity of God's reign is respected and celebrated."

Question 11:
What is the pastoral call of Christ to the church on the issue?

As Christ's continuing presence on earth, the church should do exactly what Jesus did: welcome and affirm all those whom society rejects, standing with them in their marginalization, serving their needs and advocating on their behalf, thereby bringing them into the liberating realization of their infinite preciousness to their Creator.

As the family of God, the church should become a place of inclusive, accepting, affirming love for all those who feel stigmatized and excluded by bourgeois society. As a community of those who follow the prophetic Christ, it should be in the vanguard of efforts to bring full justice and social inclusion to all minorities whose basic humanity is denied in principle or in practice by mainstream society. In those instances where the church is ready to listen to the prophetic voices of gay and lesbian Christians, every level of its ministry should be open to them, whether or not they are celibate, whether or not they are in committed relationships.

The bottom line for a church "that is increasingly losing the battle of relevancy," argues Episcopal priest Malcolm Boyd,[47] is simply this:

> Does it love unconditionally? How *much* does it love? Does it love *enough* to heal the wounds of centuries of persecution, torture and debasement? Does it love *enough* to ask for *forgiveness* for things done and left undone?[48]

If it does not, Boyd clearly implies, the church not only will fail in its calling to gays and lesbians, it will fail to be *itself*—it will fail to live out its meaning and mission as the Body of Christ the Liberator.

Question 12:

What is the political call of Christ to society on the issue?

Christ stands against the received pieties of conventional thinking today just as he did when he lived and ministered in Palestine two thousand years ago. Christ calls every society and every individual to practice the inclusive love of God and work to establish the justice of God's Eternal Reign.

Recognizing that it is morally unacceptable for anyone to be limited in fulfilling his or her God-given personhood in a free, self-determining, open and creatively participatory life, government should revoke all statutory penalties for private sexual acts between consenting adults and end all discrimination in law based on sexual orientation. Moreover, positive steps should be taken to ensure the full acceptance and participation of the L/G/B/T/Q community at every level of society. Such steps would include legal recognition of lesbian and gay relationships, provision of full health and other benefits to gay and lesbian partners, affirmative action to open employment opportunities (in particular in the public sector) to gay and lesbian people, and broad-based educational efforts to promote tolerance, diversity and respect for alternative lifestyles.

Representative Denominations and Para-Church Groups

As noted earlier, thirty years ago viewpoint 4 (Pastoral Accommodation) would have been considered the vanguard of reformative thinking in the church when it came to homosexuality—at least by liberal Christians open to such reconsideration. Within a decade, however, that perspective had been eclipsed by the more sweeping revisionism of viewpoint 5 (Affirmation), with certain radical theologians already beginning to press still further ahead toward this present viewpoint. Given a perhaps inevitable momentum toward increasingly unapologetic theological justification for gay Christian claims once these claims were allowed open discussion (along with a growing and ever more confident gay presence in both society and the church), and inspired by the widespread embrace among liberal Christians of liberation theology and the deconstructionist hermeneutic of radical Christian feminism, liberal theologians and ethicists advancing this present viewpoint have now clearly taken the lead in "progressive" Christian opinion. As a consequence, on the campuses of the mainline denominations' seminaries, within the more radical wings of these churches' lesbian and gay caucuses, in scholarly periodicals and among liberal Christian academics teaching and publishing in theology and ethics, this viewpoint is increasingly staking a claim to being the received wisdom, no longer subject to debate as to its basic assumptions.

The only major Christian body publicly identifying with this viewpoint is the Universal Fellowship of Metropolitan Community Churches (MCC).[49] Even within MCC, however, the ascendancy of this viewpoint is not entirely complete, with certain pastors and congregations reflecting a more conservative perspective akin to that outlined in the previous chapter. Among lesser-known groups, a relatively recent Episcopalian offshoot, the Evangelical Anglican Church in America (EACA)—founded in part in reaction to the slow pace of change in the Episcopal church on matters of concern to gays and lesbians—would also align itself with this viewpoint.[50]

Cross-Perspective Critique

For critics on the far right, this viewpoint is the logical conclusion of a degenerative process that begins with any deviation from that absolute condemnation which they hold to be the clear scriptural standard when it comes to homosexuality.

First, in the name of a well-meant but misguided "compassion," the deliberately chosen and culpable nature of homosexual temptation is blurred by extra-biblical notions of an unchosen homosexual "orientation" and the possibility of genuine "love" (as opposed to lust) between same-sex partners. Then the authoritative judgment of Scripture is compromised with the relativizing sophistry of biblical criticism. Add to these errors specious arguments regarding the "lesser of two evils" and "necessary" moral compromise and the next logical step, given the natural tendency of fallen human beings to defy their Creator, is open rebellion against God and God's will as revealed in Scripture.

It is precisely this spirit of rebellion which is at work here, it is argued. In order to justify their repudiation of God's mandated order for human sexuality, homosexuals and their liberal advocates reject the irrefutable evidence of nature and the self-evident biological complementarity reflected in their own bodies. They turn on the Scriptures with undisguised contempt, presuming to judge the Word of God from a position of moral superiority while rebuffing revelation as a source of moral direction in favor of their own subjective opinions and feelings. Setting themselves up in God's place as moral arbiters, they replicate the original sin of our first parents—presuming to judge for themselves what is good and what is evil. Denying God his sovereign rights over his own creation, they replace the order that he established and pronounced good with moral and spiritual chaos. The ultimate end of such thinking is made strikingly evident in statements such as those of lesbian "theologian" Sally Gearhart,[51] who—not content with claiming moral parity for homosexuality—argues its superiority to "unwholesome," socially engineered heterosexuality. Having, as Paul puts it, "exchanged the truth . . . for a lie" (Rom 1:25), those holding this view celebrate as "liberation" what is in reality their souls' deadly bondage to sin.

Moderate conservatives, while taking a somewhat less confrontational tone, question this viewpoint's unabashed assertion that a part of our task as human beings is determining for ourselves what is right for us, what is wrong. The truth is, these conservatives insist, we human beings are simply not up to the heady task radical theological thinking would assign to us: we are creatures, after all, of limited insight and understanding, bound by own our confusions, inchoate desires and sinfulness. When we attempt to claim for ourselves the prerogatives of God, we cannot help but botch the job. Such failure is inevitable precisely because we are *not* God (although we are fashioned in God's image, it is true). Those who argue that we must "claim [*our*] authority as morals agents . . . on [*our*] own terms"[52] would do well, it is suggested, to consider the words given to Yahweh by the anonymous author of Job:

> Where were you when I laid the foundations of the earth? . . . Who determined its measurements . . . who stretched the line upon it? . . . [W]ho laid its cornerstone when the morning stars sang together and all the heavenly beings shouted for joy? (Job 38:4–7 [*edited*])

The notion that "theological reflection begins not with revelation"[53] but with our own experience is contrary to fundamental premises of the Judeo-Christian understanding of reality, critics charge. Christian faith is incoherent apart from a conviction that God speaks to humankind both through word and act, that we are not left to fend for ourselves in a silent universe, that Holy Love is always reaching out to us, and that part of that loving address takes the form of divine Law, warning us against those things which can destroy the integrity and wholeness of our souls. The end result of theology which begins with our own experience, it is argued, is a God we create rather than the God who created us, as is evidenced by Goss's unapologetic refusal "to accept a God who is not identified with the . . . goals of [*the queer*] community."[54]

Moderate conservative critics also question this viewpoint's appropriation of methodological models drawn from liberation theology, in particular notions of salvation being "collective" and sociopolitical rather than ultimately individual, an intimate relationship between each human soul in its uniqueness and the God who made it. True, this relationship immediately brings one into the community of faith and is certainly intended to have consequences in the wider collective arena as well. True as well, that certain Old Testament passages ascribe a communal quality to God's covenant relationship with his people (both in terms of collective guilt and collective redemption). Nonetheless, the clear thrust of New Testament teaching is that the corporate aspect of salvation—the fact that one is reborn by faith and baptism into what recent Roman Catholic teaching often terms the "People of God"—is a consequence of personal repentance and spiritual rebirth.

Faulted as well is the enormous spiritual consequence proponents of this viewpoint tend to give to *eros*, as in, for example, Elizabeth Kaeton's statement at the Integrity Eucharist that . . . "the pathways to our spiritual selves are through our erotic selves."[55] While sexuality is certainly a powerful and significant element of human personhood, such extravagant claims, critics contend, place far too heavy a burden on *eros* and run the risk that sex—as it did for the ancient devotees of Astarte, Ishtar and the Great Mother—will become our god (or perhaps more accurately, our goddess).

Interestingly enough, some of the most sustained and thoughtful criticism of this present viewpoint has come not from the right or middle points on the spectrum but from observers identified with viewpoint 5 (Affirmation). Ralph Blair, of Evangelicals Concerned, has for years spoken and written extensively against what he considers the subjectivism, reductionism and moral permissiveness of the "new gay theology." In his review of Marvin Ellison's *Erotic Justice*,[56] for example, Blair writes scathingly of the fact that Ellison, positing all moral authority in himself, "begins with his own selective experience, self-interpreted and affirmed within the closed circle of like-minded seminary votaries." He also criticizes Ellison's "highly romanticized" picture of "'gay, lesbian, bisexual, and transgender people of color,'" charging Ellison's work with "stereotyping . . . exaggeration, selective illustration, tired tautology and jargonizing" and "set[*ting*] up one [*conservative*] straw man after another."

Bruce Bawer has been a particularly recognized and—those who share his viewpoint would contend—effective voice of opposition to the self-validating verities of the "gay subculture," including upon occasion those of its Christian contingent. Bawer rejects in the strongest terms possible the "narrow, sex-obsessed image of gay life" that the gay "community" too often presents to the wider culture as the only reality of gay experience.[57] In fact, Bawer insists:

> The gay subculture . . . disdains the notion of individual identity and takes a reductive, narrowly deterministic view of homosexuality . . . If the subculture has increasingly embraced the word "queer" in recent years, it is because the word is better than "homosexual" or "gay" at suggesting the subculture's notion of homosexuality as something that makes one essentially different, eternally the Other.[58]

Furthermore, as a philosophical conservative, Bawer rejects the automatic association of concern for gay rights with a radical political agenda (Cleaver's "solidarity with other oppressed peoples"),[59] a linkage which is dear to the hearts of many in the forefront of gay Christian advocacy. As he writes:

> Even as [*gay community spokespeople*] talk about promoting inclusiveness, they assume an exclusionary and antagonistic posture. They tie gay rights to other issues to which it has no natural relation . . . They suggest an essential connection between homosexuality and radical politics: there is no such essential connection.[60]

Bawer's criticism is not limited to secular issues. His critique of many of those writing, teaching and preaching from this current perspective serves as a fitting final word from the viewpoint nearest to it in conviction and sympathy:

> Clergymen who condemn homosexuality often argue that those who counsel acceptance of it have, in doing so, espoused trendy, secular, and relativistic notions of morality. Defenders of homosexuality are charged with having embraced the Now rather than the Eternal, with having chosen cheap gratification over costly grace. In many instances, this is indeed the case . . . [S]ome Christians frame the question in secular terms and discuss it in the vapid, fuzzy language of post-1960s leftism, speaking of sexual freedom and the right of choice. In taking this approach, they do credit neither to their

church nor to their cause. For these political categories are without spiritual meaning. As Americans we enjoy considerable temporal freedom; but those of us who are Christians believe that our only [*true*] freedom is in Christ.

The Viewpoint Responds

Contrary to charges made by conservatives, it is not gay liberation theology which misunderstands or misrepresents the message of the Scriptures. It is the individualistic, pietistic, homophobic, bourgeois "Christianity" being peddled by the churches which represents a bald-faced repudiation of the liberating call of Jesus. As Richard Cleaver writes, in what no doubt seems to critics a startling appropriation of a text often used by conservatives against those proposing liberalization of the church's teaching on homosexuality, "The church has allowed itself to subordinate the commandment of love to the demands of heterosexist culture, defying Paul's injunction 'Do not be conformed to this world, but be transformed by the renewing of your minds' (Rom 12:2)."[6]

Defenders of the church's traditional negative moral judgment on homosexuality criticize the self-serving "subjectivity" of gay liberation theological analysis. But there is, in fact, no such thing as "objective" theology. Rather, the creators and guardians of the church's moral orthodoxy have their own subjective agenda, speaking as they do for the vested interests of those "who have power that they would prefer to enjoy unmolested." But the biblical message from Exodus to Calvary again and again makes the point that legitimate theology is theology birthed in the subjective pain and travail of God's people in their oppression; it is theology forged in their struggle not only to make sense out of their condition, but to change that condition to something more closely resembling the justice of God's Eternal Reign. As gays and lesbians rediscover that scriptural message of struggle and hope, they must dare to claim it for themselves, interpreting the archetypal narratives so as to reveal the transcendent meaning of their own parallel stories. When they do so, they will discover, as Goss writes, that God is the "coempowering ground of their erotic practice and spirituality. God is in the midst of their love-making and their justice struggles . . . God is there in resistance to and protest against homophobic oppression."[62]

In this deeply practical, absolutely essential work of "doing theology" on their own behalf, lesbians and gays are in fact not laboring for themselves alone. Since the church has for so long conformed itself to this world not only by its failure to work for the liberation of lesbians and gay men but by its "consenting to become an accomplice . . . in repressing [that liberation],"[63] the church, "if it hopes to recover its prophetic role, needs lesbians and gay men, not the other way around." Indeed, the church, if it is to be the church that lives and serves in fellowship with the Spirit of Jesus, dare not ignore the gifts lesbian and gay people bring to the table of grace, gifts that exist not in spite of their gayness but which are, in fact, "the fruit of our difference." Perhaps the first fruit of that difference is the radical vision of gospel living offered by gay liberation theology, a vision that is not just for lesbians and gays, but rather represents the call of Christ the Liberator to the whole church. If the church dares to answer that call, it would become once again a revolutionary force for the justice of the Reign of God, a challenging expression of the shocking inclusivity of the Messianic banquet. Such radical faithfulness might even lead to Christians once again being criticized—as were the earliest apostles—for "turning the world upside down." (Acts 17:6)

It is no accident, proponents of this viewpoint insist, that homophobia finds its last and most congenial home in the churches. Nor is it surprising that homophobic arguments so often claim the sanction of venerable religious conviction. Bourgeois Christianity requires the alienation and consequent oppression of queer people. Queers serve as a primary exemplar of the us/them, insider/outsider, clean/unclean system of categorization that undergirds the entire system of privilege and power that this religious system exists to maintain and serve. For the straight, homophobic church, queers *must* remain exiled from the company of "respectable people," must be shut out of the community of "good Christians." Because as soon as the table of God's jubilee grace is expanded to the universal dimensions expressed and pro-claimed by Jesus—who talked theology with a sexually unconven-tional, heretical Samaritan woman and sat down and broke bread in the house of Zaccheus, a socially outcast, tax collecting swindler—then the fact that divine love is fundamentally amoral, unabashedly promiscuous in its scope, falling like rain upon the just and the unjust alike (Matt 5:45), will become inescapable. Then that love which, as Carter Heyward points out, is justice,[64] will begin to undo all the systems of oppression and exploitation which presently govern the earth.

Therefore, as Richard Cleaver puts it, if the liberating good news announced by Jesus is "[t]o reach those for whom the 'plain meaning of God's word' is hatred of homosexuality," gay and lesbian theologians must—by their words and by their *praxis* (their authentic living, their "works")—proclaim "an equally direct reading of the 'plain meaning' of the gospel of love."[65] This gospel of love which is justice is what gay liberation theology is all about; it is what the Good News is all about. Anything less is just more of the same old bad news that has kept organized religion in business since the dawn of time.

AFTERWORD

It has not been my intention in writing this book to break new scholarly ground. I lack the necessary academic training and credentials for such a task. Nor have I sought to arrive at some innovative theological insight regarding Christianity and homosexuality. If the Spirit is to bring any such fresh insight to the church, the Spirit will need to do so through Christians wiser and holier than I. My goal, as a layman with a particular interest in the subject, has been more limited: to synthesize and popularize the extensive scholarly and theological work that has been done on the question of Christian faith and the homosexual person and to render the complexity and breadth of that material accessible to others who, for pastoral or personal reasons, seek to move beyond polemics and absolutist pronouncements to a thoughtful consideration of the scope of Christian thinking on this issue.

To acknowledge these facts is not to apologize, either for my status as an amateur (in the truest sense of that term—one who works out of passion for the subject) or for my relatively modest goal. I believe it is imperative that Christian laymen and laywomen begin to accept responsibility for thinking theologically about the major issues affecting their lives—for "doing theology" as currently popular usage has it. If we are to grow into our full stature in Christ, we laity cannot leave serious moral reflection to the clergy or professional scholars as some sort of academic specialty. Nor should we be content with simply parroting a reductionist précis of whatever theological opinion is the received wisdom in our particular faith community. I do not mean to imply that well-meaning, assertive ignorance should enjoy parity with careful scholarship and informed analysis in Christian debate. I would, however, claim a place in the church's ongoing moral and theological deliberation for nonspecialists willing to do the work necessary for informed participation. If this book provides a resource for such grounded lay involvement in current Christian discussions regarding homosexuality, it will have gone a long way toward fulfilling its purpose.

That homosexuality is a profoundly immediate and personal issue for countless Christians today goes without saying. These Christians are gay or lesbian. Or their son is gay, or their daughter is a lesbian. Or one of their parents is gay. Or a beloved sibling, aunt, uncle, grandchild or friend is homosexual. (I am one of these people. What first led me to reading and reflection on the matter of Christianity and homosexuality—and eventually to writing this book—was the question of how I was to understand and live my own life as a Christian and a gay man.) These Christians, I am convinced, are not helped by simplistic answers—whether the content of those answers is liberal or conservative. They are not well served by the tendency of advocates at all points along the spectrum of opinion to ignore both the weaknesses of their own viewpoint and the strengths of other perspectives. Absolutist proof texting from the right no more constitutes a legitimate response to the pastoral need of these seeking Christians than does uncritical acceptance of the secular culture's truisms by the left. Neither polemical mischaracterizations of disputed viewpoints nor ad hominem attacks will afford these Christians the appropriate theological context for serious moral discernment.

It may be in some sense comforting for gay and lesbian critics of the ex-gay movement to assume that all ex-gays are hypocrites living in "denial," but such an assumption ignores the far more nuanced understanding of healing that ex-gays bring to their own experience. It is no doubt satisfying on a certain level for gay liberation advocates to label all Christians who disagree with them as "homophobic," but such a charge disallows the clear evidence of Christian compassion and intellectual integrity on the part of many conservatives whose convictions are based not upon fear and loathing of homosexuals but upon their scriptural hermeneutic and their understanding of biblical inspiration. Similarly, evangelicals' laudable desire to offer "hope" to the homosexual may explain their uncritical acceptance of ex-gay claims, but such good intentions do not excuse consistent refusal on the part of the movement's supporters to acknowledge the realities of ex-gay recidivism or the evidence of significant psychological and spiritual damage resulting from involvement in such ministries in a number of cases.

What traditional Catholic moral theology terms "invincible ignorance" (a willed refusal to know) is not limited to any one sector of the spectrum of Christian opinion on homosexuality. Andrew Sullivan writes[1] of going into a gay and lesbian bookstore to find a particular text written from a conservative perspective. After scrolling down the appropriate screen on the store's computer, the clerk pointed to a single word after the title Sullivan had requested: "Bad." The store would not stock or order the book. An anonymous reader's report to a publisher on my own manuscript (clearly written from a conservative perspective), while admitting that one of the scholars whose work I cite has the necessary "credentials as a theologian," added that "[he] is also a homosexual with a distinct interest at stake in exegeting Scripture to align with his lifestyle" and argued that I should specifically identify as homosexual every gay or lesbian scholar or writer I quote since that fact constitutes prima facie evidence of unreliability.

Clearly, I would not have written this present book unless I believed that there are men and women of integrity, intellectual honesty and genuine Christian faith advancing each of the viewpoints surveyed. Nor would I have taken the approach I have apart from a conviction that—if we are to love God with our "whole mind" as we approach difficult moral issues—we have an obligation to expose ourselves to and attempt to understand viewpoints which are uncongenial, even painful to us.

A number of early readers of this book in manuscript form felt I should conclude with a statement of which of the viewpoints is "right," or at least which I myself find most persuasive. Some encouraged this because they were certain I agreed with them, others because they were certain I did not and wanted my bias exposed. I remain convinced that such a verdict would not only be counterproductive in terms of my intentions for this work, it would be superfluous. Why should my judgment carry more weight than that of the many advocates of the various viewpoints I have quoted?

If I respectfully decline to pass judgment as to which of the views considered best articulates an authentic Christian perspective on homosexuality, however, then what more is there to say? Perhaps only this: having considered the arguments, the opinions, the exegesis, the interpretive paradigms, we must look beyond all such information to the trajectory of grace in individual lives. We must do this not to justify our own choices and beliefs but rather to *challenge* our own tendency to facile judgment of those with whom we disagree. Liberals must begin to acknowledge that, even if ex-gays or those who choose a life of sexual abstinence out of Christian conviction are (from the liberal perspective) mistaken in their use and exegesis of Scripture or their psychological understanding of the etiology and nature of homosexuality, the willingness of these Christians to enter into a lifelong and often painful struggle for the sake of what they perceive to be faithfulness to the call of God is not to be lightly dismissed or scorned. Indeed, such costly faithfulness (whatever one concludes about its specifics) sets an extraordinarily high standard in terms of intention which many of more liberal persuasion may well find challenging to the manner in which they go about making their own moral choices. Conservatives, on the other hand, need to move beyond superficial assessments of "the homosexual lifestyle" and begin seriously and empathically exploring the reality of gay and lesbian Christians' lives, considering whether the fruits of authentic discipleship are in evidence and affirming what they discover in those lives which reflects the Spirit of Christ.

Conservatives would do well to remind themselves that the ultimate purpose of our creation is neither the perpetuation of the species nor the preservation of the heterosexual family unit. Liberals, on the other hand, should remember that sexual and psychological fulfillment on our own terms are not the be all and end all of human existence either. These are good things, all of them—family, the bearing of children, fulfillment. Yet good as they are, each of these gifts is finally a means to something far better: our salvation, the process of being made fit for citizenship in the Eternal Reign of God. If, in our thinking about homosexuality (or any other moral issue), we fail to work out our conclusions in light of that overriding intention for our existence, then—wherever those conclusions may fall on the spectrum of conviction—they will come short of the glory of God's loving purpose for us.

APPENDIX

GENERALLY CITED BIBLICAL TEXTS

T he scriptural passages that follow are those most often cited in discussions of a Christian perspective on homosexuality.[1] As has already been made clear, it is a matter of dispute whether several of them in fact refer to homosexuality in the contemporary sense of the word at all.

Since exegesis of these texts tends to fall in one of two distinct directions—"conservative" or "liberal"—the interpretation held by any specific viewpoint is not noted, except where there is a particular reason for doing so.

In general, those who would identify with any of the first three viewpoints (Condemnation, A Promise of Healing, or A Call to Costly Discipleship) share the conservative viewpoint on these citations. Those holding to viewpoint 4 (Accommodation) also accept a relatively conservative interpretation of the passages, although their ethical paradigm allows for a somewhat more flexible application of the biblical witness when it comes to specific cases. The liberal interpretation of these texts is argued by those espousing viewpoints 5 (Affirmation) and 6 (Liberation).

The Creation Accounts

Gen 1:26(a), 27–28(a)

Then God said, "Let us make humankind in our image, according to our likeness . . .

> So God created humankind in his image,
> in the image of God he created them;
> male and female he created them.

God blessed them, and God said to them, "Be fruitful and multiply, and fill the earth and subdue it . . ."

Gen 2:18, 21–24

Then the Lord God said, "It is not good that the man should be alone; I will make him a helper as his partner." . . . So the Lord God caused a deep sleep to fall upon the man, and he slept; then he took one of his ribs and closed up its place with flesh. And the rib which the Lord God had taken from the man he made into a woman and brought her to the man. Then the man said,

> "This at last is bone of my bones
> and flesh of my flesh;
> this one shall be called Woman,
> for out of Man this one was taken."

Therefore a man leaves his father and his mother and clings to his wife, and they become one flesh. And the man and his wife were both naked, and were not ashamed.

For conservatives, these two texts establish the logical framework in which the later biblical condemnations of homosexual activity are to be understood. God's created order is heterosexual. Deviation from that created order is therefore a fundamental violation of the divine intent for sexuality. Indeed, it is often argued from the conservative side that these two affirmative texts would be sufficient to condemn all homosexual acts, even if there were no specific prohibitions of such acts elsewhere in Scripture.

Since the publication of Karl Barth's *Church Dogmatics* (Vol. III: "The Doctrine of Creation," Pt. 4)[2] in 1961, a growing number of conservatives have followed the neoorthodox giant's lead in taking the Genesis 1 text to indicate that gender differentiation or "complementarity" is not only a given of the created order but a reflection of an uncreated principle within the divine nature itself, and thus an integral component of the "image of God" in human beings. Given this understanding, homosexual acts and inclination are perceived to be not only contrary to the natural order but destructive of the divine image as well and, therefore, a significant degrading of an individual's fundamental humanity.

Liberals, on the other hand, do not believe that these passages should be taken as definitive for every possible human relationship. As Peter Gomes writes in *The Good Book*:[3] "The creation story in Genesis does not pretend to be a history of anthropology . . . It does not mention the single state, and yet we know that singleness is not condemned, and that in certain religious circumstances it is held in very high esteem." To regard the poetic, folkloric creation material in Genesis as "excluding everything it does not mention," Gomes continues, "is to place too great a burden on the text and its writers."

The Story of Sodom

Gen 18:20–21; 19:1–2(a), 4–13, 24–25

Then the Lord said, "How great is the outcry against Sodom and Gomorrah and how very grave is their sin! I must go down to see whether they have done altogether according to the outcry that has come to me; and if not, I will know." . . . The two angels came to Sodom in the evening; and Lot was sitting in the gateway of Sodom. When Lot saw them, he rose to meet them, and bowed down with his face to the ground. He said, "Please, my lords, turn aside to your servant's house and spend the night . . ." But before they lay down, the men of the city, the men of Sodom, both young and old, all the people to the last man, surrounded the house; and they called to Lot, "Where are the men who came to you tonight? Bring them out to us, so that we may know them." Lot went out of the door to the men, shut the door after him, and said, "I beg you, my brothers, do not act so wickedly. Look, I have two daughters who have not known a man; let me bring them out to you, and do to them as you please; only do nothing to these men, for they have come under the shelter of my roof." But they replied, "Stand back!" And they said, "This fellow came here as an alien, and he would play the judge! Now we will deal worse with you than with them." Then they pressed hard against the man Lot, and drew near the door to break it down. But the men inside reached out their hands and brought Lot into the house to them, and shut the door. And they struck with blindness the men who were at the door of the house, both small and great, so that they were unable to find the door . . . Then the Lord rained on Sodom and Gomorrah sulfur and fire from the Lord out of heaven; and he overthrew those cities, and all the Plain, and all the inhabitants of the cities, and what grew on the ground.

On the far right, this infamous story is understood to demonstrate incontrovertibly the seriousness of homosexual sin: sufficiently unique in its wickedness to provoke an "outcry" to God, by its very nature given to predatory violence, and provoking divine judgment of the most cataclysmic variety. More moderate conservatives acknowledge that, strictly speaking, the Sodomites' sin against Lot's angelic visitors is not homosexuality, per se, but rather attempted homosexual rape, but many would contend that the larger context of the story still portrays homosexual desire in a far from favorable light.

Liberals, following the extensive treatment of the subject in Derrick Sherwin Bailey's *Homosexuality and the Western Christian Tradition*,[4] reject this traditional reading. Sodom's sin, they contend, even if it incidentally involved possible gang rape, had more to do with violations of primitive codes of hospitality than it did with sex. In support of this interpretation they note the potentially ambiguous language used in the passage regarding the Sodomites' intentions, the contextual significance of Lot—a foreigner himself—receiving a night visit from two potentially hostile strangers, and the fact that throughout the rest of Scripture, including a reference by Jesus himself (Matt 10:15, with a parallel in Luke 10:12), the sin of Sodom is described as having to do with social injustice and inhospitality to strangers.

The Holiness Code

Lev 18:22

You shall not lie with a male as with a woman; it is an abomination.

Lev 20:13

If a man lies with a male as with a woman, both of them have committed an abomination; they shall be put to death, their blood is upon them.

Conservatives understand these Levitical prohibitions to represent a universally binding statement of the judgment of God upon male homosexual acts, although only those on the far right consider the capital penalty to be applicable today. The reference to such acts being an "abomination" is held to underscore their particular gravity.

Liberals counter that, like much else in the Levitical Holiness Code (the ban on sex during a woman's menstruation, for example), these regulations are inapplicable to Christians living not under the Law but by grace. Indeed, viewed in their historical context, these two brief statutes are clearly culturally limited, it is held: they assume that new life is transmitted whole in male semen (the "waste" of which is thus seen as tantamount to murder), they reflect a necessary nomadic Hebrew emphasis on fecundity, and—in particular—they understand (and therefore condemn) homosexual acts between males as cultic expressions of idolatrous non-Hebrew worship. This latter point is proved, it is argued, by the description of these acts as an "abomination" (to‘ebah), which is a quasi-technical term denoting acts (or things) associated with idolatry.

L. William Countryman[5] argues that the Levitical prohibitions are part of Jewish purity law which the apostolic church rescinded in its entirety for Gentile converts.

Paul's "Argument from Nature"

Rom 1:18–21(a), 24–28

For the wrath of God is revealed from heaven against all ungodliness and wickedness of those who by their wickedness suppress the truth. For what can be known about God is plain to them, because God has shown it to them. Ever since the creation of the world his eternal power and divine nature, invisible though they are, have been understood and seen through the things he has made. So they are without excuse; for though they knew God, they did not honor him as God or give thanks to him . . . Therefore God gave them up in the lusts of their hearts to impurity, to the degrading of their bodies among themselves, because they exchanged the truth about God for a lie and worshiped and served the creature rather than the Creator, who is blessed forever! Amen.

For this reason God gave them up to degrading passions. Their women exchanged natural intercourse for unnatural [*literally, "for that which is against nature"*], and in the same way also the men, giving up natural intercourse with women, were consumed with passion for one another. Men committed shameless acts with men and received in their own persons the due penalty for their error.

Conservatives see a direct link between Paul's discussion in this passage and the first chapters of Genesis, in that what is "against nature" about homosexual acts, whether on the part of men or women, is the fact that they violate the created order. Furthermore, the parallel Paul makes between rejection of the worship of the true God and turning away from "natural" sexual expression to "unnatural" makes it clear that homosexuality is always and in every conceivable context sinful, just as the refusal to acknowledge the God who self-reveals through creation is always sinful.

In *The Ethics of Sex*,[6] Helmut Thielicke, articulating the underlying rationale of the viewpoint of Pastoral Accommodation (whether or not he ultimately espouses that view's conclusions), accepts the conservative interpretation of this text, but qualifies that acceptance by noting that the matter of homosexuality is merely an illustrative reference within Paul's larger argument, not the point of the passage. Given this subordinate theological emphasis, he contends, we have a "certain freedom to rethink the subject."

On the liberal side, the contemporary applicability of this passage is rejected on a number of grounds: the explicit link between homosexual acts and idolatry renders the passage irrelevant to the question of Christian gays and lesbians who are not idolaters; the emphasis on the lustful nature of the sexual relations described eliminates loving, consensual relationships from consideration; Paul's use of "nature" in this and other passages cannot support the traditional link to an overriding natural order of creation; and, most importantly, the very logic of Paul's argument indicates that he has in mind homosexual acts by people he at least presumes to be heterosexual, which means the passage cannot speak to the situation of people who are homosexual in orientation. Furthermore, since Paul could not have known what we now know to be true about the existence of an unchosen, immutable homosexual orientation, even if he intended to condemn all homosexual acts, we must respectfully reject his ignorance on this point and admit that he was wrong.

Paul's ΜΑΛΑΚΟΙ and ΑΡΣΕΝΟΚΟΙΤΑΙ

1 Cor 6:9–11

Do you not know that wrongdoers will not inherit the kingdom of God? Do not be deceived! Fornicators, idolaters, adulterers, μαλακοί (*malakoí*), ἀρσενοκοῖται (*arsenokóitai*), thieves, the greedy, drunkards, revilers, robbers—none of these will inherit the kingdom of God. And this is what some of you used to be. But you were washed, you were sanctified, you were justified in the name of the Lord Jesus Christ and in the Spirit of God.

1 Tim 1:9–10(a)

. . . the law is laid down not for the innocent but for the lawless and disobedient, for the godless and sinful, for the unholy and profane, for those who kill their father or mother, for murderers, fornicators, ἀρσενοκοίταις . . .

The interpretation of these two disputed terms is debated. Conservatives, following popular readings of the older translations, have tended toward the view that whatever μαλακοî and ἀρσενοκοîται might specifically mean separately, together they are best understood as referring to all males who engage in homosexual acts, whatever the context, or, more specifically, the passive and active partners in such acts. Such thinking was presumably the basis of the Revised Standard Version's lumping together of both terms under the single English word "homosexuals."

The liberal viewpoint is that these two words have a considerably more specific and limited meaning. Μαλακοî, according to this point of view, might best be rendered "hedonists" or "sybarites" in contemporary parlance, while ἀρσενοκοîται[ς] should probably be understood as "male prostitute" or "hustler." Robin Scroggs, in his *The New Testament and Homosexuality*, argues that the two words refer to effeminate, aging boy prostitutes and their older customers respectively. In any case, neither passage, it is held, can be taken to condemn responsible, caring, committed relationships between gay and lesbian people today.

Many conservatives cite the conclusion of the Corinthian passage—"And this is what some of you used to be. But you were washed, you were sanctified, you were justified in the name of the Lord Jesus Christ and in the Spirit of God" (verse 11)—as explicit biblical evidence that healing is the Christian answer for homosexuality.

SELECTED ANNOTATED BIBLIOGRAPHY

Given the extent of publication in the area of Christianity and homosexuality over the past thirty years, the following list is of necessity extremely selective. The books included were chosen in part on the basis of how representative any given work is of a particular viewpoint within the church. An additional consideration was the wide readership and influence of certain titles.

It will be noted that, with the possible exception of Andrew Comiskey's *Pursuing Sexual Wholeness*, I have favored theological, theoretical works over biographies (hence the exclusion, for example, of the Reverend Troy Perry's *The Lord Is My Shepherd and He Knows I'm Gay*, the Reverend Mel White's *Stranger at the Gate: To Be Gay and Christian in America*, and John Paulk's *Not Afraid to Change: The Remarkable Story of How One Man Overcame Homosexuality*). This decision was not due to any lack of appreciation for the significance and impact of personal witness, but rather to the fact that, in general, such books merely flesh out the convictions given more systematic treatment in the titles included. I have also limited the selection to works devoted in their entirety to the question of Christianity and homosexuality, omitting as a result books such as Lewis Smedes's *Sex for Christians: The Limits and Liberties of Sexual Living*, L. William Countryman's *Dirt, Greed and Sex: Sexual Ethics in the New Testament and Their Implications for Today* and Peter Gomes *The Good Book: Reading the Bible with Mind and Heart*. These and other more general works contain valuable material, however, and full bibliographical information is included where these and similar titles are cited in the text.

It will be noted that, in terms of publication dates, the balance of the listings leans toward the "first generation" of contributions to the topic. This is to be accounted for by the fact that—with the exception of the Queer Liberation elements of viewpoint 6 (Liberation)—the general terms of the debate were set out relatively early in the ongoing discussion.

Atkinson, David. *Homosexuals in the Christian Fellowship.* Grand Rapids: Eerdmans, 1979.

After surveying various viewpoints held by Christians on the issue, the evangelical author comes to conclusions which fall somewhere between viewpoints 2 (A Promise of Healing) and 3 (A Call to Costly Discipleship): while healing is a possibility for many, some gays or lesbians may be unable to change; those who cannot are called to a life of celibacy.

Bahnsen, Greg L. *Homosexuality: A Biblical View.* Grand Rapids: Baker Book House, 1978.

Bahnsen argues viewpoint 1 (Condemnation) out of a rigorously Reformed perspective: orientation and acts are equally damned, one cannot be a Christian and at the same time a homosexual either in inclination or action; homosexual desires (which Bahnsen insists are always "lusts") are learned and can be unlearned; God has given the state the obligation to suppress and punish unrighteousness, therefore homosexuality should be subject to criminal penalties.

Bailey, Derrick Sherwin. *Homosexuality and the Western Christian Tradition.* London: Longmans, Green & Co., 1955.

While Bailey was not the first to question conventional interpretations of those scriptural passages traditionally deemed to condemn homosexuality and homosexuals, this scholarly study was a watershed in the field. Everything written after it of necessity refers back to Bailey's analysis, the impact of which was particularly significant on treatment of the story of Sodom and its sin. Given his subsequent importance to more liberal exegetes, Bailey's conclusions on many points are surprisingly conservative.

Barnhouse, Ruth Tiffany. *Homosexuality: A Symbolic Confusion.* New York: Seabury Press, 1979.

Barnhouse, a therapist and an Episcopalian, argues that the homosexual's "choice" for sexual aberration—even if it took place subconsciously at a very early age—is still something for which he or she is morally culpable. She considers that choice, in fact, to be a form of "original sin." Believing homosexuality to be both mental illness and moral evil, she insists that homosexuals have an obligation to try to become heterosexuals (through traditional therapy). Those who find they cannot change, and for whom celibacy would be too difficult, should attempt to form stable homosexual relationships, however. The book is particularly important for its treatment of the symbolic dimensions of human sexuality and has been a theoretical source for a number of other works from a conservative perspective.

Batchelor, Edward, Jr., ed. *Homosexuality and Ethics.* **New York: Pilgrim Press, 1980.**

Batchelor's anthology includes relevant entries from the writings of Aquinas, Thielicke, Barth, Reuther, Pittenger, Barnhouse and others.

Blair, Ralph. *With Sunshine and Rainfall for All: An Evangelical Affirmation of Gay Rights; Hope's Gays & Gays' Hopes; Ex-Gays; Homosexualities: Faith, Facts & Fairy Tales;* **etc. New York: Ralph Blair, dates various.**

Blair, a psychologist and the founder of Evangelicals Concerned, affirms—from what he contends is a solidly evangelical viewpoint—the sexual, psychological and spiritual health of gay men and lesbians. He encourages homosexuals to develop same-sex life partnerships which are monogamous and Christ-centered. Blair has extensively documented and critiqued the claims and difficulties of the ex-gay movement.

Boswell, John. *Christianity, Social Tolerance and Homosexuality.* **Chicago: University of Chicago Press, 1980.**

A basic text for those arguing viewpoint 5 (Affirmation), Boswell's work has been criticized by conservatives as being neither as objective nor as scholarly as has been claimed by his admirers (the book was a winner of the 1981 American Book Awards for History). Of particular interest to many are Boswell's apparently exhaustive word studies on specific disputed terms such as ἀρσενοκοῖται (although a more recent work by Scroggs—see below—offers a radically differing opinion on the derivation and meaning of this Pauline term).

Cleaver, Richard. *Know My Name: A Gay Liberation Theology.* Louisville: Westminster John Knox Press, 1995.

Cleaver makes an impassioned argument for viewpoint 6 (Liberation), working out of a liberation theology paradigm which calls gay men to solidarity with other oppressed groups in prophetic resistance to homophobia, sexism, heterocentrism, racial discrimination, economic inequality, militarism and Western capitalist exploitation of Third World nations and peoples. Identifying himself unequivocally as a Christian and making use of a number of scriptural stories to illustrate his arguments, Cleaver writes that "gay male liberation is our part of the whole revolutionary project of our times."

Comiskey, Andrew. *Pursuing Sexual Wholeness: How Jesus Heals the Homosexual.* Lake Mary, Florida: Creation House, 1989.

Comiskey acknowledges his indebtedness to the theories and practice of Leanne Payne and Elizabeth Moberly (see below). What is most distinctive about this book is the author's often painful candor regarding the nature of the healing process to which those he terms "homosexual strugglers" are called: "We cannot expect to experience a complete absence of sexual struggles in this lifetime . . . the homosexual struggler may still experience homosexual temptations. [*This does not*] minimize . . . God's healing power. It simply places that healing in the dynamic process of *becoming* whole, a process that will never end until we see Jesus in heaven." Comiskey is the founder and director of Desert Stream, an ex-gay ministry of the Vineyard Christian Fellowship.

Goss, Robert. *Jesus Acted Up: A Gay and Lesbian Manifesto.* San Francisco: HarperSanFrancisco, 1993.

While one conservative reviewer claimed it was difficult to find anything good to say about this book (and others have noted Goss's penchant for post-modernist jargon), *Jesus Acted Up* vigorously argues the cutting edge of "Queer Christian" thinking and "discourse": the biblical God is the God of the marginalized and oppressed, therefore gay and lesbian Christians must band together in "base communities" of prophetic resistance to the homophobia of church and society. They also "need to re-vision God as erotic power and . . . companionship," as "love-making and justice-doing," and acknowledge the "sacramentality" of their "queer experience," looking to "Jesus the Queer Christ [*who*] fights for gay men and lesbians . . . and . . . struggles to liberate them from the effects of homophobic oppression and . . . internalized homophobia." Goss, a former Jesuit and a priest, is a member of Act-Up and Queer Nation.

Jones, H. Kimball. *Towards a Christian Understanding of the Homosexual.* **New York: Association Press, 1966.**

Kimball, writing from a liberal Protestant perspective, provides a thoughtful presentation of the arguments of viewpoint 4 (Pastoral Accommodation). Given the movement of the theological debate regarding homosexuality in the more than thirty years since his book appeared, Kimball's work will seem dated to many. The pastoral approach he advocates is probably practiced more widely than is generally supposed, however, in particular by liberal evangelical and Roman Catholic clergy and therapists.

Lovelace, Richard F. *Homosexuality and the Church: Crisis, Conflict, Compassion.* **Old Tappan, New Jersey: Fleming Revell Co., 1978.**

Lovelace is careful to avoid inflammatory polemics and antigay stereotypes. He does not believe, however, that compassion for homosexuals justifies jettisoning the conservative understanding of biblical authority. Hope for the homosexual, Lovelace argues, lies in the recovery ministries of the ex-gay movement, which he discusses in some detail.

Macourt, Malcolm, ed. *Towards a Theology of Gay Liberation.* **London: S.C.M. Press, 1977.**

The essays in this relatively short volume argue the two most liberal viewpoints on the spectrum (Affirmation and Liberation)—although without the radical liberation model represented by the work of Cleaver and Goss (see above). Particularly noteworthy are: W. Norman Pittenger's "What It Means to Be Human," a useful supplement to the argument he advances in *A Time for Consent?* (see below); Michael Keeling's "A Christian Basis for Gay Relationships," which grounds Keeling's ethical proposals for Christian gays in what he contends are the larger moral "themes" of Scripture; and Rictor Norton's "The Biblical Roots of

Homophobia," an unapologetic, no-holds-barred denunciation of conventional understandings of the scriptural witness.

McNeill, John J. *The Church and the Homosexual*. Mission, Kansas: Sheed, Andrews and McMeel, Inc., 1976.

Articulating a view mingling viewpoints 4 (Pastoral Accommodation) and 5 (Affirmation) from the perspective of traditional Roman Catholic moral theology, this work has had wide influence. McNeill, a Jesuit priest at the time the book was published, has since been expelled from his order under pressure from the Vatican due to his refusal to be silenced on the subject. He was one of the founders of Dignity, the national organization for gay and lesbian Catholics.

Moberly, Elizabeth R. *Homosexuality: A New Christian Ethic*. Cambridge: James Clark & Co., 1983.

Moberly's book—a basic text for the ex-gay movement—argues that "same-sex attachment ambivalence" in homosexuals results in a failure to achieve complete sexual identity with their own gender. The homosexual's erotic attraction to same-sex partners, therefore, has at its root a good thing: a "reparative drive" to attain the same-sex bonding which was not achieved in childhood. Believing that same-sex ambivalence must (and can) be healed—since homosexual identity is by definition incomplete and homosexual acts are immoral—Moberly proposes a two-pronged therapeutic approach—a deeply felt nonsexual relationship with a same-sex friend or counselor and various forms of healing prayer.

Payne, Leanne. *The Broken Image: Restoring Personal Wholeness Through Healing Prayer*. Westchester: Crossways Books, 1981.

Writing anecdotally from her extensive practice of inner healing for "sexual brokenness" of all kinds, Payne contends that "There is no such thing as a 'homosexual person.' There are only those who need healing of old rejections and deprivations, deliverance from the wrong kind of self love and the actions that issue from it, and . . . the knowledge of their own higher selves in Christ." Payne's method of healing prayer draws from diverse sources: on one hand she utilizes the holy water and the oil of chrism of historic Christianity; on the other, she encourages those to whom she ministers to create "faith pictures" of healing encounters with the dead. Contrary to Moberly's opinion, she insists that homosexuality "as a condition for God to heal . . . is . . . remarkably simple."

Pittenger, W. Norman. *A Time for Consent? A Christian's Approach to Homosexuality.* **London: S.C.M. Press, 1967 (rev. eds. 1970, 1976).**

This influential work is dependent both upon Process Theology and the "Situation Ethics" of Joseph Fletcher, who holds that the morality of any particular act can only be evaluated in terms of its context. Pittenger argues that, for homosexuals as for heterosexuals, the erotic and affectional aspects of love—which gays and lesbians are capable of experiencing fully only with a same-sex partner—are to be judged by their degree of conformity to the Christian ethic of other-centered, self-emptying love. The question mark in Pittenger's title was dropped in the second and third editions.

Scanzoni, Letha & Virginia Ramey Mollenkott. *Is the Homosexual My Neighbor? Another Christian View.* **San Francisco: Harper & Row, 1978.**

This was the first widely read presentation of the arguments of viewpoint 5 (Affirmation) from an evangelical perspective and it continues to be popular. While dealing with the usually cited scriptural materials and theological arguments, the book focuses particularly on the painful experience of gays and lesbians in relation to a church which has—as the authors view the matter—violated the gospel imperative of inclusive love by rejecting and demonizing them.

Schmidt, Thomas E. *Straight and Narrow? Compassion and Clarity in the Homosexual Debate.* **Downers Grove: Inter-Varsity Press, 1995.**

Schmidt's expressed aim is to provide a new, compassionate but soundly biblical perspective on the issue, and several conservative reviewers have hailed his work as the definitive statement of evangelical opinion on the question of homosexuality. Critics, on the other hand, have charged that there is little that is new in Schmidt's analysis and that his determination to be compassionate is undermined by a refusal to acknowledge the affectional elements of same-sex attraction and a failure to understand the difference between a call for abstinence outside of marriage for the heterosexual and the demand of lifelong celibacy and absence of coupled intimacy for the homosexual. As does Lovelace, Schmidt proposes the ministry of the ex-gay movement as the church's answer for the homosexual.

Scroggs, Robin. *The New Testament and Homosexuality: Contextual Background for Contemporary Debate.* Philadelphia: Fortress Press, 1983.

Scroggs's basic argument is that the only model for homosexual behavior known to New Testament writers was classical pederasty (with its attendant abuses and lack of reciprocity) and that, therefore, biblical evidence cannot be applied to the quite different realities of modern homosexual practice—a premise challenged by a number of conservative scholars. Scroggs's treatment of the problematical ἀρσενοκοῖται—tracing it to Jewish tradition (via the Septuagint) rather than pagan Greek usage—is potentially discouraging to evangelicals attempting to reconcile Christian discipleship and active homosexual expression, since it ties Paul's use of the word directly to the Levitical prohibitions.

NOTES

![black bar]

Preface

1   The word "etiology" is commonly employed to frame this question. Since, however, etiology is primarily a medical term for the origin of a disease or abnormal condition, its use in this context occasions strong objection from many gay and lesbian apologists who contend that it implies an a priori negative judgment on homosexual orientation.

2   This issue offers two advantages for comparative purposes. First, it avoids the extraordinary emotional *frisson* that seems inevitably to accompany discussions of sexual morality. Also, although the fact is rarely noted, pacifism is an issue on which "conservative" Christians find themselves in what is in fact the "liberal" viewpoint. However the disputed scriptural evidence is interpreted, it is clear that, in its first centuries, the church was pacifistic, with the accommodation of involvement in war being a "novelty" introduced at a later stage.

3   Attempts to trace the derivation of "gay" as a designation for the male homosexual pose a thorny but, at least for those interested in etymology, fascinating challenge. Writing in the early 1950s, Donald Webster Cory admitted in *The Homosexual in America* (New York: Greenberg [Ayer Publishers], 1951) that, "How, when, and where this word originated, I am unable to say." Noting that some "experts"—whom he does not identify—claim that the usage began in French as early as the sixteenth century (*gaie*—the feminine form of the word being applied to males), Cory contends that it first appeared in English shortly after World War I, and adds that he has personal knowledge of psychiatrists whose homosexual patients were referring to themselves as "gay" by the 1920s. Cory stresses the value of the term as a code word for use in public conversation at a time when identification as a homosexual could have serious consequences: since "gay" in more general parlance meant vivid, amusing and/or lighthearted, a homosexual could mention that a particular event,

person, bar or restaurant was "very gay" and be confident that only another homosexual would understand what was meant.

More recently, George Chauncey, in *Gay New York: Gender, Urban Culture, and the Making of the Gay Male World, 1890–1940* (New York: Basic Books [HarperCollins Publishers, Inc.], 1994), traces the usage in English from its original reference to pleasurable things in general, to (by the seventeenth century) *immoral* pleasures in particular, to (by the nineteenth century) a lewd woman or prostitute. At the same time, "gay" in common idiom could refer to something brightly colored or a person showily dressed (which, in the homosexual underground, was an accurate description of the style adopted by many "fairies," or effeminate homosexuals). The confluence of these various layers of meaning in both the general heterosexual culture and the homosexual subculture is well expressed in a lurid novel by Lew Levenson, *Butterfly Man* (New York: Macaulay, 1934), from which Chauncey cites the following rather extravagant speech put in the mouth of a young homosexual chorus boy: "I'm lush. I'm gay. I'm wicked. I'm everything that flames." Like Cory, Chauncey recognizes the usefulness of the term as a coded *double entendre*, as in a 1951 advertisement for a New York restaurant which dubbed itself knowingly as the place "Where the Gay Set Meet [sic] for Dinner."

4   Although "queer" has often been assumed to be a particularly offensive epithet for homosexuals, Chauncey, op. cit., documents the fact that most non-effeminate (or "butch") homosexual men referred to themselves by that term from the first decades of this century until well into the 1930s, distinguishing themselves by it from effeminate homosexuals who were called "fairies," "faggots" or "queens" in the homosexual subculture.

5   Self-described "queer Christian" and former Jesuit Robert Goss writes in this regard: "*Queer* has become an empowering symbol for living sexual differences . . . [an] inclusionary term for gay men and lesbians and people of color who believe that the words *gay* and *lesbian* are 'white' political labels." *Jesus Acted Up: A Gay and Lesbian Manifesto* (San Francisco: HarperSanFrancisco, 1993).

6   Frank du Mas, *Gay is Not Good* (Nashville: Thomas Nelson, 1979)—*emphasis added*.

7   On this point, it was instructive to note that those readers who complained most vigorously of what they took to be bias against their own viewpoint in my handling of critical material had no complaint whatsoever when I applied the same critical approach to viewpoints they opposed.

Introduction

1   Chicago: University of Chicago Press, 1980; see bibliography.

2   Ibid.

3   "Buggery" is usually interpreted as anal intercourse between males, although some dictionaries simply define it by the equally nonspecific "sodomy." The word has its root in the Middle English *bougre*, which can mean either heretic or sodomite, or both, and is a variant upon the medieval Latin *Bulgarus*, which literally means a male from Bulgaria. Thus, not only were heretics and those who committed homosexual acts commingled in the common mind, the medieval conceptual mix also included the whole notion of "foreignness." A number of usually reliable sources are content with the presumption that Bulgarians were so completely "other" in language, religion (being Orthodox, not Catholic) and mores that they were logically suspect both theologically

and sexually. The actual etymology of the term is considerably more complex, however. In eighth-century Bulgaria, a strongly dualistic (affirming two eternal, equal principles—one good, one evil—and rejecting the material creation as an evil prison for the spirit) heretical sect called the Bogomils came into prominence, its teachings spreading as far west as Italy and France. Three hundred years later, a strikingly similar movement posed a significant threat to Catholic Christianity in Northern Italy, where its rigorously ascetic followers were nicknamed Cathari ("the pure"), and Southern France, where its adherents were commonly called Albigenses. Scholars are divided on the question of whether the Albigensian heresy was a direct offspring of Bogomil teaching or an independent development. Whichever was the case, the parallels between the two sects were recognized at the time, with the result that, in popular usage, the Albigenses were sometimes sneeringly referred to as "*bougres*"— Bulgarians. Since one Albigensian distinctive was the repudiation of sexual relations even between spouses, it was charged that its males found sexual release with each other. Hence the connection between heresy and homosexual acts, a connection which, over time, became a truism assumed of all heretical movements.

4   Among Foucault's major works are *Power/Knowledge* (New York: Pantheon Books, 1980) and *History of Sexuality*, Vols. I, II & III (New York: Vintage Books, 1990). Foucault's analysis, as Robert Goss (*Jesus Acted Up*, op. cit.) puts it, "proceeds from a sociological perspective of conflict" (i.e., the assumption of an ongoing power struggle which is the human condition) and asserts that any "knowledge," so called, is in fact a social construct which functions to legitimize the power of those who have and disseminate that knowledge through public "discourse" and practice. Foucault proposes deconstruction of such oppressive truth claims by means of a "genealogical method" which recovers and raises to articulation "subjugated knowledges" and "dangerous memory" (aberrant argument and experience which are suppressed or dismissed by the dominant universal truth construct). Of particular importance to constructionists is Foucault's argument that the heterosexual/homosexual/bisexual paradigm represents a "medicalization" (Goss's term) of the human sexual capacity created by the medical/psychiatric community in the interest of expanding its power and control over sex in general and the sexually deviant in particular.

5   Richard Cleaver, *Know My Name: A Gay Liberation Theology* (Louisville: Westminster John Knox Press, 1995; see bibliography). It should be noted that Cleaver describes himself as being "incline[d] to the constructionist view."

6   *Jesus Acted Up*, op. cit.

7   The word was not translated into English until 1892.

8   The institute library was looted and the collection burned by the Nazis on May 6, 1933.

9   Founded by Harry Hay (a now legendary figure in knowledgeable gay circles) and several other former Communist Party activists in Los Angeles, the organization's original name was The Mattachine Foundation. After several years, the radically tainted founders were purged and the group reorganized under the title The Mattachine Society.

10   Lev 20:13.

11   Whether this state of affairs was a gross injustice or a perfectly legitimate societal restraint upon vice is, of course, a debated point among Christians.

12   Patrick Merla, ed.; New York: Avon Books, 1996.

13   In the late 1980s, "outing"—the exposure of prominent closeted homosexuals by other gays—became an issue in the gay and lesbian community. It remains a highly controversial tactic even within that community. Some argue that *any* act of outing is justified, since the greater the number of famous people known to be gay, the more likely it is that social perceptions of homosexual marginalization will begin to change. In a sense, this logic runs, if these people will not do their duty to their community, then the community has the right to do it for them. Others, taking a more moderate viewpoint, argue that outing is only legitimate in cases where a hypocritically closeted individual is doing actual harm to gay and lesbian people, through political or religious means. Still others remain convinced that coming out is by definition the most personal of decisions and one which no person may rightly make for another, whatever the perceived strategic advantage of doing so.

14   "Transgender" is the currently preferred designation for those who were formerly termed "transsexuals": men or women whose experience of their true, psychological gender does not conform to their external sexual characteristics and who therefore seek medical intervention—hormone therapy, "sex change" surgery—to remedy this perceived incongruity.

15   Lev 20:13.

16   Gen 18:20 – 19:25.

17   Ours is hardly the first generation since the "triumph" of Christendom in which concern has been expressed over an apparent increase in homosexual behavior, however. In the eighteenth century, *Plain Reasons for the Growth of Sodomy in England* was published. The "plain reasons" adduced included the drinking of tea and the "pernicious influence of Italian opera."

18   Rom 1:18–28.

19   Op. cit. Conservatives would be quick to argue that, contrary to Boswell's implication, the fact that there may have been homosexuals in the church throughout its history in no way establishes the moral legitimacy of homosexual acts or impulses, since there have always been sinners as well as saints in every Christian community.

20   London: Longmans, Green & Co., Ltd., 1955; see bibliography. Bailey's exegesis of the relevant biblical materials has been the foundation of everything that has followed in the way of reconsideration of the traditional viewpoint, even though, on a number of points, he remains essentially conservative in his conclusions.

21   *Know My Name,* op. cit.

22   Johann Baptist Metz, *The Emergent Church*, translated by Peter Mann. (New York: Crossroad, 1981).

23   *Know My Name,* op. cit.

24   These terms are in and of themselves the subject of heated discussion—see chapter 2—hence the quotation marks.

25   Figures for summer 1998, reported in John Leland & Mark Miller, "Can Gays Convert?" (*Newsweek,* August 17, 1998).

26   Sponsors of the ads were identified as: Alliance for Traditional Marriage — Hawaii, American Family Association, Americans for Truth About Homosexuality, Center for Reclaiming America, Christian Family Network, Christian Coalition, Citizens for Community Values, Colorado For Family Values, Concerned Women for America, Coral Ridge Ministries, Family First, Family Research Council, Liberty Counsel, National Legal Foundation and Kerusso Ministries.

27 Leland & Miller, "Can Gays Convert?" (op. cit.).

28 With Tony Marco (Mukilteo, Washington: WinePress Publishing, 1998).

29 Comiskey is Director of the Vineyard Christian Fellowship's Desert Stream ministry.

30 Rom 1:18–28.

31 The notion of some sort of congenital or physical explanation for homosexuality became less persuasive to most theorists during the middle years of the twentieth century with the ascendency of Freudian psycho-dynamic models. Nonetheless, some researchers continued to explore biological factors. Studies of twins were utilized by some, with ambiguous and often contradictory results. Others sought a morphological determinant, with sometimes bizarre results. One researcher insisted that he had never come across a fat homosexual and concluded that male homosexuals are generally slender or athletic with triangular or egg-shaped faces (Donahue, in *One*, December, 1961). Others over the years claimed to have found further consistently appearing physical characteristics in gay men which might be indicators of a physical cause: they were generally slighter and more female in body type than heterosexual males (Weil, 1924); they had smaller penises than normal heterosexual men (Henry & Gailbraith, 1934); they had larger penises than heterosexual men (Nedoma & Freund, 1961)—all cited by Ralph Blair in *Etiological and Treatment Literature on Homosexuality* (New York: National Task Force on Student Personnel Services and Homosexuality, 1972).

32 While it would be difficult to overstate the impact of Freud's theories upon contemporary psychotherapeutic theory and practice, as well as upon the self-understanding of most late-twentieth-century Western Europeans and Americans, it should be noted that he is not without his critics both within and outside of the scientific community. In recent years, various aspects of Freud's teaching have come under fire from detractors as disparate as feminists on the left and conservative evangelical Christians on the right.

33 The letter, to an anonymous correspondent, is dated April 9, 1935.

34 London: Hogarth, 1905.

35 *The Bulletin of the New York Academy of Medicine*, 40, 1964.

36 Edmund Bergler, *One Thousand Homosexuals: Conspiracy of Silence or Curing and Deglamorizing Homosexuals?* (Patterson: Pageant Books, 1959).

37 Bergler, *Homosexuality: Disease or Way of Life?* (New York: Collier, 1956).

38 Irving Bieber, *et al. Homosexuality: A Psychoanalytic Study* (New York: Basic Books Inc., 1962).

39 Evelyn Hooker, "Adjustment of the Overt Male Homosexual," *Journal of Projective Techniques*, Vol. 21, No. 1, 1957.

40 This alternative viewpoint gradually began to be voiced in the published works of psychotherapeutic professionals as well, perhaps most notably in George Weinberg's provocatively (for its time) titled *Society and the Healthy Homosexual* (New York: St. Martin's, 1972).

41 Today, even many Christian churches which do not accept the moral legitimacy of homosexual acts consider homophobia a reality and view it as a sin against both charity and justice. Some Christians, however, insist that what contemporary culture labels "homophobia" is in fact nothing more than a natural, morally proper revulsion toward blatant rebellion against the created order.

42 In July 1994, the American Psychological Association released a statement on homosexuality which included the following:

The research on homosexuality is very clear. Homosexuality is neither mental illness nor moral depravity. It is simply the way a minority of our population expresses human love and sexuality. Study after study documents the mental health of gay men and lesbians. Studies of judgment, stability, reliability, and social and vocational adaptiveness all show that gay men and lesbians function every bit as well as heterosexuals. Nor is homosexuality a matter of individual choice. Research suggests that the homosexual orientation is in place very early in the life cycle, possibly even before birth. . . . Research findings suggest that efforts to repair homosexuals are nothing more than social prejudice garbed in psychological accouterments.

43　Since this theory of etiology and treatment is discussed at length in chapter 2, a brief summary will suffice here.

44　Like the classic American Freudians of the 1940s and '50s, reparative therapists tend to focus their attention and build their etiological model almost exclusively upon gay men.

45　Martin A. Silverman, M.D., "Gender Identity Disorders in Boys: A Complemental Series," from "Collected Papers," NARTH Annual Conference, May 4, 1996.

46　Ibid.

47　Quoted in Leland & Miller, "Can Gays Convert?" (op. cit.).

48　The American Psychological Association released a similar resolution in August 1997.

49　APA Online Press Release No. 98–56, December 14, 1998.

50　*Los Angeles Times*, December 12, 1998, in a story from the Associated Press.

51　*Love Undetectable: Notes on Friendship, Sex, and Survival* (New York: Alfred A. Knopf, 1998).

52　For Sullivan, such honesty about the discomforting accuracy of certain elements of reparative therapy theory in no way requires acceptance of the entirety of reparative therapists' claims. Indeed, the burden of Sullivan's extended and lapidary essay is to refute reparative therapy's assertions of gay pathology, the moral and psychological inferiority of homosexual to heterosexual love, the unworkability of gay relationships and possibilities of "cure."

53　The most commonly mentioned figure—10 percent—is based on projections from research done in the 1950s by Alfred Kinsey and his Institute for Research in Sex, Gender and Reproduction. Kinsey's research methodology and conclusions (particularly as to the prevalence of men who have engaged in homosexual acts) have been the subject of considerable debate of late, with not only Kinsey's competence but even his integrity being challenged by some conservative scholars, e.g., Judith A. Reisman & Edward W. Eichel, *Kinsey, Sex and Fraud: The Indoctrination of a People: An Investigation Into the Human Sexuality Research of Alfred C. Kinsey, Wardell B. Pomeroy, Clyde E. Martin and Paul H. Gebhard* (Lafayette, Louisiana: Lochinvar-Huntington House Publishers, 1990) and Reisman, *Kinsey, Crimes and Consequences: The Red Queen and the Grand Scheme* (Arlington, Virginia: Institute for Media Education, 1998). While conservative writers repeatedly cite Reisman as proof that Kinsey's "findings" are unsubstantiated, the attitude of the mainstream therapeutic and academic communities toward such revisionism is generally dismissive.

54　The Genesis story of the creation of Eve from Adam's rib would be seen as a variant on this myth, with the noteworthy difference that it replaces the parity of sexual principles depicted in the original form of the story with the supremacy of the masculine principle (in that the male is made first and the female is then made from him). Despite this significant revision, the Genesis material retains, in somewhat more subtle form, the imagery of both male and female being initially one in Adam, who is—in and of himself—fully and completely human.

55 Such an etiological model obviously has resonance with that propounded by reparative therapists, although it lacks reparative therapy's carefully honed concepts of gender identity deficit and defensive detachment from the father. In either case, homosexual advocates reject such theorizing as little more than what they consider the venerable fallacy of gay men being "sissies" and lesbians not being "real women." While it is true that some male homosexuals are effeminate or evidence stereotypically feminine interests and personality traits, others, they point out, are extremely masculine. There are gay truck drivers who love football just as there are gay florists with a passion for Barbra Streisand. Similarly, there are extraordinarily feminine lesbians as well as "bull dykes."

56 New York: New American Library, 2nd ed., 1987.

57 Most Christians holding to a conservative perspective on the issue of homosexuality reject the idea that the condition might have a genetic source (indeed, many deny the existence of a homosexual "condition" at all). The minority open to the possibility of a genetic element in causality argue, however, that—even if it were someday proved that there is a genetic component predisposing some people to homosexuality—those so predisposed would have no more justification for homosexual behavior than those with a genetic predisposition to violence have for antisocial behavior.

58 Many gay Christians use theological language to assert much the same thing, professing that God created them gay, or that their orientation is a gift of God and God only gives good gifts.

59 It should be noted again, however, that this point is disputed by some conservative Christians.

60 Such "nature" (as opposed to "nurture") explanations for homosexuality would presumably account for the relatively common phenomenon of one child in a family growing up to be gay while his or her siblings, raised in the same family dynamic, are straight.

61 In fact, even leading reparative therapist Joseph Nicolosi, a Roman Catholic psychologist, acknowledges that there are homosexuals who "are inappropriate for reparative therapy because they show no signs of gender identity deficit and do not match our developmental model." Nicolosi, *Reparative Therapy of Male Homosexuals: A New Clinical Approach* (North Vale, New Jersey: Jason Aronson, 1991).

Chapter 1: Condemnation

1 Since it goes to the matter of potentially significant authorial bias, I should again explicitly acknowledge that, as noted in the preface, this present book must be regarded from such a viewpoint as not only unnecessary but pernicious. To those of this opinion, the suggestion that there might be more than one perspective held by Christians on the question of homosexuality, or the encouragement to consider such perspectives with an open mind, would be understood to constitute, in and of itself, a rejection of the clear and incontrovertible teaching of the Word of God.

2 Higher criticism is the study of the literary methods employed in, and the historical development and sources of, scriptural materials. The term is used to distinguish such scholarship from "lower" or textual criticism, which attempts to establish the most accurate form of the text through comparison of extant

versions. The higher critical method is rejected by fundamentalists and many conservative evangelicals, who argue that its application of general historical principles to the Bible of necessity denies the inspiration and inerrancy of Scripture.

3   Greg Bahnsen, *Homosexuality: A Biblical View* (Grand Rapids: Baker Book House, 1978; see bibliography), for this and following quotations.

4   Aquinas, in his *Summa Theologica*, actually posits several related explanations of "nature" as it relates to human beings, including a cogent distinction between essential (metaphysical) nature and actual (physiological) nature. He never reduces the concept to the literalism of the "key-lock" model (penis fits vagina) that his argument from nature is sometimes taken to be. Nor does he start simply with the raw data of biology. Rather, he begins with a conviction that all of the created order is imbued by its Creator with purpose and therefore has a tendency to move toward its appointed end, which is completeness, which is good. That being the case, the "naturalness," in the contemporary empirical sense of the word, of any particular act does not determine its goodness. Rather, as Pim Pronk puts it in *Against Nature? Types of Moral Argumentation Regarding Homosexuality* (trans. John Vriend; Grand Rapids: William B. Eerdmans Publishing Co., 1993), it is the other way around: "the good is criterion for [an act's] naturalness." As to how we know the good that defines nature, and the moral conclusions to be drawn therefrom ("natural law"), Aquinas argues that this understanding is given us in the very structures of our human reason, what he terms the "first principles of the intellect" which are "infused" in us with our creation. As Pronk notes, in this Aquinas is an "intuitionist: he believes that the commands of natural law are self-evident in the same way as the principles of logic."

5   Pronk (op. cit.), for example, cites a 1939 statement made by F.A.H. van de Loo (official representative from the archdiocese of Utrecht), before a congress of Dutch Catholic physicians discussing homosexuality. Presenting the position of the church, van de Loo articulated the "natural law" argument against homosexuality in its most reductionistic form: the "nature" of the sex act is evident from the biological structure and reproductive function of the genitals and that nature is directed to procreation.

6   J. Douma, cited in Pronk, op. cit.

7   Carl F.H. Henry, "In and Out of the Gay World," in W. Dwight Oberholtzer, ed., *Is Gay Good? Ethics, Theology and Homosexuality* (Philadelphia: Westminster Press, 1971).

8   *Homosexuality: A Biblical View*, op. cit.

9   The church does allow birth control by the "rhythm method," which limits sexual activity to the wife's less fertile periods in her monthly cycle. While this exception would seem to violate the logical premise of its opposition to birth control—that every licit sexual act should be at least potentially open to conception—the church argues that, by virtue of its being "natural," the rhythm method is morally acceptable so long as it is not abused with the aim of limiting the size of one's family for selfish reasons.

10   As the entry on homosexuality in the 1967 edition of the *New Catholic Encyclopedia* states: "The homosexual act by its essence excludes all possibility of transmission of life; such an act cannot fulfill the procreative purpose of the sexual faculty and is, therefore, . . . a very grave transgression of the divine will. It is also a deviation from the normal attraction of man for woman, which leads to the foundation of the basic stable unit of society, the family." John F. Harvey, "Homosexuality," *New Catholic Encyclopedia*, Vol. 7 (New York: McGraw Hill, 1967).

11   Although Luther held (on the basis of Old Testament example) that a husband, denied his legitimate spousal rights by either the disinclination or disability of his wife, was entitled to take a concubine.

12   While at one time many Protestants questioned the probity of birth control, family planning is now seen even by the vast majority of fundamentalists as not only a right but a Christian responsibility.

13   Bahnsen, op. cit.

14   Ibid., citing Rom 5:12, 18–19, which reads in pertinent part: "Therefore. . . sin came into the world through one man, and death came through sin, and so death spread to all because all have sinned . . . one man's trespass led to condemnation for all. . . by the one man's disobedience the many were made sinners . . ."

15   Bahnsen, for example, op. cit., warns that "[t]he practice and theorizing of many schools of psychology entail questionable assumptions such as the cogency of 'subconscious' notions, the understanding of man that is utilized, [and] the moral and evaluative presuppositions that are applied . . ."

16   On this point, Bahnsen, op. cit., insists that even if one or another "psychogenic" explanation of homosexuality is accepted, all these explanations presume that the homosexual propensity is the result of a "personal reaction" to familial dysfunction. And, Bahnsen notes, "Scripture always holds men accountable for how they react to their circumstances. No circumstance makes someone unavoidably sinful in his reactions, for there is always a way of escape pleasing to God." That being the case, "homosexual desire is something for which men are held responsible by God."

17   *Homosexuality: A Biblical View*, op. cit.

18   Bahnsen provides numerous examples of this principle, among them Prov 6:16–18 (plotting evil against a neighbor), Matt 5:21, 22 (anger leading to violence), Eph 4:31 (malice), Ps 37:1, 7 (envying the dishonest), Amos 8:5 (planning deceit), and Matt 5:27–29 (looking on a woman with lust).

19   The translations are Bahnsen's own. The NRSV renders the terms "lusts" (Rom 1:24) and "degrading passions" (Rom 1:26).

20   Bahnsen, op. cit.

21   Ibid.

22   As Harvey's article on homosexuality in the *New Catholic Encyclopedia*, op. cit., notes: "All true love is a going-out of oneself, a self giving; but, all unconsciously, homosexual love is bent back upon the self in a closed circle, a sterile love of self, disguised in apparent love for another. What seems like ideal love to the homosexual must be shown to be narcissism."

23   Bahnsen, however, is careful to note that "Not all homosexuals can be classified as seductive corruptors of little children." Op. cit.

24   Paul Cameron, a psychologist and the head of the conservative Family Research Institute, has written that the perversity of homosexuality is so profound that homosexuals even show a disproportionate propensity to murder and be murdered ("Murder and Homosexuality," *Family Research Report*, May–June 1994). Although Cameron was expelled from the American Psychological Association on a charge of ethics violations and is personally controversial among conservatives themselves, his studies are repeatedly cited as authoritative in materials dealing with homosexuality from the perspective of the "Christian Right" (Didi Herman, *The Antigay Agenda: Orthodox Vision and the Christian Right* [Chicago: University of Chicago Press, 1997]).

25   Former U.S. Congressman William Dannemeyer, a conservative Republican from Southern California closely identified with the Christian Right, argues on

this point that "militant" homosexual activists (which he treats as agents of all gays and lesbians) represent a "well-planned and well-financed attack on our civilization." *Shadow in the Land: Homosexuality in America* (San Francisco: St. Ignatius, 1989).

26 Bahnsen, op. cit.

27 e.g., Dannemeyer, op. cit.; Chuck & Donna McIlhenny, with Frank York, *When the Wicked Seize a City: A Grim Look at the Future and a Warning to the Church* (Lafayette, Louisiana: Huntington House, 1993).

28 Roger Grindstaff, writing under the pseudonym "Roger Dean," *Gay* (Brooklyn: Teen Challenge, n.d.).

29 Bahnsen, op. cit., for this and following quotations.

30 The Greek words in question are μαλακοί (*malakoí*) and ἀρσενοκοῖται (*arsenokóitai*). For discussion of the debate surrounding the actual meaning of these two terms, see viewpoint 5, "Affirmation," pp. 157–161.

31 Bahnsen adds that the common bisexuality of many homosexuals, the "free adaptation" of heterosexuals to homosexual behavior in prisons, and the "actual results of proper pastoral counseling" (for which he offers no documentation) "demonstrate that homosexuality is not an irreversible fixation. It is a willful orientation and adopted way of life that can be changed." Op. cit.

32 Clyde Narramore, *The Psychology of Counseling* (Grand Rapids: Zondervan, 1960). It should be noted that, with the rise of ex-gay ministries in the 1970s (see Viewpoint Two, "A Promise of Healing"), the general trend of conservative thinking has been to embrace ex-gay claims as the pastoral solution to the individual homosexual's "problem."

33 Bahnsen, op. cit.

34 On this point, Bahnsen writes that it is "especially necessary in this day to lay to rest the myth of constitutional homosexuality." Op. cit.

35 Bahnsen, op. cit.

36 Ibid. Bahnsen cites Ps 119:53 in support of this admonition: "Hot indignation seizes me because of the wicked who forsake thy law." (RSV)

37 Unattributed editorial, "The Laws Against Homosexuals," *Christianity Today*, 14, 3 (1969).

38 Lindsell, "Homosexuals and the Church," *Christianity Today*, 17, 25 (1973).

39 Bahnsen, op. cit., for this and following quotations.

40 Ibid, for this and following quotations.

41 While he argues forcefully for the criminalization of homosexuality, Bahnsen is careful to note that such civil penalties should apply only to homosexual *acts*, not inclinations, since the "civil issue of homosexuality has nothing to do with homosexual lust or internal attitudes of the heart (any more than heterosexual lust is a matter within the state's province), for the civil magistrate deals only with external, public behavior, with offenses discernible as overt acts." Furthermore, Bahnsen insists, civil penalties against homosexuality should be administered justly; that is, accused homosexuals should be entitled to due process and should not be subject to entrapment or other extra-legal methods of enforcement.

42 Whether homosexuality should be a capital offense is a matter of some dispute among those holding this viewpoint. Some have called for the reinstitution of the death penalty for homosexual acts, basing these demands on Lev 20:13. The Reverend Walter Alexander, for example, of Reno's First Baptist Church, has stated for the record that "we should do what the Bible says and cut their throats." (Quoted in Bruce Bawer's *A Place at the Table: The*

Gay Individual in American Society. New York: Poseidon Press, 1993). Others argue that—in a secular, culturally diverse society—all that can reasonably be required are serious non-capital criminal penalties. Bahnsen, curiously enough, while devoting an entire chapter to the argument that homosexuality is not only a sin but a crime, never states what the penalty for that crime should be.

43   E.g., Gloria Copeland, *God's Will Is Prosperity* (Tulsa: Harrison House, Inc., 1978) and Markus Bishop, *Our Covenant of Prosperity* (Tulsa: Harrison House, Inc., 1997).

44   Brian Bouldrey, editor. New York: Riverhead Books, 1995.

45   Malcolm Macourt, editor. London: SCM Press Ltd., 1977.

46   Except for the exegetically problematical and variously interpreted "sin against the Holy Spirit"—Matt 12:32; Mark 3:29; Luke 12:10.

47   For discussion of the Pauline argument that homosexual "passions" and acts are "against nature," see viewpoint 5, "Affirmation."

48   Pronk, op. cit., notes that while the ancient concept of nature as normative may begin with empirical observation, it goes on to philosophical speculation. This is because "nature" is taken to be not the raw idiosyncratic data of any particular individual member of the class under consideration (in the case of human beings, *this particular person*), but rather the "true being" of the class considered in the abstract (*humankind*). "Nature" thus stands, as it were, above the specifics of any particular individual and this, Pronk points out, comes very close to the Platonic notion of pre-existent "idea."

49   Douma, in Pronk, op. cit.

50   *Against Nature?* (op. cit.); Bahnsen, ironically, also cites the "naturalistic fallacy" (*Homosexuality: A Biblical View*, op. cit.). But where Pronk ascribes that fallacy to those who would censure homosexuality as unnatural—and therefore immoral or pathological—on an appeal to biology or majority human experience, Bahnsen attributes it to those who would "attempt to generate a valid Christian ethic out of modern scientific research" and on that basis claim that, since homosexuality is a consistent fact of human experience or an immutable, innate "orientation" (what, arguably, *is*), it must be natural and therefore morally acceptable (what *ought to be*).

51   On the latter point, it is noted that the majority of children raised by two gay or lesbian parents turn out to be straight, which would seem to argue strongly against the claim that children are more likely to be drawn into homosexuality if they are exposed to positive gay role models.

52   Bahnsen, op. cit., for this and following quotation.

53   Lindsell, "Homosexuals and the Church," op. cit.

Chapter 2: A Promise of Healing

1   See introduction, pp. 21–22.

2   Even Protestants rejecting sacramental theology on principle will generally agree that there are few better or more rigorous schools in maturity, mutuality and self-emptying love than marriage and family, and—Catholics note—it is precisely for growth in these things that the sacramental grace of marriage is given.

3   Lewis, *The Screwtape Letters* (London: Geoffrey Bles, 1942). To avoid confusion, it should be noted that Lewis's own understanding of homosexuality does not appear to have included a hope for cure (his death in 1963 predated

by nearly a decade the rise of the ex-gay movement). Therefore, although his views on the eternal consequences of sexual intercourse and the transcendence of gender are consistent with this present position, his overall perspective fits more naturally with viewpoint 3, "A Call to Costly Discipleship."

4 Comiskey, *Pursuing Sexual Wholeness: How Jesus Heals the Homosexual* (Lake Mary, Florida: Creation House, 1989; see bibliography).

5 Stern, *The Flight from Woman* (New York: Farrar, Straus & Giroux, 1965).

6 Novelist Robert Siegel, quoted by Leanne Payne without citation in *Crisis in Masculinity* (Westchester, Illinois: Crossway Books, 1985).

7 Payne, *Crisis in Masculinity;* op. cit.

8 C. S. Lewis, *That Hideous Strength* (New York: Collier, 1962).

9 Op. cit.

10 Barth, *Church Dogmatics*, Vol. III: "The Doctrine of Creation," Pt. 4 (Edinburgh: T&T Clark, 1961).

11 Ibid.

12 *Pursuing Sexual Wholeness,* op. cit.

13 Those holding to this view reject the arguments of some contemporary feminists that gender is nothing more than a difference in "plumbing," with everything else typically associated with gender differentiation being simply a matter of social convention and conditioning. As Comiskey puts it in *Pursuing Sexual Wholeness* (op. cit.): "Gender isn't merely a cultural prescription."

14 This is not to argue for a kind of bullying domination for the male who "calls all the shots" or a sickly passivity for the female who simply "does what she's told." Nor is it to deny the fact that there are situations in which the female, acting upon her own secondary "masculine principle," must initiate, or times when the male, expressing his subordinate "female principle," is called to respond. Indeed, it is held, in our relationship with God, we are all responding feminine to God's initiatory masculine.

15 Comiskey gives concrete examples throughout his book, both directly and through anecdote, of how these universally applicable characteristics of masculine and feminine gender identity are to be lived out. Properly gender-identified males will approach life with "gusto, not timidity," whereas a truly feminine woman will exhibit "softness," "vulnerability" and "gentle responsiveness." Masculine identity is expressed through delight in "rough and tumble" activity, and an "ability to initiate, to effect change, to fight and lose and fight again, to relish the prospect of victory and push through every resistance until it's achieved." Appropriately feminine identity, on the other hand, calls for "gentle receptivity," "deep feeling" and a "cautious approach to life." (*Pursuing Sexual Wholeness,* op. cit.)

16 *The Flight from Woman,* op. cit. Comiskey obviously has a similar masculine paradigm in mind when he writes of his own gender identity history: "The 'fighting spirit' of boyhood was nearly defeated in me before it had a chance to develop." (*Pursuing Sexual Wholeness,* op. cit.)

17 *The Flight from Woman,* op. cit.

18 Barnhouse, *Homosexuality: A Symbolic Confusion* (New York: Seabury Press, 1979; see bibliography).

19 John W. Dixon, Jr., "The Sacramentality of Sex," *Male and Female*, Ruth Tiffany Barnhouse and Urban T. Holmes, III, eds. (New York: Seabury Press, 1976).

20 Op. cit.

21 Westchester, Illinois: Crossways Books, 1981; see bibliography.

22 Quoted without citation in Ralph Blair's *Homosexualities: Faith, Facts & Fairy Tales* (New York: R. Blair, 1991). It should be noted that Blair—a psychotherapist and the founder of Evangelicals Concerned (a national organization of "Christians addressing the integration of Christian lifestyle and homosexuality")—is generally not writing for an academic audience. As a consequence, standard source citations are almost always omitted from his works. Nonetheless, Blair's various self-published booklets, which include extensive monitoring and reporting of ex-gay ministries and their publications, constitute a unique information resource—albeit one with a very distinct point of view. That caveat being made, I would add that, while Blair's critics sometimes fault him for bias in his selection of evidence or the conclusions he draws from that evidence, I have found no allegation that anything he has reported is untrue, misquoted or fabricated.

23 Comiskey, *Pursuing Sexual Wholeness*, op. cit.

24 Cambridge: James Clark & Co., 1983; see bibliography.

25 Moberly was for a number of years active in the work of Exodus International, the ex-gay umbrella organization. Early in 1998, however, she announced a "change in ministry" to focus on "prayer for world evangelization," "an informal ministry of listening and encouragement," "alternative" approaches to cancer-related issues and "critiquing Darwinism."

26 Westchester, Illinois: Crossways Books, 1985.

27 The reasons for such alternative nomenclature appear to be at least two. In the first place, it is felt that to speak of a "homosexual orientation" is to come too close to the pernicious notion of an *innate* and *unchangeable* homosexual orientation (which concept one Exodus document labels as simply "pro-homosexual propaganda"—Sy Rogers & Alan Medinger, *Homosexuality and the Truth*, as quoted in Blair, *Homosexualities*, op. cit.). Secondly, the term is rejected by some as implying a kind of legitimizing parity between homosexual and heterosexual orientations. No matter how similar the two might appear to casual observation, it is argued, with the only difference being the matter of target, homosexual passions and affections are not the psychological, emotional or moral equivalent of heterosexual desires and attachments. They are, even at their best, a bent (to use Payne's term) or immature (to use Moberly's) misuse of erotic love.

28 At various points in her published works, Payne includes among these causative injuries (for male homosexuals): an overly protective mother whose intimacy with her son is such that he is unable to separate his sexual identity from hers; the "best little boy in the world" syndrome, in which the son so struggles to please the mother that he is unable to detach properly from her at puberty; lack of a warm, loving father after whom the boy can pattern himself; deprivation of "father-love, father-touch, father-communication," which later erupts in compulsions to touch and be touched by other men; a cruel or antagonistic father leading to the suppression of masculine identity; a father who fails to affirm his son's masculinity; rejection of one's own body; homosexual rape in childhood; exposure to pornography and/or group masturbation during puberty; inordinate self-love; compulsive masturbation as a form of adolescent narcissism continuing into adulthood; and spiritual rebellion. She also alleges, in at least one case, that a client was pushed toward homosexual yearnings (while in college) by "current homosexual propaganda." The roots of lesbianism, according to Payne, are often far less complicated. Typically, she argues, lesbian desire is actually no more than eroticized need "for a mother's arms." Other etiological factors can include: fear or hatred of an abusive or distant father which is then generalized to all men; over-identification with an

admired father, so that the young woman fails to develop a sense of herself as feminine; a possessive, devouring mother who provides a false model for the nature of love which is then reproduced in an obsessive attachment to another woman; and "extremes in feminist political rhetoric" which "not only open the mind to hatred [*of men*], but also to lesbian sexuality." Finally, Payne argues, either male or female homosexuality can sometimes be based in traumatic rejection by or estrangement from one or both parents in infancy, or in childhood "vows" in which the child rejects the same-sex parent and, at the same time, his or her gender identity with that parent.

29   The idea of the "cannibal compulsion" appears in Payne's work without attribution. Comiskey, in his own *Pursuing Sexual Wholeness* (op. cit.), specifically refers to the concept as being Payne's insight. Be that as it may, it is remarkably similar to C. Tripp's notion of "import/export" as the motivator for sexual attraction (*The Homosexual Matrix*, op. cit.), the only difference being that Tripp views the phenomenon as operative in *all* sexual relations, not just homosexual ones.

30   Payne, *Crisis in Masculinity*, op. cit.

31   The mother, Payne insists, cannot affirm either a son or a daughter in his or her gender identity, only a father can. This is because the child's gender identity, along with the rest of his or her selfhood, is developed in a process of separation *from* the mother.

32   *Homosexuality: A New Christian Ethic*; op. cit.

33   Ibid.

34   Moberly also notes that, whatever the cause of the original breach of attachment, not all children will react to it by defensive detachment. Some will continue to reach out to the same-sex parent (or some substitute therefor) for fulfillment of same-sex needs and will, as a result, not reject that parent and, with the parent, their own gender identification. Given this fact, Moberly insists, there is no "determinism" in these matters. She does not, however, go so far as does Ruth Tiffany Barnhouse (*Homosexuality: A Symbolic Confusion*, op. cit.), who asserts that the "choice" to reject one's own gender identity—even if it took place subconsciously at a very early age—is something for which a person is morally responsible and represents, in fact, one aspect of original sin.

35   Unlike Payne, Moberly does not consider a broken relationship with the father to be a decisive factor in both male and female homosexuality. Detachment from the father as a love-source is a fundamental issue for gay men; detachment from the mother is what is significant for lesbians. Moberly also diverges from Payne in that she sees the determinative developmental stage for creation of same-sex ambivalence as very early childhood (with potential for reinforcement from peer relationships later on), whereas Payne cites the puberty/adolescence cusp as the formative moment for gender identity problems. Both agree, however, that—whatever the etiological pattern—the end result in homosexuals is an inappropriate (and sinful) attempt to meet unfulfilled gender identity needs through erotic means created for entirely different purposes.

36   *Pursuing Sexual Wholeness*, op. cit.

37   At one point Comiskey writes: "The ultimate end of sin is death. For the homosexual struggler, this means first an end to his line because of lack of children."

38   Comiskey uses these terms, drawn from the charismatic movement, without ever explaining precisely what he means by them. From context, it would seem that "blessing" or "covering" a child's gender identity is the equivalent of—in psychological terms—"affirming" it.

39   *Pursuing Sexual Wholeness*, op. cit.

40   On this point, Comiskey notes a study by George Rekers—reported in Rekers's *Shaping Your Child's Sexual Identity* (Grand Rapids: Baker Books, 1982)— which asserts that the degree of closeness with the same-sex parent is more important to secure gender identity than the actual gender attributes modeled by that parent. In other words, a markedly effeminate father who was nevertheless closely bonded with his son would produce a stronger masculine gender identification in that son than might a stereotypically macho but distant father.

41   *Pursuing Sexual Wholeness*, op. cit., for this and following quotes.

42   For Payne, the homosexual compulsion, like all forms of sexual brokenness, is a result both of being sinned against (by the failures of parents, other significant adult figures and same-sex peers) and of sinning (by one's reaction to those failures). Consequently, one who is beset with homosexual desires, whether or not these desires are acted upon, would be understood to be at least to some extent in a state of unresolved sin.

43   *Pursuing Sexual Wholeness*, op. cit.

44   *Homosexuality: A New Christian Ethic*, op. cit.

45   Payne, *The Broken Image*, op. cit.

46   *Homosexuality: A New Christian Ethic*, op. cit.

47   Nevertheless, she notes that defensive detachment, while specific to the homosexual's relationship to his or her own sex, has consequences of a more global nature: a generalized sense of inferiority and rejection, depression, fear, insecurity and loneliness.

48   Payne, *The Broken Image*, op. cit.

49   Ibid.

50   *Pursuing Sexual Wholeness*, op. cit.

51   On the other hand, Comiskey himself sometimes seems to view homosexual sin as particularly heinous, as when he writes: "Satan especially delights in homosexual perversion because it not only exists outside of marriage, but it also defiles God's very image reflected as male and female." (*Pursuing Sexual Wholeness*, op. cit.)

52   *The Broken Image*, op. cit.

53   Bahnsen, *Homosexuality: A Biblical View*, op. cit.

54   As it is termed by Richard Lovelace in *Homosexuality and the Church: Crisis, Conflict, Compassion* (Old Tappan: Fleming Revell Co., 1978; see bibliography). Moberly specifically notes her disagreement with Lovelace on this point.

55   By this argument, Moberly in no way intends to excuse or legitimize homosexual acts; she merely means to place the desires out of which those acts arise in the proper moral perspective. Since same-sex attachment needs are a fact of our nature as created by God, we are entitled to have those needs met. If they are not met at the proper developmental stage, and the lingering deficit expresses itself erotically after puberty, this does not somehow make the needs themselves illegitimate through lack of "timeliness." Rather, it is the manner by which the postpubescent psyche attempts to meet these *still legitimate* needs—through sexual and romantic attachment—that is inappropriate.

56   *Homosexuality: A New Christian Ethic*, op. cit.

57   *One Nation under God*, (Teodoro Maniaci & Francine M. Rzeznik, directors. 3Z/Hourglass Productions, Inc. New York: First Run Features, 1993). This widely viewed and controversial documentary has been criticized by defenders

of the ex-gay movement for its evident bias against the idea that homosexuals should or can successfully change their orientation. That the film has such a point of view is unarguable, and the film's directors make no particular pretense of neutrality. On the other hand, while it is true that editing of interviews can to some extent distort or color the statements presented, the fact remains that the quotations cited here and elsewhere in this chapter were made by those interviewed.

58 William H. Masters & Virginia E. Johnson, *Homosexuality in Perspective* (Boston: Little Brown, 1979).

59 What Rogers and Exodus mean by "recovery," according to Michael Bussee, one of the organization's founders, is that "it is possible to go from gay to straight." *One Nation under God*, op. cit.

60 Payne, *The Broken Image*, op. cit., for this and following citations.

61 In the case history of a diagnosed lesbian with which Payne begins *The Broken Image*, these repressed memories include sexual abuse in very early childhood by the father, with the mother discovering father and daughter *in flagrante delicto* and hysterically throwing the child against a wall. Through one session of healing of memories, this unfortunate young woman is reported to have forgiven both parents, been released from her own abiding sense of generalized guilt and shame, and been freed not only from lesbian feelings but also from an addiction to cigarettes and compulsive overeating. "A new person from this day on," this young woman did need to go through a "learning process," however, in terms of developing healthier attitudes toward herself and others.

62 In one case, this involved picturing Jesus in attendance at the client's *in utero* and birth trauma, which—Payne recounts—both she and the client "saw" and experienced vividly.

63 In one instance, a lesbian was directed to see herself "handing to Jesus" the various aspects of her broken sexuality; in another, a gay man was led to picture himself taking on a new "masculine identity" as he made his will one with the perfect masculinity of Christ.

64 Payne attributes the loss of the gift of psychological healing within the church to the ascendancy of Aristotelian categories through the theology of St. Thomas Aquinas. Unlike Plato, she notes, Aristotle only accepted the functions of the rational mind (reasoning, experience) as means for perceiving truth. In so doing, he (and Aquinas and the Western church after him) ignored the intuitive heart or "deep mind" (what we now call the subconscious), which is the seat of the creative imagination, memory, dreams, visions, metaphor, symbol, myth, love and the gifts of the Holy Spirit.

65 *Homosexuality: A New Christian Ethic*, op. cit.

66 Ibid.

67 Op. cit. for this and all following quotations.

68 As Comiskey notes, he has "nothing invested in covering my difficulties." Such honesty, he adds, "frees me to be wholly authentic with others about my 'unhealedness.'"

69 "This realignment of desire is fundamental to the healing process," Comiskey notes. "Perhaps this explains the relative lack of success achieved by traditional psychotherapy in 'curing' homosexuals. A person wrestling with a life-dominating network of desires and distorted self-perceptions cannot be healed by mere analysis of the soul. That soul needs to be encountered by its Creator and bathed in His love . . ."

70 Comiskey comments that many who come to his programs for help ultimately "find the cost of obedience too great, its rewards too intangible. They may

desire to be free from homosexuality at some level, but at a more profound level, their hearts remain aligned with homosexual pursuits. The threat of loss is too overwhelming. Yielding control over their desires and inner brokenness may be too much. As a result, their willingness remains weak, repentance is shallow, and their hearts grow divided between the pursuit of God and the immediate returns of homosexual pursuits."

71   On this point, Comiskey stands in marked disagreement with Payne's assurances of relatively rapid healing. In fact, despite her having written the glowing Preface to his book, Comiskey would seem to indirectly issue a caution regarding Payne's sort of ministry when he writes: "Some helpers. . . insist on the pivotal role of healing in the restoration of the sexually broken. That healing more often than not occurs over a short, intensive period that is outside one's local church context. But often the healed return home to a fellowship context that supplies no real relational structure on which their growth can be supported." (*Pursuing Sexual Wholeness*, op. cit.)

72   Comiskey reports that, after forgiving his father and the male childhood peers who had rejected him, he discovered for the first time a deep desire in his soul for male acceptance and friendship which he could affirm without shame: "I didn't want sex or romance from men—I wanted buddies!"

73   While Moberly would seem to indicate that celibacy within an achieved heterosexual identity could also be a viable choice for the healed homosexual, Comiskey's personal commitment to the significance of marriage and family leads him to focus on that result of the healing process to the near-exclusion of long-term celibacy as an alternative option.

74   While some ex-gay ministries report immediate results along the lines of the Payne model, most hold that it usually takes two or more years before the recovery process reaches its goal of a same-sex gender identity sufficiently strong for one to choose to pursue heterosexual relationships.

75   Quoted without citation in Blair, *Homosexualities*, op. cit.

76   Kevin Linehan, quoted without citation in Blair, ibid. Such statements would appear to indicate that, to those in the movement, becoming ex-gay is on one level primarily a matter of a shift in cognitive perspective: one makes the choice to see oneself as God is understood to see one, through the perfect heterosexual humanity of Jesus. That being done, the continuation of homosexual feelings is irrelevant to one's identity because, on the higher level of spiritual truth, the fact is that one is heterosexual.

77   This is the case not only because of scriptural prohibitions but because of the overarching cosmic significance of male-female complementarity. As Ruth Tiffany Barnhouse writes (*Homosexuality: A Symbolic Confusion*, op. cit.): "Homosexuality constitutes a rejection, either partial or total, of the possibility of union with the other sex. Very clearly, the wholeness of the sacred order is neither symbolized nor approximated by sexual practices which are thus grounded in the denial of half of the image of God."

78   *Homosexuality: A New Christian Ethic*, op. cit.

79   Payne, *The Broken Image*, op. cit.

80   *One Nation under God*, op. cit.

81   Begun in 1977 as a twenty-five minute weekly radio broadcast by conservative Christian child psychologist and author James Dobson (after the extraordinary success of his book, *Dare to Discipline* [Wheaton, Illinois: Tyndale House Publishing, 1970]), Focus on the Family has grown into an international organization with a wide range of ministries. It sponsors numerous publications, films, television programs, videos, professional support groups, pastoral print resources and political action activities.

82   Ex-gay John Paulk—who, with his wife, former lesbian Anne, gained wide media coverage for the ex-gay movement in the summer and fall of 1998 (see introduction, page 14)—is now on the Focus on the Family staff, hired to represent the organization on issues relating to homosexuality.

83   "Focus on the Family Position Statement on Homosexual Rights," released October 1, 1998, *emphasis added.*

84   This argumentation is significant for those holding this view, since, if it can be demonstrated that homosexuals are not as a class legitimately qualified to claim civil rights protection, then the legal protections they seek must be—by definition—"special rights."

85   "Focus on the Family Position Statement on Violence Against Homosexuals," released October 1, 1998.

86   The Right Reverend William Wantland (Eau Claire, Wisconsin) has stated that there are "thousands" of homosexuals "who have been able to be changed in their orientation" through the efforts of ex-gay ministries and live "happy, productive lives as heterosexuals" (quoted by Ralph Blair in *The Record*, the newsletter of Evangelicals Concerned. Summer, 1996).

87   Love in Action is now directed by John Smid, who—in 1988, while the organization was still located in California—was instrumental in John Paulk's release from homosexuality. Love in Action's previous longtime head, ex-gay Frank Worthen, has remained in San Rafael, where he and his wife now lead New Hope Ministries.

88   Blair contends such problems have troubled the "ex-gay" movement from its inception—and "at the top." Among the examples documented in his *Homosexualities: Faith, Facts & Fairy Tales* (op. cit.) are: Guy Charles, who claimed to have been "delivered" from the "lusts, the desires, the fantasies, [and] the acts" of homosexuality, but who, in 1977—after numerous complaints about his having sex with the young men coming to his Liberation in Jesus Christ "ex-gay" program—justified his same-sex activity on a claim that it represented not homosexuality but rather "David and Jonathan" relationships sanctioned by scriptural example; Colin Cook, whose *Homosexuality: An Open Door?* (Boise: Pacific Press Pub. Assn., 1985) was hailed by Richard Lovelace of Gordon-Conwell Seminary as an "authentic theological masterpiece. . . a jewel. . . a theological pearl," but who, in 1986, was forced to resign from leadership of his "ex-gay" program after it was discovered he had been sexually involved with more than a dozen of the young men coming to him for treatment over a six year period (Cook, in retaliation, publicly alleged that "sexual improprieties between leaders and counselees occur" throughout the "ex-gay" movement); and Doug Houck, founder of the Seattle-based Metanoia Ministries, who was forced by his Board in 1990 to remove himself as Director of that organization due to continued "homosexual acting out" over a three year period (Houck blamed his "moral lapse" on a "heavy workload" that had so "consumed" him that he was no longer able to "fully understand my actions").

89   Nearly all of the early movement leaders who claimed to have been changed to "ex-gay" have now left the movement, Blair writes. Among these dropouts are Roger Grindstaff (alias "Roger Dean") of Disciples Only and Teen Challenge (see page 256, note 28), John Evans (alias "Ted") of Love in Action, Jim Kasper of Melodyland's Exit ministry, Greg Reid of EAGLE ("Ex-Active Gay Liberated Eternally"), Rick Notch of Open Door, Jeff Ford and Ed Hurst of Outpost and Michael Bussee and his late life-partner Gary Cooper, who were among the founders of both Exit and Exodus International. After nearly a decade of presenting themselves as "ex-gay," marrying, having children, and counseling hundreds of people through their ministries, Bussee and Cooper

admitted they had fallen in love with each other, left their wives and were joined in a union which they held to be the equivalent of a marriage. Bussee now asserts that "[s]exual orientation is forever. I was so sincere. I tried so hard, but I wasted years of my life misleading myself and misleading others." (Quoted by Mel White in *Stranger at the Gate: To Be Gay and Christian in America* [New York: Simon & Schuster, 1994]). In another context, Bussee has stated: "The bottom line is, the 'ex-gay' process doesn't work." (Quoted without citation in Blair, *Homosexualities,* op. cit.)

90   Payne, Preface to Comiskey's *Pursuing Sexual Wholeness,* op. cit.

91   "Ex-gay" defenders counter that most of those arguing that change *doesn't* happen are people who believe it should *not* happen.

92   As already noted, L.I.F.E. Ministry's Joanne Highley promises "a transformation of one's orientation" and Episcopal Bishop William Wantland speaks of homosexuals "who have been able to be changed in their orientation." Similarly, Dallas Seminary professor Kenneth Gangel claims that the homosexual "propensity can be changed by the power of Jesus Christ" and argues that those Christian leaders who do not promise complete change in orientation "stop short of the real power of the gospel." (Quoted without citation in Blair, *Homosexualities,* op. cit.)

93   Such a change would presumably be evidenced by the "ex-gay" eventually no longer having to struggle against persistent homosexual erotic or emotional drives (since no true heterosexual has to deal with such issues) and instead, like any other heterosexual, experiencing sexual and affectional attraction to and satisfaction with the opposite sex.

94   Reported without citation by Blair, ibid. Kenney became involved in the "ex-gay" movement after her fiancé announced he was gay and ended their engagement and she has been quite open about her difficulties in finding a suitable husband within "ex-gay" ranks. In comments quoted by Blair, Kenney explains, with remarkable candor: "Being in ex-gay ministry often has meant that I've. . . met and fallen in love with men from gay backgrounds." Such attachments did not have the results Kenney hoped for, however, so "I finally asked God to bring a man into my life who could appreciate me as a woman."

95   Blair (*Homosexualities,* op. cit.) documents the following sampling: Frank Worthen, former director of one of the oldest "ex-gay" ministries, Love in Action, admits that "one of the most difficult battles ex-gay men and women face is working through attractions we often have to members of the same sex"; Alan Mediger of Regeneration and Exodus International comments that "when an ex-gay is trying to help a struggling homosexual, the temptation to fall is great"(former "ex-gay" Rick Notch notes in this regard the particular hazards posed by "ex-gay" conventions such as those sponsored by Exodus); and Outpost's Joe Hallett acknowledges that: "[e]x-gays [*are*] people who choose not to act out homosexuality and yet feel its pull."

96   Comiskey, *Pursuing Sexual Wholeness,* op. cit. It has been noted that, along with this ongoing struggle against homosexual desires, Comiskey—while attesting to feeling sexual and emotional attraction for his wife—never alludes to any even passing heterosexual attraction outside of his marriage.

97   Op. cit.

98   Blair, ed., *Review: A Quarterly of Evangelicals Concerned,* Fall, 1991; Vol. 16, No. 1.

99   *Pursuing Sexual Wholeness,* op. cit.

100   Payne and others, of course, are considerably bolder than Comiskey, leaving assertions that "there is no such thing as a homosexual" undocumented and undefended (Payne, *Crisis in Masculinity,* op. cit.).

101 Payne, *The Broken Image*, op. cit.

102 Some "ex-gay" spokespersons have appeared to come close to making just such a shift when they have compared homosexual "recovery" to the recovery of alcoholics through Alcoholics Anonymous Twelve Step programs. What has not been made explicit by "ex-gays" using the AA analogy, however, is the fact that AA members are always adamant on the point that, no matter how long they have been sober, they are and always will be alcoholics.

103 Comiskey points out (*Pursuing Sexual Wholeness*, op. cit.) that God himself proclaims "it is not good for man to be alone" (Gen 2:18); Comiskey adds that human beings are meant for touch, intimacy and partnership.

104 Should this last observation seem overly cynical, critics note that "ex-gay" advocates have at times not been above a certain level of cynicism of their own, demonstrated in particular by their use of various questionable "proofs" that change truly is possible for the homosexual. A much quoted and supposedly "scientific" study by two Christian psychologists claiming to document change of sexual orientation is a case in point. Published in 1980, the study by Dr. Mansell Pattison and his wife Myrna Loy Pattison ("Religiously Mediated Changed in Homosexuals," *American Journal of Psychiatry*, Vol. 137, No. 12, Dec. 1980) deliberately "stacked the deck" on its research from the start. As Michael Bussee and Gary Cooper report in interviews in the film *One Nation under God*, the Pattisons came to them (while they were still active in "ex-gay" ministry) asking for referrals to successfully changed "ex-gays" who could be used as subjects for their study. After searching the 400 to 800 files of individuals who had been through their ministries' programs, Bussee and Cooper came up with thirty people who, they believed, offered the best evidence of successful reorientation (as Cooper notes in the interview, this is extremely bad science, since "we were deliberately trying to affect the results"). After interviewing those thirty individuals, the Pattisons indicated in their published study that eleven had shown significant "change" and, on that basis, claimed there was proof for the effectiveness of religiously-based conversion of sexual orientation. Ironically, two of the "success stories" cited in the article were Bussee and Cooper themselves, both of whom later repudiated their "ex-gay" testimonies and admitted they had never stopped being homosexual. Even after Bussee and Cooper publicly disavowed their claimed "recovery" and exposed the unscientific nature of the Pattisons' work, however, "ex-gay" proponents have continued to cite the Pattison study to support claims of "change" (most recently, Joseph Nicolosi in his 1991 book, *Reparative Therapy of Male Homosexuals*, op. cit.). In an example cited by Blair, the respected evangelical publisher Logos International reissued Love in Action founder Kent Philpott's *The Third Sex? Six Homosexuals Tell Their Stories* (Plainfield, New Jersey: Logos International, 1975), one of the earliest books to assert "ex-gay" claims, even after all six of the book's subjects had renounced their purported healings. Blair also documents a number of instances in which reputable conservative Christian authors have quoted "ex-gay" testimonials in their own works to support "ex-gay" claims, but have carefully edited out admissions of continuing temptation and struggle that appear within these affirmations of "release" from homosexuality (Blair, *Ex-Gay* [New York: Ralph Blair, 1982]).

105 Blair, interviewed in *One Nation under God*, speaks of the "ex-gay" movement's "rehash of dated psychoanalytical ideas."

106 *One Nation under God*, op. cit., and *Homosexuality: A New Christian Ethic*, op. cit.

107 *Reparative Therapy of Male Homosexuals*, op. cit.

108 Blair, *Review*, op. cit.

109   "The Personalization of Sex," in *From Machismo to Mutuality*, Ruether &
      Eugene Bianchi, eds. (New York: Paulist Press, 1976). If Ruether's character-
      ization seems to overstate "ex-gay" arguments on this point, it should be
      remembered that Karl Stern, whose views Payne promotes in her own highly
      influential teaching, actually speaks even more extravagantly on the question
      of appropriate gender drives and attributes. Similarly, Comiskey's less florid
      statements regarding suitable gender traits at least come very close to those
      stereotypes Ruether is attacking.

110   *Pursuing Sexual Wholeness*, op. cit.

111   *Homosexuality: A Symbolic Confusion*, op. cit. Barnhouse does qualify her judg-
      ment by adding that, at least in some cases, "even though the homosexual dis-
      position itself constitutes an immaturity, it surely ranks well below other
      immaturities in the amount of social or moral harm which is done."

112   "Out-Takes," in *Boys Like Us*, op. cit.

113   There have been numerous proposals as to precisely what does constitute the
      imago Dei in humans: free will (Gregory of Nyssa, died c. 395; John of Damas-
      cus, died c. 749); a reflection of God's triune nature in the three "powers" of
      the human mind—memory, intellect and will (Augustine); humans' superiority
      over the rest of creation; human reason; immortality; and the capacity of the
      soul for God which makes it possible for human beings to be brought into
      union with their Creator. The consensus of the pre-Reformation western
      Church seemed to be that the image of God had to do with human reason and
      free will, which, though damaged by the Fall, were not completely destroyed.
      The Protestant Reformers tended toward a more pessimistic view: Luther,
      while agreeing with Rome that the image of God in man was free will, argued
      that, *post lapsum*, this freedom had been lost in everything but name only.
      Calvin taught that the image of God was an "integrity" whereby the passions
      were governed by reason so that human nature functioned as a harmoniously
      ordered whole. For Calvin, this image was not annihilated by the Fall, but was
      "so corrupted that whatever remains is but a horrible deformity." A recent
      Roman Catholic reference work (Richard P. McBrien, ed., *The HarperCollins
      Encyclopedia of Catholicism* [San Francisco: HarperCollins, 1995]) succinctly
      summarizes the range of possibilities raised within the Christian tradition as
      to what constitutes the image of God in humans: reason, intellect, the capacity
      for moral decision, the ability to rule over creation, free will, and—more gener-
      ally—the "special kinship" which exists between God and humankind. Nota-
      bly absent from this listing, as critics of Barth's argument would be quick to
      point out, is any reference to male-female complementarity.

114   Even so great an advocate of God's healing power as Kathryn Kuhlman was
      always careful to note that many who came to her meetings left without find-
      ing the healing they sought, and she considered this painful reality a part of
      the unknowable mystery of God's ways with His children.

115   *The Broken Image*, op. cit.

116   It has been noted that nearly all those promoting the possibility of "healing"
      for the homosexual specifically acknowledge their indebtedness to the work
      and witness of Agnes Sanford. Despite the nearly incalculable impact of San-
      ford's ministry on the church over the past thirty or more years, as well as that
      of the School of Pastoral Care she founded with her husband, the Reverend
      Edgar Sanford, Ms. Sanford's teaching has never been without its critics and
      her views are still far from uncontested in many circles. To further complicate
      the matter, there are those who promote Sanford's inner healing teachings but
      nevertheless do not see homosexual relationships as necessarily sinful or
      homosexuals as being in need of "healing" of their orientation. Episcopal
      priest and author Morton Kelsey, for example, has for years been one of the

most widely read of Sanford's disciples. Nevertheless, in *Sacrament of Sexuality: The Spirituality and Psychology of Sex*, coauthored with his wife Barbara (Warwick, New York: Amity House, 1986), Kelsey argues that, "[w]here people really feel that their truest expression is to accept a permanent homosexual lifestyle, [*Christians*] should encourage them to live it in the most loving, creative way, just as the best heterosexual partners do, and we can help integrate them into the Church's life."

117   *Stranger at the Gate*, op. cit.

118   Blair, *Homosexualities*, op. cit.

119   *Stranger at the Gate*, op. cit.

120   *Homosexualities*, op. cit.

121   I place "Eastern" in quotation marks because the Orthodox church does not consider itself to be a denominational or regional "part" of a larger whole that is the Christian church. Rather, Orthodoxy understands itself as *the* continuing reality of that "one, holy, catholic and apostolic church" founded by Christ's redemptive work and his commissioning of the apostles, from which "Western" Christianity (first Roman Catholicism, then, subsequently, Protestantism) is in schism. Hereafter, I will follow Orthodoxy's own usage and omit "Eastern" from the designation.

122   Mathewes-Green's comments were made in personal correspondence with the author. Mathewes-Green herself, it should be noted, tends toward closer identification with viewpoint 3, "A Call to Costly Discipleship," than with the present viewpoint. Nevertheless, she believes intellectual integrity requires a respectful hearing by the church of the witness of those affirming that they have experienced significant healing in what they perceive to be sexual brokenness.

Chapter 3: A Call to Costly Discipleship

1   There is a certain irony to the fact that this letter is generally known only because Vanauken released it to Leanne Payne for publication in her *The Broken Image*, op. cit. Payne avoids the fact that Lewis obviously assumes the homosexual's condition is immutable by introducing the letter as an example of how God can use such a "wound. . . even before the psychological healing comes."

2   And a question, furthermore, which most of this viewpoint would argue is never addressed in revelation.

3   An interesting example of the use of such an exegetical paradigm that does not deal with sexual morality is the treatment of Paul's statement in 1 Cor 6:10, that "drunkards. . . will never inherit the kingdom of God." With the present medical understanding of alcoholism as a disease, most Christians would no longer argue that a faithful Christian who struggles unsuccessfully with alcoholism throughout his or her life (e.g., C. S. Lewis's beloved brother Major Warren Lewis) will necessarily be excluded from the company of the redeemed.

4   C. S. Lewis, however, whose opinions on homosexuality—at least as expressed in his letter to Vanauken cited above—would seem clearly to place him within this viewpoint, nonetheless is one of those who has written eloquently of the transcendent nature of gender, in particular in his novel *That Hideous Strength*, op. cit.

5   In theological terms the "end" of a particular act is both a *descriptive term*—the result achieved when that act is properly performed without interference or misdirection—and a *prescriptive term*—the *intended* result of the act, the purpose for which it was created by God in the first place (as with the descriptive and normative meanings of "nature," the latter is often extrapolated from the former). The end of eating, for example, is nourishment and bodily health. Given that end, gluttony is a sin not only because it entails greed and economic injustice, but because it contravenes the end of eating (bodily health) by actually doing injury to the body.

6   In *Casti connubii*, his 1930 encyclical on Christian marriage, Pius XI explicitly argued the subordination of the unitive to the generative end of the sexual act, and as recently as the late 1950s Catholic moral theologians continued to uphold this viewpoint. Michael J. Buckley, for example, in his *Morality and the Homosexual* (London: Sands & Co., 1959; published in America the following year by Newman Press [Westminster, Maryland]), sees a direct relationship between this subordination and maintenance of the church's moral stand against homosexuality: "[To] put sexual fulfillment and mutual help and companionship on an equality with the primary purpose of procreation . . .play[s] into the hands of homosexuals. If sexual pleasure and companionship are regarded as equally primary. . . the force of the argument against homosexual unions in which there is genuine affection is enormously weakened."
     Rosemary Radford Ruether in a sense proves Buckley's point when she writes, seventeen years later: "If sex/love is centered primarily on communion between two persons. . . then the love of two persons of the same sex need be no less than that of two persons of the opposite sex. Nor need their experience of ecstatic bodily communion be less valuable." ("The Personalization of Sex," op. cit.)

7   Lewis, *The Screwtape Letters*, op. cit.

8   Gerard Weber & James Killgallon (San Francisco: HarperCollins, 1996).

9   This term was used rather than the more authoritative "pastoral letter" because the document was approved by the administrative board of the bishops' conference, not by a vote of the entire national episcopacy.

10   Although Bahnsen (*Homosexuality: A Biblical View*, op. cit.) appears to do so.

11   As an example of such scientific overreaching, proponents of this view would cite the common claim that, because there is evidence of homosexuality in virtually every human culture, homosexuality is a "natural" part of human experience and therefore cannot be morally objectionable.

12   McBrien, ed., op. cit.

13   The bishops were careful to distinguish between homosexual orientation and homosexual acts, however, cautioning that the statement should not be taken as an "endorsement of what some would call a 'homosexual lifestyle.'" Despite this caveat, the bishops' message stands in a certain tension with an October 1, 1986 "Letter to the Bishops of the Catholic Church on the Pastoral Care of Homosexual Persons" issued by the Vatican's Congregation for the Doctrine of the Faith. That letter argues—in reaction to certain "overly benign interpretations" of the homosexual condition by Catholic theologians and pastors—that while the homosexual condition "is not a sin, it is a more or less strong tendency ordered toward an intrinsic moral evil and thus the inclination itself must be seen as an objective disorder."

14   Robert M. Friday, "Homosexuality," *The New Dictionary of Theology*, Joseph A. Komonchak, et al., eds. (Wilmington, Delaware: Michael Glazier, 1987).

15   McBrien, ed., *HarperCollins Encyclopedia of Catholicism*, op. cit.

16 They can also, conversely, be as broken, immature and unstable as are some heterosexuals. Whatever psychological deficits a homosexual may suffer are not elements of his or her sexual orientation per se, although—as is the case with many heterosexuals—neurosis may well involve sexuality along with other elements of the personality.

17 That all this is held to be true is not understood to justify homosexual acts, however.

18 See page 269, note 13.

19 *The Screwtape Letters,* op. cit.

20 Field, *The Homosexual Way* (Downers Grove: Inter-Varsity Press, 1979).

21 White, *Eros Defiled* (Downers Grove: Inter-Varsity Press, 1977).

22 Ibid.

23 "Jesus doesn't expect us to commit sexual suicide" was a commonly advanced argument among certain members of Integrity, the Episcopalian organization for gays and lesbians, in the mid-1970s.

24 This and the previous quotation are also recorded in parallel passages in Matt 10:37–39 and 19:29.

25 Weber & Killgallon, eds. op. cit.

26 This was not the first time Creech had been the focus of public controversy regarding ministry to homosexuals. In 1990, Creech was forced to resign his pastorate of the Fairmont United Methodist Church in Raleigh, North Carolina, after he and other local clergy founded the Raleigh Religious Network for Gay and Lesbian Equality and subsequently marched in Raleigh's 1988 Gay and Lesbian Pride Parade.

27 Thomas McAnally, quoted in "Methodists Tighten Ban on Gay Unions," Don Lattin, *San Francisco Chronicle,* August 12, 1998.

28 Chief officiant at the union was the Reverend Don Fardo, Barnett's and Charlton's pastor at Sacramento's St. Mark's United Methodist Church. Fardo's bishop, the Reverend Melvin G. Talbert, a past president of the National Council of Churches who had gone on record as supporting same-sex unions, stated that—despite his own personal convictions—as a bishop he was required to uphold church law and that, consequently, if a formal complaint were filed against Fardo, he would have no choice but to set in motion the disciplinary procedure which could result in Fardo's being defrocked.

29 Termed "our Selma" by some supporters of the blessing of same-sex unions, the Barnett-Charlton ceremony attracted extensive media coverage, a "circle of love" of supportive clergy and laity who remained outside to ward off protestors, and a contingent of picketers from the Reverend Fred Phelps's Westboro Baptist Church of Topeka, Kansas, one of whom carried a large sign reading "Brides of Satan." (Phelps and his congregants have for a number of years made a practice of demonstrating around the country at the funerals of well-known homosexuals who have died of AIDS.)

30 In an attempt to avoid further division, the Judicial Council in November 1998 ordered the denomination's congregations and regional conferences to cease identifying themselves as "reconciling" (i.e., supportive of gay unions and the ordination of non-celibate homosexual clergy) or "confessing" (upholding the church's traditional and still official position).

31 Citing conflicts over gay issues and scriptural authority, the Fellowship's president, the Reverend John Christie, resigned from the United Methodist Church in the fall of 1998 to accept the pastorate of a Baptist congregation.

32 Under Presbyterian polity, not only clergy, but local congregational elders and deacons are ordained.

33 In 1985, the General Assembly's Permanent Judicial Commission began to take selective action against certain More Light churches for violation of the 1978 policy statement, ruling that a More Light "pledge" endorsed by these congregations was illegal under church law. Nonetheless, the More Light Church Network has continued to show slow but steady growth into the 1990s, so that in 1996 there were approximately fifty More Light congregations in the United States (Keith Hartman, *Congregations in Conflict: The Battle Over Homosexuality* [New Brunswick, New Jersey: Rutgers University Press, 1996]).

34 The following year, a church court revoked the appointment of the Reverend Janie Spahr, a lesbian in a committed partnership with another woman, as co-pastor of a Rochester, New York, congregation.

35 Nonetheless, some Presbyterian clergy quietly continued to officiate at such ceremonies and, in early 1999, the Hudson River Presbytery (New York) voted 105 to 35 to allow its clergy the freedom to decide individually whether or not they would bless gay unions. The decision was expected to be challenged by conservatives through the denomination's courts.

36 Homosexual candidates committed to celibacy continued to be eligible for ordination.

37 The Reverend Barry Stopfel has since been ordained to the priesthood. With his life partner, Will Leckie, he has published *Courage to Love: A Gay Priest Stands Up for His Beliefs* (New York: Doubleday, 1997).

38 The Reverend Richard C. Crocker, an Episcopal priest from Iowa, quoted in "Episcopalians Narrowly Reject Call to Bless Same Sex Unions," Larry B. Stammer, *Los Angeles Times*, July 20, 1997.

39 The Reverend Jane N. Garrett of Vermont, quoted in Stammer, ibid.

40 The resolution in fact won a simple majority in the House of Deputies. However, under the rules of the House, passage required fifty-seven affirmative votes from each group within it, lay and clergy. The final tally was fifty-six lay votes in favor, forty-one opposing, and fifty-six clergy votes in favor, thirty-seven opposing. In short, the measure lost in the lower house by only two votes.

41 Quoted in Stammer, op. cit.

42 The conference, which occurs once every ten years, gathers together the worldwide bishops of the Anglican communion (all those national churches in communion with and tracing their origins to the Church of England) under the leadership of the Archbishop of Canterbury, primate of the English church. It takes its title from Lambeth Palace, the archbishop's official residence.

43 Quoted in "Lambeth Takes Conservative Stance on Human Sexuality," James H. Thrall, Anglican Communion News Service (on line), ACNS LC094, 6 August 1998.

44 The resolution was approved by a vote of 526 bishops in favor, 70 opposing and 45 abstentions. (American Presiding Bishop Frank T. Griswold III was among those bishops who abstained.) Commentators noted not only the uncommon rancor attending the matter (Archbishop Carey described the session devoted to the resolution as "difficult and painful" Thrall, ibid.), but also the fact that the more strongly conservative amendments added from the floor were spearheaded by third-world bishops who for the first time were in the majority at the conference. That more might be at stake than scriptural authority or traditional morality seemed clear when several American bishops voting against the resolution were jeered and hissed as "colonialist" and "white" (as was reported by Lambeth participant the Right Reverend William

Swing, Bishop of the Diocese of California, in a speech given at a day of theological reflection upon the Lambeth resolution on sexuality held at the Church Divinity School of the Pacific in Berkeley, California, February 27, 1999).

45 Recently, however, concern has been expressed in some conservative Catholic quarters over an alleged "homosexualization" of the priesthood, the claim being that qualified heterosexual men are kept from considering pastoral ministry as a vocation due to the preponderance of gay men in the priesthood and the tacit acceptance of a "gay mentality" in many seminaries.

46 See page 269, note 13.

47 Hartman, *Congregations in Conflict*, op. cit. After the expulsion of Dignity from church property, the American hierarchy established Diocesan Gay/Lesbian Outreach ministries, which provides officially sanctioned liturgies for homosexual Catholics willing to affirm church teaching on sexuality and accept the discipline of abstinence. In combination with the loss of Catholic churches and priests for Dignity services, this move split many exiled Dignity chapters and resulted in a decline in Dignity membership nationwide. Pat Windsor, "Dignity, Church Find Ways to Peacefully Coexist," *National Catholic Reporter* 27 (August 16, 1991).

48 Chapters in any particular diocese may be organized only with the consent of the local bishop.

49 Telephone interview with Courage staff member, June 10, 1996.

50 Thielicke, trans. John W. Doberstein, *The Ethics of Sex* (New York: Harper & Row, 1964).

51 Bawer, *A Place at the Table*, op. cit.

52 Lewis letter to S. Vanauken, published in Payne, *The Broken Image*, op. cit.

53 Thomas Schmidt, Westmont College *Horizon*, 4/10/86.

54 There is particular irony to Lewis's statement in that he was, in fact, one of those who found love and married quite late in life. Further, even though both Lewis and author Joy Davidman Gresham had previously written that, in accordance with scriptural and Western church teaching, divorced Christians are not free to remarry so long as their former spouse is alive, they were married in a canonically irregular ceremony (by a nonresident Anglican priest without the required permission of the local bishop) despite the fact that Mrs. Gresham was herself a divorcee with a still living ex-husband.

55 *A Place at the Table*, op. cit.

56 German feminist theologian Uta Ranke-Heinemann's *Eunuchs for the Kingdom of God*, (trans. Peter Heinegg; New York: Doubleday, 1990), gives extensive evidence of what Ranke-Heinemann considers the near-pathological fear and loathing of the feminine and all things sexual that permeates the writings of those early theologians whose views were instrumental in establishing the church's elevation of celibacy and virginity as morally superior states.

57 Grand Rapids: W. B. Eerdmans, 1978; cited in Blair's *Homosexualities*, op. cit.

58 *Homosexualities*, op. cit. Blair is referring to the often-quoted (and disputed by some conservatives) Kinsey projection of the percentage of homosexuals in the general population.

59 Quoted without citation in Blair, ibid.

60 Ibid.

61 *A Place at the Table*, op. cit.

62 Ibid.

63 *Straight and Narrow? Compassion and Clarity in the Homosexual Debate* (Downers Grove: Inter-Varsity Press, 1995); see bibliography.

64 As Bawer writes, "Homosexuality, at the deepest, truest level, is not a matter of *doing* something. It's a matter of *being* something. (*A Place at the Table*, op. cit.)

65 Ibid.

66 Schmidt's *Straight and Narrow? (op. cit.)* contains what some contend is a particularly striking example of this double standard in the treatment of scriptural materials. Although insisting that, when it comes to homosexuality, "Scripture must be the primary and final authority for. . . morality," Schmidt then raises another issue condemned in Scripture, usury (the lending of money at interest), but denies the contemporary relevance of what he admits are "repeated" biblical prohibitions of this practice, arguing that changing cultural realities (a simple vs. a complex economy, private vs. corporate lenders) have so altered the *meaning* and *consequences* of usury that scriptural proscriptions have been rendered obsolete.

67 *A Place at the Table*, op. cit.

68 Ibid.

Chapter 4: Pastoral Accommodation

1 *The Ethics of Sex*, op. cit.

2 Smedes, *Sex for Christians: The Limits and Liberties of Sexual Living* (Grand Rapids: William B. Eerdmans, 1976).

3 Curran, "Homosexuality and Moral Theology: Methodological and Substantive Considerations," *The Thomist*, Vol. 35, No. 3 (July 1971); Washington: The Thomist Press.

4 *The Ethics of Sex*, op. cit.

5 *Sex for Christians*, op. cit.

6 The Code also, it should be noted, proscribes other acts which the majority of Christians still hold to be sinful—adultery (Lev 18:20; 20:10), for example, and bestiality (Lev 18:23; 20:15).

7 *Sex for Christians*, op. cit.

8 Thielicke's always labored language (at least as it reads in translation) is particularly problematical here in that, strictly speaking, Leviticus says nothing at all about "homosexuality" (which term designates both orientation and act) but only refers to sexual *activity* between two men. Moreover, there is no mention at all of "pederasty"—generally understood as anal intercourse with an adolescent boy—in the text, although pederasty could certainly fall under the far more general Levitical language, which speaks of "a man ly[ing] with a male as with a woman." (Lev 20:13)

9 *The Ethics of Sex*, op. cit.

10 *Sex for Christians*, op. cit., for this and following quotation.

11 *The Ethics of Sex*, op. cit.

12 Ibid, for this and following quotation.

13 . . . "Christ is the head of every man, and the husband is the head of his wife, and God is the head of Christ. Any man who prays or prophesies with something on his head disgraces his head, but any woman who prays or prophesies with her head unveiled disgraces her head—it is one and the same thing as having her head shaved. . . . For a man ought not to have his head veiled,

since he is the image and reflection of God; but woman is the reflection of man.. Indeed, man was not made from woman, but woman from man. Neither was man created for the sake of woman, but woman for the sake of man. For this reason a woman ought to have a symbol of authority on her head, because of the angels." (1 Cor 11:3–5, 7–10).

14   While Thielicke does not go on to spell out what these conventions were, they would certainly include: prostitutes went out in public with their hair uncovered and the priestesses and oracles of certain of the ecstatic mystery religions prophesied without veils, whereas respectable women were not seen outside of their own homes with heads bared.

15   Protestant Thielicke ignores the fact that, among traditionalist Roman Catholics and old-school Orthodox, it is still expected that women will cover their heads in worship.

16   *The Ethics of Sex*, op. cit., for this and following quotations. There is a certain irony to the fact that, since Thielicke wrote these words in 1964, many Christians have come to question not only Paul's illustration but his *point* in this passage as well, contending on both biblical and extra-biblical grounds that the differentiation of the sexes does not require the subordination of the woman to the man but rather the loving submission of each to the other and both to Christ.

17   Although given only cursory discussion by Thielicke himself, this point becomes extremely significant to the arguments of the next viewpoint ("Affirmation").

18   Thielicke exemplifies this principle in the fact that, with the rise of the democracies, the meaning and application of the scriptural texts relating to the governing authorities must perforce undergo rethinking—one cannot settle all questions regarding political issues and the duties of citizens by recourse to a proof text. Ibid.

19   Curran, "Homosexuality & Moral Theology," op. cit.

20   While many conservatives would no doubt see in such an approach an untenable abridgement of scriptural authority, proponents of this viewpoint point out that, in fact, conservatives themselves apply such interpretive qualifications to the biblical text all the time. Few evangelical women, for example, feel that the writing of St. Peter on the point of appropriate female adornment (1 Pet 3:3) forbids them from wearing make-up or jewelry, nor do most mainstream Protestants believe that women should "remain silent in church," despite St. Paul's statement to that effect (1 Cor 14:34). Similarly, conservative Roman Catholics and Anglicans do not feel bound by the Pentateuch's prohibition of "graven images" (Exod 20:4) as aids to devotion.

21   Smedes, for example, writes forcefully that "It seems utterly clear to me that the Bible from beginning to end views the heterosexual union as God's intention for sexuality." *Sex for Christians*, op. cit.

22   H. Kimball Jones, in his *Towards a Christian Understanding of the Homosexual* (New York: Association Press, 1966), quotes with apparent approval Sylvanus M. Duvall's comment that "from the standpoint of nature, the purpose of sex is to lure people into behavior which will perpetuate the race." Duvall, *Men, Women and Morals* (New York: Association Press, 1952).

23   This is not to say that viewpoints 1 through 3 entirely ignore or discount this element; the distinction is primarily one of emphasis.

24   Smedes, *Sex for Christians*, op. cit. Anglo-Catholic Michael Ramsey, Archbishop of Canterbury from 1961 to 1974, makes much the same point when he writes, "Sex is the bond of a union between two persons in their totality as persons; that is its true meaning." *Canterbury Pilgrim* (London: S.P.C.K., 1974).

25 Smedes, *Sex for Christians,* op. cit.

26 *The Ethics of Sex,* op. cit.

27 Smedes also questions whether homosexual relations can even be truly unitive. While admitting that "homosexual persons sometimes do. . . achieve deeply personal associations over a long period of time" and that "[h]omosexual people often do seem to relate to each other in deeply personal unions," Smedes feels it is legitimate to ask whether the gay person has "a built-in obstacle to meaningful sexual relations in which physical sex is integrated into a total personal union." Furthermore, he raises the possibility that the integration of sexual development within the wholeness of individual personhood, which is "hard enough for heterosexuals," is "perhaps impossible for homosexuals." *Sex for Christians,* op. cit.

28 Jones, *Towards a Christian Understanding of the Homosexual,* op. cit.

29 It should be noted that Curran's theory is not limited in application to questions of sexual morality.

30 "Homosexuality and Moral Theology," op. cit.

31 The most significant of these realities would be that respectable women had no "place" in ancient Levantine society apart from the protections of a husband or father, and the related fact that there were often not enough eligible men to go around.

32 As will be developed more fully through the questions that follow, this viewpoint always insists that its arguments are applicable only to the truly "constitutional" homosexual, that is, the person who is exclusively homosexual in orientation, unable to make a heterosexual adjustment or to "change," and lacking the specific charism of celibacy. Those holding that no one is truly homosexual or that any homosexual can change if he or she is willing to submit to God's healing work would obviously dispute the premises underlying such an approach.

33 *Sex for Christians,* op. cit.

34 This is not to say that such a person cannot in many instances function in heterosexual intercourse, just as many heterosexuals can under certain circumstances (isolation in a same-sex prison population, for example) function homosexually while remaining fully heterosexual in orientation.

35 Smedes, however, asserts that it is "stupid to suppose that we can get clear information on homosexuality from homosexual people: their understanding of their sexuality is just as limited as heterosexuals' understanding of theirs. They may be experts on what they suffer, but they are not necessarily experts on what they are." Smedes, *Sex for Christians,* op. cit. Aside from his rather intemperate use of "stupid," Smedes fails to address the wider epistemological ramifications of a denial of the validity of first person experiential evidence as a basis for psychosocial understanding. In that regard, gays and lesbians have complained for years of purported scientific "experts" who describe them and their lives in terms that bear little relationship to the reality they themselves experience.

36 Curran notes the difficulty this diversity of opinion among scientific professionals poses for the Christian ethicist: "Ethics can never make the mistake of absolutizing any one of the empirical sciences, such as psychology or psychiatry . . . If the experts. . . are divided, how can someone without that particular expertise make a competent judgment? The ethicist cannot merely follow the majority opinion, for history constantly reminds us that majority opinions are not necessarily true." "Homosexuality and Moral Theology," op. cit.

37 *Sex for Christians,* op. cit.

38   Thielicke, *The Ethics of Sex,* op. cit.

39   Smedes, *Sex for Christians,* op. cit.

40   *The Ethics of Sex,* op. cit.

41   *Towards a Christian Understanding of Homosexuality,* op. cit.

42   Curran, "Homosexuality and Moral Theology," op. cit.

43   Jones, *Towards a Christian Understanding of the Homosexual,* op. cit.

44   Smedes, *Sex for Christians,* op. cit.

45   *The Ethics of Sex,* op. cit.

46   Smedes, *Sex for Christians,* op. cit.

47   Ibid.

48   "Homosexuality and Moral Theology," op. cit.

49   *The Ethics of Sex,* op. cit., for this and following quotations.

50   "Homosexuality and Moral Theology," op. cit.

51   *Sex for Christians,* op. cit.

52   Thielicke, *The Ethics of Sex,* op. cit.

53   Jones, *Towards a Christian Understanding of the Homosexual,* op. cit.

54   Smedes, *Sex for Christians,* op. cit., for this and following quotation.

55   Jones, *Towards a Christian Understanding of the Homosexual,* op. cit.

56   Curran, "Homosexuality and Moral Theology," op. cit.

57   *Sex for Christians,* op. cit., for this and all the following quotations from Smedes. As should already have become obvious, Smedes, like the other authors considered in this section, casts his discussion of homosexuality exclusively in terms of the male gender. Rather than attempt to wrest his and their syntax into an inclusive form, I take it to be understood that all statements quoted apply equally to gay men and lesbians.

58   While Smedes does not give a name to the condition of a person who has made such a "conversion" from homosexuality but not to heterosexuality, it must be presumed he is proposing asexuality as preferable to active homosexuality.

59   Smedes suggests behavior modification techniques as one aid in this struggle.

60   "Homosexuality and Moral Theology," op. cit.

61   West, *Homosexuality* (Middlesex: Penguin Books, 1960), as quoted in Jones, *Towards a Christian Understanding of the Homosexual,* op. cit.

62   *Towards a Christian Understanding of the Homosexual,* op. cit., for this and the following quotations.

63   *The Ethics of Sex,* op. cit., for this and all the following quotations from Thielicke. Such sublimation—which Smedes also encourages under other names—is flatly rejected by Jones as leading to neurosis.

64   On this point, Thielicke sees a "certain analogy" between the situation of the constitutional homosexual and that of humankind after the Flood, noting that, in the post-deluge Noachic covenant (Gen 1:9ff.), "God in the way in which he deals with the fallen world places himself on the basis of [*that*] disordered world," which is to say, God starts with the given and makes the best of it that can be made (e.g., illegal force will be restrained by legal force).

65   Thielicke notes that celibacy cannot be mandated for all homosexuals unable to achieve reorientation, since "celibacy is based upon a special calling."

66   *The Ethics of Sex,* op. cit.

67 If charged with maintaining an indefensible second class citizenship for the gay Christian in a committed relationship (good enough for church membership, but not good enough for leadership), proponents of this viewpoint can point to a precedent in two epistles attributed to St. Paul. This precedent, while never articulated directly, can be deduced from both 1 Tim 3:2 and Titus 1:6–7, where it is stated that an επισκοπος, which is variously translated "bishop," "superintendent," or "overseer" and—in the Titus passage—treated as equivalent to πρεσβυτερος ("elder"), should be "the husband of one wife." Here a distinction is clearly being made between appropriate candidates for Christian leadership and others—the divorced/remarried, (less plausibly) the widowed/remarried, and (possibly, given historic context) polygamists—who, while members of the Christian community, were at the same time considered ineligible for leadership.

68 *Crisis in Masculinity*, op. cit.

69 *Homosexuality: A New Christian Ethic*, op. cit.

70 Eph 5:10–17 (an extended analogy between a Roman soldier's armor and Christian virtues); 2 Tim 2:3–4 (a metaphorical description of the Christian as a "good soldier" of Jesus Christ).

71 Matt 8:5ff.; Luke 7:1ff. (the cure of the centurion's servant); Matt 27:54; Mark 15:39; Luke 23:47 (the centurion at the cross); Acts 10:1ff. (the centurion Cornelius and his family become the first gentile Christians).

72 "Homosexuality and Moral Theology," op. cit.

73 *The Ethics of Sex*, op. cit.

74 *Sex for Christians*, op. cit.

75 "Heterosexism" or "heterocentrism" (an alternative usage currently gaining in popularity) is "the claim that heterosexuality is more than simply a *part* of God's good creative design, that it is the. . . only normative form of human sexuality, the only orientation which can be proclaimed good." Patricia Beattie Jung, "Heterosexism, Justice and the Church," *The Witness*, Vol. 80, No. 6 (6/97).

76 *The Ethics of Sex*, op. cit.

77 *Towards a Christian Understanding of the Homosexual*, op. cit.

78 *Sex for Christians*, op. cit.

79 Thielicke, *The Ethics of Sex*, op. cit.

80 *Sex for Christians*, op. cit.

81 Such moral selectivity becomes more difficult to maintain in the extreme situations created by war or political despotism, it is true, but certainly there were many pious German believers during the rise of the Nazi tyranny, for example, who continued to live out their lives as conventional "good citizens" of the Reich without inquiring too deeply into the moral meaning of their complicity with the state.

Chapter 5: Affirmation

1 David Blamires, "Recent Christian Perspectives on Homosexuality—The Context For Debate," *Towards a Theology of Gay Liberation*, op. cit.

2 W. Norman Pittenger, *A Time for Consent*, 3rd rev. ed. (London: S.C.M. Press, 1976).

3 Silva, "Contemporary Theories of Biblical Interpretation," *The New Interpreter's Bible* (Nashville, Tenn.: Abington, 1995).

4   Gomes, *The Good Book: Reading the Bible with Mind and Heart* (New York: William Morrow & Co., 1996) for this and following quotation.

5   Indeed, biblical proof texts have been used at various times in Christian history to justify slavery, polygamy, genocidal warfare against indigenous peoples, the oppression of women, South African apartheid and a host of other evils which nearly all Christians would now condemn on the basis of *biblical* principles (what Michael Keeling terms the "fundamental moral structures" of the Scriptures ["A Christian Basis for Gay Relationships," *Towards a Theology of Gay Liberation,* op. cit.]).

6   This, liberal critics charge, is precisely the failing of fundamentalist exegesis. Fundamentalists, like everyone else, interpret the "raw" scriptural data. However, since they are on principle unable to acknowledge the fact that they do so, they must refuse to avail themselves of most of the useful data offered by reason, textual studies, Christian history and the sciences, with the result that their interpretive process is informed by little more than their own prejudices and unstated assumptions.

7   That is to say, through a complicated process of composition, collection and redaction that mingles the strands of various oral and written traditions, the geographically specific God of the patriarchs is seen to slowly evolve into the preeminent—albeit still strictly partisan—God of exodus and conquest. This God—through the witness and vision of the prophets—gradually comes to be understood as the One to whom all the nations will be drawn and through whom all tribes and peoples, not just the chosen race, will be redeemed. This vision of God is still further expanded not only by the fact of the Incarnation, through which the transcendent One becomes palpably immanent, but by the specific teaching of Jesus, in which we are invited to approach our Creator with the affectionate trust of a child and call God "*Abba* (Papa)." Through the writings of the first generation of Christians, in particular St. John, this understanding is further enriched by a profound awareness that the God proclaimed throughout Scripture is, in the divine essence, nothing less than eternal self-emptying Love (1 John 4:8–10, 16[b]).

8   Or, as Martin Luther put it in a homely metaphor, the Scriptures are the manager that holds the Eternal Word.

9   Also known and revered (in particular among fundamentalists, who often give this translation quasi-inspired status) as the King James Version. There is a certain historical irony in the fact that King James I was himself a highly complex person in terms of his sexual/affectional leanings—and quite publicly so. While at least in practice bisexual (he fathered children), James's passionate feelings appear to have been reserved for his male favorites, the most notable of whom was George Villiers (later created Duke of Buckingham). So fervent were the King's feelings for Villiers that—anticipating certain theological speculations of this present century by 350 years—he declared in open Council in 1617: "I love. . . Buckingham more than anyone else . . . Jesus Christ did the same and therefore I cannot be blamed. Christ had his John and I have my George." The King's pet name for Villiers was "Steenie," after St. Stephen, who at his martyrdom—according to Acts 6:15—had the "face of an angel."

10   Deut 23:17; 1 Kgs 14:24; 15:12; 22:46; 2 Kgs 23:7.

11   We have little information as to the precise nature of the cultic services provided by these *qadeshim* in Canaanite religion. The most common view is that these sacred male whores were also transvestites who "played the woman's role" in ritual temple sex—which could also be a part of the explanation for the Law's prohibition of cross-dressing (Deut 22:5). It is now generally agreed, however, that whatever the form of their duties, the *qadeshim* (and the biblical condemnations of their activities) have no more relevance to questions

regarding homosexuality per se than do denunciations of female cult prostitutes to heterosexuality. (Bahnsen, op. cit., is an exception when he equates the *qadeshim* with homosexuals in general and argues that, since Deut 23:18 refers to their earnings from prostitution as the "wages of a dog," God "calls [*homosexuals*] dogs.")

12   The RSV's lead in translating the two separate Greek words by a single English word or phrase is followed by a number of subsequent versions, including the New English Bible New Testament of 1961 ("[*those*] guilty of homosexual perversion") and the New American Bible of 1970 ("sodomites").

13   The 1989 revision of the RSV, the New Revised Standard Version Bible (NRSV), perhaps as a result of forty years of widespread criticism on this point, reverts to two separate English words in its translation of 1 Cor 6:9: "male prostitutes" (for μαλακοί) and "sodomites" (for ἀρσενοκοῖται), neither of which can be construed to refer to nonpracticing homosexual persons.

14   The AV translation raises a new difficulty, however, in that the meaning of "effeminate" has changed considerably since it was chosen to translate μαλακοί in 1611. To generations of ordinary Christian readers, "effeminate" has pointed unambiguously to the "nelly queen" of conventional stereotype, the "he-she" whose mannerisms and interests are a grotesque, overdrawn caricature of femininity. To the AV's translators, however, calling a man "effeminate" said nothing whatsoever about the direction of his sexual appetites. Rather, following quite literally upon the basic meaning of the Greek, to describe a man as "effeminate" was to say that he was—through sensual excess of all kinds, including but certainly not limited to the sexual—"soft." An effeminate man was a voluptuary. The most thoroughly heterosexual rake, trailing in his wake a string of seduced and despoiled women, could thus be described as "effeminate" on account of his pampered, overrefined, self-indulgent and sybaritic lifestyle. The New Jerusalem Bible of 1985 catches something of this meaning in its translation of μαλακοί as "the self-indulgent."

15   John J. McNeill, *The Church and the Homosexual* (Mission, Kansas: Sheed, Andrews and McMell, Inc., 1976; see bibliography).

16   That this interpretation of μαλακοί is not without etymological foundation is indicated by the fact that, in contemporary Greek slang, μαλάκας—a derivative of μαλακός (which still means "soft," as a baby's skin is soft)—is used as a term of contempt indicating its object is a compulsive masturbator ("wanker" would be something of an English equivalent, at least in Britain).

17   *The Church and the Homosexual*, op. cit.

18   *Homosexuality and the Western Christian Tradition*, op. cit.

19   Scroggs, *The New Testament and Homosexuality: Contextual Background for Contemporary Debate* (Philadelphia: Fortress Press, 1983; see bibliography). Scroggs's depiction of these effeminate call boys bears certain similarities to the "mollies" of eighteenth- and nineteenth-century New York, see introduction, page 5.

20   Although the consensus of contemporary biblical scholarship is that 1 Timothy is of post-Pauline authorship (Scroggs reflects the mainstream of that opinion in dating it "toward the beginning of the second century CE"), for simplicity's sake I shall treat it according to its self-designation as part of the Pauline corpus.

21   *Christianity, Social Tolerance and Homosexuality*, op. cit., for this and following references to and quotations from Boswell.

22   In fact, he makes specific acknowledgment of his debt to Boswell's then-unpublished work. McNeill, *The Church and the Homosexual*, op. cit.

23   Op. cit. for this and following quotations.

24 Scroggs sees both in the lack of a "recoverable history" for the word prior to Paul's use of it and in the very clumsiness of the Greek construction indications that ἀρσενοκοῖται is a translation of a foreign term.

25 *Homosexuality and the Western Christian Tradition*, op. cit.

26 Moffat's wording is repeated in the 1966 Jerusalem Bible, but abandoned in that version's 1985 revision in favor of "the self-indulgent [*and*] sodomites."

27 *Christianity, Social Tolerance and Homosexuality*, op. cit.

28 *The Church and the Homosexual*, op. cit.

29 The story of the outrage at Gibeah (Judges 19) raises nearly all the same issues as that of Sodom and biblical scholars are agreed that—whatever its basis in historical fact—the Gibeah narrative is deliberately structured so as to bring out its parallels to the Sodom account. Given this clear dependency, Judges 19 is rarely afforded independent discussion by commentators in terms of scriptural references applicable to the question of homosexuality.

30 E.g., Bahnsen's *Homosexuality: A Biblical View*, op. cit.

31 Westmont College *Horizon*, op. cit.

32 Op. cit.

33 The word is *yādhă* ("to know"), which is the term used for what the men of Sodom intend to do to the angelic strangers sheltered in Lot's house ("send them out to us so that we may know them"). It appears 943 times in the Old Testament without modifier and (apart from this passage and the derivative Gibeah account) in only ten of these instances does it refer to copulation, and then only to heterosexual intercourse. (It is used an additional five times in combination with *mishkāb* ["lying"] to refer to heterosexual relations. Thus, Bailey contends, if *yādhă* is to be understood in a coital sense in this particular passage ("send them out to us so that we may have sexual intercourse with them"), such an interpretation must be seen as an exception to the general (though not universal) Old Testament usage. A far more usual understanding would be some nonsexual form of knowledge along the lines of "send them out to us so that we may interrogate them." Bailey does admit, however, that *yādhă* is also used later in this same passage in a clearly sexual sense ("two daughters who have not known man"). Without commenting directly on the implicit grammatical parallelism, Bailey argues that Lot's offer of his daughters does not require a sexual reading of the Sodomites' intentions. Rather, he writes, "no doubt the surrender of his daughters was simply the most tempting bribe that Lot could offer on the spur of the moment . . ." While on its face this comment would seem to stretch plausibility well beyond its natural limit, it is true that contemporary Westerners no doubt find it nearly impossible to appreciate the extraordinary seriousness with which ancient peoples of the Levant took the obligations of hospitality—or the remarkably low value they placed on females.

34 It has been suggested (though not by Bailey) that whatever sexual component there may have been to the Sodomites' demand to "know" Lot's visitors was less a matter of homosexual desire than it was a determination to symbolically subjugate and humiliate the potentially dangerous strangers by forcing them to "play the woman" sexually—a not unknown practice in the Middle East even into recent centuries.

35 While the "abominable things" referred to could conceivably be sexual in nature, there is no indication that they were specifically homosexual. It is noteworthy, as well, that they are cited at the end of the list of Sodom's transgressions and given no particular emphasis in the catalogue of vices for which the city stands condemned.

36   *Homosexuality: A Biblical View,* op. cit.

37   Majority scholarly opinion holds that the Holiness Code probably did not reach the final form in which it appears in Leviticus until after the Exile (although it includes a good deal of earlier material). For purposes of this brief discussion, however, I treat it on its own terms.

38   The Code includes, among other things: regulations for the slaughtering of sacrificial animals (chapter 17) and standards of selection for such animals (22:17–30); purity rules for the priestly caste (chapter 21), including the barring of men with certain physical defects from serving in the priesthood (21:16–23); a liturgical calendar of major feasts (chapter 23); procedures for consumption of sacrificial meals (19:5–8); regulations relating to socioeconomic justice, limits on slavery and periodic redistribution of property (19:9–18; 19:35–37; 25:8–17, 23–55); rules against "mixing of kinds," e.g., sowing two types of seed in one field, mating different species of domestic animals or wearing clothing made of two sorts of fabric (19:19); kinship delineations related to prohibitions of incest (18:6–18; 20:11–14, 19–21); laws banning idolatry (19:4) and other Canaanite religious practices (including child sacrifice [18:21; 20:2–5], magic, divination and necromancy [19:26, 31; 20:6, 27], tattooing [19:28], and certain forms of hair and beard trimming [19:27]); and condemnation of various sexual acts including adultery (18:20; 20:10), homosexuality (18:22; 20:13), bestiality (18:23; 20:15, 16), and intercourse with a menstruating woman (18:19; 20:18).

39   McNeill, *The Church and the Homosexual,* op. cit.

40   This interpretation of the Levitical prohibitions regarding sex acts between males is argued by, among others, McNeill (*The Church and the Homosexual,* op. cit.), Boswell (*Christianity, Social Tolerance and Homosexuality,* op. cit.), James B. Nelson (*Embodiment: An Approach to Sexuality and Christian Theology* [Minneapolis: Augsburg Publishing, 1978]), Richard Woods (*Another Kind of Love: Homosexuality and Spirituality,* 3rd ed. [Ft. Wayne, Indiana: Knoll Publishing Co., Inc., 1988]), and numerous biblical commentaries (e.g., *Leviticus and Numbers: The New Century Bible* [London: Nelson, 1967], in which Norman H. Smith writes, "Homosexuality here is condemned on account of its association with *idolatry*" [emphasis in original]).

41   *To'ebah* sometimes literally means "idol" in Old Testament usage (e.g., Isa 44:19; Ezek 7:20; 16:36). It is also employed to denigrate a wide variety of acts and objects connected with idolatrous practice: the precious metals of which idols are made (Deut 7:25), cross-dressing (Deut 22:5), and the offering paid to a sacred cult prostitute (Deut 23:18). In other instances it is used for things which, while they are not specifically related to idolatry, are not viewed as uniquely heinous either: nonkosher food (Deut 14:3) and unjust measures (Deut 25:16).

42   Countryman, *Dirt, Greed & Sex: Sexual Ethics in the New Testament and Their Implications for Today* (Philadelphia: Fortress Press, 1988), for this and following quotations.

43   In fact, Countryman notes that it is simplistic to attempt to explain the whole of the purity code through reference to non-Hebrew cultic associations. In terms of the matter of clean and unclean animals, for instance, swine, which were reckoned unclean, had connections to Canaanite rites, it is true, but so did oxen and doves, both of which are designated as clean.

44   Jewish Christians, on the other hand, were permitted to continue its observance insofar as this did not require abridging table fellowship with Gentile Christians.

45   This "limit" would argue against the once-common practice among some fun-
      damentalists of opening the Bible at random and taking whatever phrase or
      passage their eyes fell upon as God's "word" to them in terms of a particular,
      immediate question or situation.

46   For many, predictive prophecy would be the exception to this particular
      exegetical rule. For example, when Isaiah writes that a young woman—*almah*
      in the Hebrew—will conceive and bear a son (Isa 7:14), he does not appear to
      have parthenogenesis in mind, since *almah* indicates nothing as to virginity or
      lack thereof. It is only some seven hundred years later that the full significance
      of Isaiah's words, as they have traditionally been construed by Christians, is
      revealed: Matthew, reflecting on the Septuagint's translation of *almah* by the
      Greek παρθένος, which *does* specifically connote a woman without sexual expe-
      rience, understands Isaiah to be prophesying the virgin birth of Jesus (Matt
      1:23). Conservative commentators have often noted the "double" nature of
      biblical prophecy: a more immediate fulfillment anticipated by the prophet
      himself and a larger fulfillment further in the future which is discernable only
      in retrospect. More liberal exegetes tend to be suspicious of such an approach,
      however—in particular, as in the case cited here, when it involves reading back
      into a passage concepts unsupported by the language of the text itself.

47   I.e., the scriptural proof texts conventionally used to condemn homosexuality.
      The term appears extensively in Evangelicals Concerned literature and is also
      the title of an always-popular seminar Blair leads at the annual "Connections"
      conferences sponsored by EC on both the East and West coasts.

48   It is, in fact, the only scriptural reference to same-sex acts between women.

49   Of the sort prevailing in ancient brothels and twentieth-century gay bath-
      houses, for example.

50   While the practice in the Greco-Roman culture to which Paul's comment is
      addressed was for mature men to cut their hair relatively short, the custom
      among Palestinian Jews at the time was quite different: men wore their hair
      long (oiled and pulled back in a bun at the nape of the neck), a custom which
      Jesus no doubt followed, which would mean, if Paul's statement were to be
      taken literally, that Jesus himself acted "against nature."

51   Countryman points out, however, that such an understanding of φύσις in the
      context of Romans 1 would completely defeat the point of Paul's argument,
      since "'widespread social usage' in the Greek world in fact accepted homosex-
      ual intercourse." *Dirt, Greed, and Sex,* op. cit.

52   In this, Jewish anthropology appears to have differed from the Greco-Roman
      understanding, which, as Countryman puts it, "seems to have assumed that
      human beings are attracted sexually both to their own and the opposite sex."
      Nonetheless, Countryman continues, both viewpoints "lacked even a behav-
      ior-based category for people who showed a fixed preference for partners of
      the same sex." Ibid.

53   Gomes, in *The Good Book,* op. cit., argues along these lines in his discussion of
      Romans 1. The passage cannot be applicable to constitutional homosexuals,
      he contends, since its entire point is to denounce "people who know what is
      right but who, because of their arrogant willfulness in their fallen state, choose
      to act contrary to that knowledge." Since such willful rebellion against reality
      is the point of Paul's argument, Gomes continues, the apostle's denunciations
      must be aimed at constitutional heterosexuals who are turning away from
      what would normally satisfy them to perform homosexual acts contrary to
      their spontaneous sexual urges. Boswell makes the same argument: "the per-
      sons Paul condemns are manifestly not homosexual: what he derogates are
      homosexual acts committed by apparently heterosexual persons. The whole

point of Romans 1, in fact, is to stigmatize persons who have rejected their calling, gotten off the true path they were once on. It would completely undermine the thrust of the argument if the persons in question were not 'naturally' inclined to the opposite sex in the same way they were 'naturally' inclined to monotheism." (*Christianity, Social Tolerance and Homosexuality*, op. cit.).

54 Countryman takes a different approach to Romans 1, however, arguing that while Paul, at least for rhetorical purposes, is willing to grant that the homosexual activity common among Gentiles is "unclean" in the sense of violating Jewish purity codes, it is "not in itself sinful, but had been visited upon the Gentiles as recompense for sins, chiefly the sin of idolatry but also those of social disruption." *Dirt, Greed and Sex*, op. cit.

55 Liberal Christians note that proponents of the conservative viewpoint have a tendency simply to ignore those scriptural passages which even they themselves would have to admit reveal authorial misapprehension. St. Paul, for example, when writing of the Parousia to the church at Thessalonika, clearly assumes that this event will take place within the lifetime of at least some of his initial readers (1 Thess 4:15–17). It is difficult to imagine anyone who would not acknowledge, with however much hedging and qualification, that on this detail (which is certainly not the point of the passage) the apostle was wrong. It has also been pointed out that Paul's statement in Rom 13:3 that government is "not a terror to good conduct, but to bad. . . do what is good, and you will receive. . . approval," if taken literally and applied universally, is manifestly untrue, contradicted not only by Paul's own martyrdom during the Neronian persecution, but also by the state's execution of Jesus—not to mention the suffering and murder of thousands of fundamentally, sometimes even heroically, decent people at the hands of various governments down through the centuries and continuing to our own day.

56 *The Good Book*, op. cit.

57 E.g., Eph 6:5.

58 E.g., 2 Tim 2:11–12.

59 Bahnsen (*Homosexuality: A Biblical View*, op. cit.), along with some other conservatives, would disagree, arguing that all the specific regulations of the Jewish law pertaining to sexual conduct are subsumed in the seventh commandment, "You shall not commit adultery." (Exod 20:14)

60 *The Good Book*, op. cit.

61 Gomes writes of a message of ever-widening "inclusivity," in which all people (women, slaves, racial outcasts, homosexuals) are invited into the loving freedom of the eternal reign of God, made particular in time in the Christian community (*The Good Book*, op. cit.). Ralph Blair speaks in one of his publications of "major biblical themes such as justice, grace and mercy" (*What's the Bible?* [New York: Blair, 1989]). A study document prepared by the Commission on Homosexuality of the Episcopal Diocese of Michigan cites "an understanding of God we have derived. . . from Scripture, a God who has revealed himself in a spirit of love which seeks the lost," and notes St. Paul's teaching that Christians live not under the letter of the law but by its spirit (Commission on Homosexuality, Episcopal Diocese of Michigan, *Report of the Task Force on Homosexuality* [Detroit: Episcopal Diocese of Michigan, 1973]). Michael Keeling refers to the "fundamental moral structures" or themes of the Bible which "exercise control over the varying moral advice [*in specific scriptural passages*] which may or may not represent these themes in any particular situation." The first of these "structures," according to Keeling, is that of covenant, or more particularly, covenant grounded in love—first with a chosen people

but ultimately "with the whole of humanity" ("A Christian Basis for Gay Relationships," *Towards a Theology of Gay Liberation,* op. cit.).

62   *A Place at the Table,* op. cit.

63   Gomes, *The Good Book,* op. cit.

64   "A Christian Basis for Gay Relationships," op. cit., for this and following quotation.

65   "What It Means to Be Human," *Towards a Theology of Gay Liberation,* op. cit., for this and following quotations from Pittenger.

66   In *A Time for Consent,* op. cit., Pittenger argues that, for the homosexual person, this sort of relationship is only possible with a partner of the same sex: "The male homosexual is able to give himself, whole and entire, only to another man; the female homosexual, [*only*] to another woman."

67   Rainer Maria Rilke, trans. M. D. Herter Norton, *Letters to a Young Poet* (New York & London: W. W. Norton & Co., 1934).

68   "What It Means to Be Human," *Towards a Theology of Gay Liberation,* op. cit.

69   "Coming Out of the Closet," *Footsteps: Newsletter of the Mercy of God Community,* June–July 1997.

70   *A Time for Consent,* op. cit.

71   Not all speakers and workshop presenters at EC "Connections," much less all EC members, share Blair's view on this point.

72   Peggy Campolo, "The Holy Presence of Acceptance," *The Other Side,* 30 (March–April, 1994). Campolo's very public stand is noteworthy for the fact that her husband disagrees with her on the morality of such same-sex unions and yet they have supported each other's right to their divergent convictions on this point—often, Peggy Campolo notes, at considerable personal cost.

73   *Report of the Task Force on Homosexuality,* op. cit. Others of this viewpoint are less absolute on the question of monogamy. Michael Keeling, for example, comments that "something 'relational' may happen even in the briefest of encounters," but then goes on to admit that "I have to say also that the model of 'communal salvation' does imply that long-term—even if not lifelong—relationships are a moral aim." ("A Christian Basis for Gay Relationships," *Towards a Theology of Gay Liberation,* op. cit.)

74   *A Time for Consent,* op. cit.

75   Or, as Bruce Bawer puts it in *A Place at the Table,* op. cit., certain people "happen to have been born gay."

76   Which, we tend to forget, was until this century itself considered "abnormal," even "sinister" (from the Latin *sinister,* "on the left side"), with left-handed children being forced—often at considerable psychological cost—to use their "right" hand.

77   The latter option does not, of course, mean such a person ceases to be homosexual, any more than a sexually active heterosexual prison inmate whose only outlets are homosexual ceases to be heterosexual in fundamental orientation.

78   *A Place at the Table,* op. cit., for this and following quotation.

79   Christopher Bryant, *The Heart in Pilgrimage* (London: Darton, Longman & Todd, Ltd., 1980).

80   *A Place at the Table,* op. cit.

81   Gomes, *The Good Book,* op. cit.

82   *A Time for Consent,* op. cit., for this and following quotations.

83   *The Good Book,* op. cit.

84 *Another Kind of Love,* op. cit. Woods adds that "[s]omething less may be far from depravity or even sinfulness, but it nevertheless falls below the level of what every human person deserves and desires . . ."

85 Ibid.

86 Peggy Campolo writes on this point that she and her husband Tony "are both angered by the terrible lies about gays and lesbians propagated by some church leaders, lies which have led to cruel mistreatment and great injustice. We both pray for the church to repent." Campolo also reports that she writes "letters to newspapers and magazines, from carefully worded polite corrections of erroneous information in our local paper to the angry protest I sent to the Christian magazines that published [*a*] homophobic, full-page ad . . ." "The Holy Presence of Acceptance," op. cit.

87 *Report of the Task Force on Homosexuality,* op. cit.

88 Cited in Bawer, "Lecture at St. John's Episcopal Cathedral," in Bruce Bawer, ed., *Beyond Queer: Challenging Gay Left Orthodoxy* (New York: The Free Press [Simon & Schuster], 1996), without further attribution. The recommendation has not, at this point, been accepted by that denomination (see discussion on pages 111–113).

89 "Lecture at St. John's Episcopal Cathedral," op. cit.

90 Ibid.

91 *Report of the Task Force on Homosexuality,* op. cit.

92 *A Place at the Table,* op. cit., for this and following Bawer quotations.

93 Legal protections afforded by civilly recognized gay marriage would include property and inheritance rights, custody rights for jointly raised children, tax and insurance benefits and visitation rights as "next of kin." (See *Lesbian and Gay Marriage* [Cambridge, Massachusetts: The Coalition for Lesbian and Gay Civil Rights, n.d.]).

94 A four-day conference of approximately 250 Episcopalians held in April 1997 in Pasadena, California, for example, was entitled "Beyond Inclusion: Celebrating Gay and Lesbian Commitments and Ministries in the Episcopal Church." True to its name, the conference encouraged participants to work for the blessing of gay unions and the ordination of non-celibate gay men and lesbians to the diaconate and priesthood of the Episcopal church.

95 "Connections" keynoters have included Peggy Campolo, Lewis Smedes, Rosalind Rinker, Ken Medema, Virginia Ramey Mollenkott, Letha Dawson Scanzoni, Nancy Hardesty, Phyllis Hart and Chip and Nancy Miller.

96 Indeed, as has been pointed out by a number of historians, one of the primary attractions to Judaism for first-century "God fearers"—Gentiles who accepted Jewish monotheism and the Jewish moral law, but did not take on the full burden of Jewish ritual regulations—was the self-evident ethical superiority of Jewish sexual and family morality to the prevalent corruption of pagan society. Early Christian apologists made a similar contrast between Christians' moral standards and those of the wider culture.

97 The first listed of these "works," critics note, is πορνεία (*pornēa,* usually translated "fornication" or "sexual immorality"), which many exegetes contend is a generic term for *any* sexual behavior contrary to the Jewish law. If this interpretation is accurate, πορνεία would therefore include male homosexual acts.

98 That this is true becomes obvious when one considers the following hypothetical example. Even if a brother and sister loved each other with the fullest possible maturity, mutuality and commitment, sexual relations between them would be wrong, not because of any subjective failure in love on their part, but because of an objective fact completely independent of their subjective attitudes: the sibling relationship by its very nature precludes, or should preclude, a sexual relationship. The same is true, it is argued, for homosexuals. No

matter how deeply felt and self-giving the love between two members of the same sex might be, the objective fact that they are of the same gender means that a sexual relationship can never be appropriate between them.

99   Lewis, *The Problem of Pain* (London: Geoffrey Bles, Centenary Press, 1940).

100   Bawer makes this explicit when he writes, "If homosexuality is wrong, who is wronged by it. . . ?" *A Place at the Table*, op. cit.

101   Pittenger, "What It Means to Be Human," op. cit.

102   Pittenger, *A Time for Consent*, op. cit.

103   Indeed, as C. S. Lewis points out in *The Screwtape Letters*, op. cit., it is the "sublime" fornications and adulteries which are often the most spiritually destructive—those relationships in which two people, drawn into an all-consuming "mutuality," are unwilling to let anything stand in the way of their unitive obsession.

104   Op. cit.

105   Guenther Haas, "Exegetical Issues in the Use of the Bible to Justify the Acceptance of Homosexual Practice," *Christian Scholar's Review* XXVI:4 (Summer 1997). I am particularly indebted to Haas's excellent summary and thorough citations for the critical material in this section.

106   Ibid.

107   See pages 159–160.

108   David F. Wright, "Homosexuals or Prostitutes: The Meaning of ἀρσενοκοῖται (1 Cor 6:9; 1 Tim 1:10)." *Vigiliae Christianae* 38 (June 1984).

109   David F. Wright, "Translating ἀρσενοκοῖται (1 Cor 6:9; 1 Tim 1:10)," *Vigiliae Christianae* 41 (December 1987).

110   Wright, "Homosexuals or Prostitutes," op. cit. Countryman, on the other hand, argues that Wright "has succeeded only in removing much of Boswell's evidence without in fact proving his hypothesis untenable or demonstrating another hypothesis in its place. What Wright has demonstrated is that antagonism on the part of some Christians toward those who engage in homosexual intercourse goes back to at least the second century and almost certainly shows direct continuity with the same sentiment in Hellenistic Judaism." *Dirt, Greed, and Sex*, op. cit.

111   See pages 160–161.

112   Wright, "Homosexuals or Prostitutes," op. cit.

113   Haas's term; "Exegetical Issues in the Use of the Bible to Justify the Acceptance of Homosexual Practice," op. cit.

114   Mark D. Smith, "Ancient Bisexuality and the Interpretation of Romans 1:26–27," *Journal of the American Academy of Religion* 64 (Summer 1996).

115   D. F. Wright, "Review of *The New Testament and Homosexuality* by Robin Scroggs," *Scottish Journal of Theology* 38 (March 1985).

116   *Homosexuality and the Western Christian Tradition*, op. cit.

117   See pages 162–163.

118   "Exegetical Issues in the Use of the Bible to Justify the Acceptance of Homosexual Practice," op. cit.

119   Ibid.

120   Countryman, however, argues that the retention of the ban on adultery is based on its involving violation of a "property right," not on its being a matter of sexual purity per se. Moreover, he rigorously follows the logic of his interpretive scheme to its limit by asserting that occasional acts of bestiality

resulting from youthful experimentation or lengthy isolation (as distinguished from the acting out of a pathological condition) are morally negligible. *Dirt, Greed, and Sex,* op. cit.

121   Haas, "Exegetical Issues in the Use of the Bible to Justify the Acceptance of Homosexual Practice," op. cit., for this and following quotation.

122   *Dirt, Greed, and Sex,* op. cit.

123   The rhetorical device, in Countryman's view, being simply a setup for turning judgment back upon the Jewish readers among Paul's intended audience themselves: "Therefore you have no excuse, whoever you are, when you judge others' for in passing judgment on another you condemn yourself . . ." (Rom 2:1)

124   For example—after what Haas describes as "a thorough study of the key terms that Paul uses in his discussion of same-sex relations in Rom 1:24–27," including their use not only in that passage, but in the rest of the New Testament and the writings of Hellenistic Judaism as well—Schmidt (*Straight and Narrow?,* op. cit.) concludes that, while Paul does not specifically use the word "sin" in reference to same-sex desires and acts, objective analysis of his language in Romans 1 makes it inescapably clear that he considers such desires and acts sinful.

125   "Exegetical Issues in the Use of the Bible to Justify the Acceptance of Homosexual Practice," op. cit.

126   *Straight and Narrow?,* op. cit.

127   *Homosexuality and the Western Christian Tradition,* op. cit.

128   E.g., Schmidt, *Straight and Narrow?,* op. cit.; Richard B. Hays, "Relations Natural and Unnatural: A Response to John Boswell's Exegesis of Romans 1," *Journal of Religious Ethics* 14 (Spring 1986); James B. DeYoung, "The Meaning of 'Nature' in Romans 1 and its Implications for Biblical Proscriptions of Homosexual Behavior," *Journal of the Evangelical Theological Society* 31 (December 1988).

129   *Christianity, Social Tolerance and Homosexuality,* op. cit.

130   *Dirt, Greed, and Sex,* op. cit.

131   "Exegetical Issues in the Use of the Bible to Justify the Acceptance of Homosexual Practice," op. cit.

132   Ibid, for this and following quote.

133   This experience could be the result of either family dysfunction or some other impediment to normal patterns of development. It is noted that even one widely read gay author has recently acknowledged that such a connection exists, at least in the lives of many gay men (Andrew Sullivan, *Love Undetectable,* op. cit.—see introduction, page 23).

134   "The Loving Opposition," *Christianity Today,* 7/19/93, cited in Gomes, *The Good Book,* op. cit., for this and following quotations.

135   *Know My Name,* op. cit.

136   The conservative requirement of generativity in this case being replaced by an equally circumscribing demand for "unitive intention."

137   *Know My Name,* op. cit., for this and following quotation.

138   Gomes, *The Good Book,* op. cit., for this and following quotation.

Chapter 6: Liberation

1 Since I make a similar *caveat* in regard to viewpoint 1 (Condemnation), it should be noted that some arguing this present viewpoint would consider the approach I take in this book to be itself fatally enmeshed in the "homophobic discourse" of institutional Christianity, in that I propose for consideration on their "objective" merits viewpoints which are seen as a part of the church's "cultural discourse of hatred" and its "institutional practice. . . of oppressing those who are sexually different." (Goss, *Jesus Acted Up*, op. cit.)

2 Indeed, gay liberation theologian Richard Cleaver goes further: not only is morality not individualistic, salvation itself is not "personal" in the traditionally understood sense. Rather, "Salvation is collective. By covenanting, we choose to be part of a gathered people, a people called out of the undifferentiated mass of humanity." For Cleaver, this accepting of a covenantal relationship with God—which *is* salvation—is "the choosing of peoplehood over individual salvation, over atomization." *Know My Name*, op. cit.

3 Ibid.

4 In order to get an accurate sense of the sort of people attracted to Jesus, it is suggested, we should consider that—were he to come among us today—he would surround himself not only with a handful of small businessmen (as were the fishermen Peter, James and John) and a few independently wealthy women who would support his work out of their own resources (as did Mary of Magdala), but also with street hustlers, transvestite prostitutes, junkies, people with AIDS (the lepers of our day), homeless street kids with thick rings dangling from their noses and queers.

5 Goss argues that "[i]f Jesus the Christ is not queer, then his. . . message of solidarity and justice is irrelevant. If the Christ is not queer, then the gospel is no longer good news but oppressive news for queers. If the Christ is not queer, then the incarnation has no meaning for our sexuality." *Jesus Acted Up*, op. cit.

6 Early in the gay Christian movement there were various attempts to discern hints of a gay subtext within the biblical stories of David and Jonathan ("your love to me was wonderful, passing the love of women"—2 Sam 1:26, AV), Ruth and Naomi ("whither thou goest I will go"—Ruth 1:16, AV) and even in Jesus' relationship with the Apostle John (the disciple "whom Jesus loved" who leaned upon his chest while reclining at the Last Supper—John 13:23). These proposals are now generally recognized as being little more than romanticized misreadings of the far different cultural conventions of ancient societies—similar, in fact, to the venerable (but scripturally unsupported) notion that Mary Magdalene was "in love" with Jesus.

7 *Jesus Acted Up*, op. cit.

8 "When the Lord your God brings you into the land that you are about to enter and occupy, and he clears away many nations before you. . . then you must utterly destroy them." The Jerusalem Bible translates 2(b) more literally: "you must lay them under ban." What this divinely sanctioned "ban" (Hebrew, *herem*) meant in practical terms is made clear in the horrific description of the capture of Jericho: "They enforced the ban on everything in the town: men and women, young and old, even the oxen and sheep and donkeys, massacring them all." (Josh 6:21, Jerusalem Bible translation)

9 Valente, *Sex: The Radical View of a Catholic Theologian* (New York: Macmillan Publishing Co., 1970), for this and following quotations.

10 Goss writes similarly: "All biblical texts are social constructions of androcentric patriarchal culture and history. The Bible. . . has served and

continues to serve to legitimate [*men's*] clerical, social, and political power." *Jesus Acted Up*, op. cit.

11   *Erotic Justice: A Liberating Ethic of Sexuality* (Westminster: John Knox, 1996).

12   As Goss puts it, "Queer Christians refuse to leave the Bible in the hands of the powerful to be used as a weapon against themselves." *Jesus Acted Up.*, op. cit.

13   Elisabeth Schüssler Fiorenza, *Bread Not Stone* (Boston: Beacon Press, 1984).

14   Goss, *Jesus Acted Up*, op. cit., for this and following quotation.

15   James Cotter, "The Gay Challenge to Traditional Notions of Human Sexuality," *Towards a Theology of Gay Liberation*, op. cit.

16   *Sex: The Radical View of a Catholic Theologian*, op. cit.

17   Cotter, "The Gay Challenge to Traditional Notions of Human Sexuality," op. cit.

18   Neale Secor, "A Brief for a New Homosexual Ethic," *The Same Sex: An Appraisal of Homosexuality* (New York: United Church Press, 1969).

19   *Erotic Justice*, op. cit. Richard Cleaver, drawing on the work of Uruguayan Jesuit Juan Segundo, details one liberation model for "doing theology" that begins with "experiencing our experience": the "hermeneutic circle." This four step process (1) originates in the experience of oppression, suffering or pain which renders conventional moral or theological answers insufficient. This (2) leads to "suspicion" of those pious truisms, which in turn (3) leads us to search the scriptures "in a new way, our perceptions sharpened by our suspicions." This prayerful search uncovers scriptural truth which, while always there, was overlooked so long as we were "comfortable. . . content with the old verities." In the final step of the circle, we (4) use the message we have discovered in scripture to interpret the reality that sent us to the scriptures in the first place—in other words, we create a new theological paradigm. *Know My Name*, op. cit.

20   Goss, *Jesus Acted Up*, op. cit., for this and following quotations.

21   *The Courage to Love*, op. cit.

22   *Sex: The Radical View of a Catholic Theologian*, op. cit.

23   "The Gay Challenge to Traditional Notions of Human Sexuality," op. cit.

24   *The Courage to Love*, op. cit.

25   Recognition of this reality presumably lies behind the vows used in some Metropolitan Community Church union services, vows in which the traditional "till death us do part" is replaced with "so long as our love shall last."

26   "The Gay Challenge to Traditional Notions of Human Sexuality, op. cit., for this and following quotations.

27   "A Christian Basis for Gay Relationships," op. cit.

28   *Erotic Justice*, op. cit.

29   *Sex: The Radical View of a Catholic Theologian*, op. cit.

30   Ibid.

31   Reacting against the tone of victimization and apology felt to be inherent in a claim that gays and lesbians "can't help being what they are" because their orientation is "unchosen," some gay and lesbian theologians have begun to question what was until recently one of the fundamental tenets of all but the most conservative viewpoints—that homosexuals cannot be faulted for their orientation because it is something over which they have no control. Cleaver reflects this shift when he writes that "the distinction between choosing our sexuality and being chosen by it is less clear in real life than in philosophy. It is also less important to how we do theology than we think." (*Know My Name*, op. cit.) Some recent gay liberation theologians go even further, identifying

with social constructionist Michel Foucault when he argues that "sexuality is something we create ourselves." (Quoted in "Sex and the Politics of Identity: An Interview with Michel Foucault," Bob Gallagher & Alexander Wilson, *Gay Spirit*, Mark Thompson, ed. [New York: St. Martin's Press, 1987].)

32   Cleaver argues that the distinction between homosexual orientation and acts is "based on a false dichotomy between being gay and acting gay; it assumes that 'acting gay' is merely a matter of sexual activity in the narrowest genital sense . . . But gayness is as much a matter of culture as a choice of sexual object." *Know My Name*, op. cit.

33   *The Courage to Love*, op. cit.

34   See introduction, page 9.

35   Sally Gearhart, "The Miracle of Lesbianism," in Gearhart & William R. Johnson, eds., *Loving Women/Loving Men* (San Francisco: Glide Publications, 1974), quoted in Cleaver, *Know My Name*, op. cit.

36   "The Gay Challenge to Traditional Notions of Human Sexuality," op. cit.

37   Ibid.

38   As Goss writes, "Gay/lesbian liberation forcefully articulate[s] the significance of the erotic and the pleasurable . . ." *Jesus Acted Up.*, op. cit.

39   See page 112.

40   Reported by Frederica Mathewes-Green in her column for "United Voice," a conservative caucus within the Episcopal Church—text from the Internet (www.episcopalian.org/eu).

41   *Know My Name*, op. cit.

42   "Heterosexism, Justice and the Church," op. cit.

43   Goss, *Jesus Acted Up*, op. cit.

44   Cleaver writes that lesbians and gays, as part of their spiritual development, must come to the consciousness of being an "oppressed class." *Know My Name*, op. cit.

45   Goss, *Jesus Acted Up*, op. cit., for this and following quotations.

46   In accordance with the Latin American theologians who coined the term (and participated in creating the model for Christian community which it describes), Goss defines a "base community" as a "biblically centered affinity group, reflecting on biblical truth in the midst of social oppression." (*Jesus Acted Up*, op. cit.)

47   Boyd's *Are You Running With Me, Jesus?* (New York: Avon Books, 1965) was enormously popular in the 1960s; he came out as a gay man in the 1970s.

48   "If We Unlock Church Doors, Will Anyone Come?" *The Witness*, Vol. 80, No. 6 (6/97).

49   MCC was founded in 1968 by the Reverend Troy Perry. Although MCC is often referred to as the "gay denomination," MCC spokespersons point out that while the church is predominantly gay and lesbian (or, in certain urban areas, L/G/B/T/Q) in membership, most congregations also include at least a few heterosexuals, often single parents with children—many of whom state that what drew them to an MCC church was the nonjudgmental support and welcoming love they found there.

50   One EACA priest working among homeless youth and street sex workers in San Francisco expresses well the core conviction of this viewpoint: "The heart of the biblical message is that God is a God of Liberation, a God who identifies with those who are the have-nots . . . For us in the Gay/Lesbian/Bi/Transgender/ Questioning Community, this month [*June*] is Pride Month

when we celebrate our heritage of liberation and the power of the Spirit in that liberation." (Fr. C. River Sims, "Journal of an Alien Street Priest," *Peniel* [6/97]).

51 See pages 210-211.

52 Ellison, *Erotic Justice,* op. cit.

53 Ibid.

54 *Jesus Acted Up,* op. cit.

55 See pages 212-213.

56 Op. cit., critiqued in the Spring 1997 issue of *Review* (Vol. 21, No. 3).

57 Bawer himself remained celibate for years not out of Christian conviction (he felt he no longer had a place in the Christian community once he discovered himself to be gay) but rather through commitment to what he terms a "godless virtue" ("Devotions," *Coast to Coast: Poems by Bruce Bawer* [Brownsville, Oregon: Story Line Press, 1993]). He came back to faith as a result of his relationship with his life-partner.

58 *A Place at the Table,* op. cit.

59 *Know My Name,* op. cit.

60 *A Place at the Table, op. cit,* for this and following quotation.

61 *Know My Name,* op. cit. for this and following quotation.

62 *Jesus Acted Up,* op. cit.

63 *Know My Name,* op. cit., for this and following quotations.

64 Carter Heyward, *The Redemption of God: A Theology of Mutual Relation* (Lanham, Maryland: University Press of America, 1982).

65 *Know My Name,* op. cit.

Afterword

1 *Love Undetectable,* op. cit.

Appendix

1 I do not include Jude 7, which refers to the citizens of Sodom and Gomorrah "going after strange flesh" (NRSValternate reading), since most scholars are agreed that—in light of the previous verse which cites angels who left their "proper dwelling" (apparently a reference to Gen 6:1-4 in which the "sons of God" mate with the daughters of men)—the point of this passage is the inappropriateness of "cross-species" coupling, not homosexuality per se. I have also omitted 2 Pet 2:6-11. Although this text figures peripherally in some fundamentalist treatments of the subject, most scholars are in agreement that its reference to the "depraved lusts" (2:10) of the Sodomites is too generic a condemnation to figure significantly in a discussion of the biblical treatment of homosexuality. Conservatives note, however, that the clear assumption of both these passages is that the Sodomites' sin was sexual in nature.

2 Op. cit.

3 Op. cit.

4 Op. cit.

5 *Dirt, Greed, and Sex,* op. cit.

6 Op. cit.

INDEX OF SCRIPTURE CITATIONS

Index of Scripture Citations